# PERFORMANCE ANXIETIES

# Performance anxieties

*Re-producing masculinity*

David Buchbinder

ALLEN & UNWIN

*For my father*
Sam Buchbinder



First published in 1998 by
Allen & Unwin
9 Atchison Street, St Leonards NSW 2065 Australia
Phone: (61 2) 9901 4088
Fax: (61 2) 9906 2218
E-mail: frontdesk@allen-unwin.com.au
URL: http://www.allen-unwin.com.au

National Library of Australia
Cataloguing-in-Publication entry:

Buchbinder, David, 1947– .
Performance anxieties: re-producing masculinity.

Bibliography.
Includes index.
ISBN 1 86448 425 x.

1. Men. 2. Men's studies. 3. Masculinity (Psychology).
4. Sex role. I. Title.

305.31

Set in 10/11.5pt Garamond by DOCUPRO, Sydney
Printed and bound by SRM Production Services Sdn Bhd, Malaysia

10 9 8 7 6 5 4 3 2 1

# *Contents*

# *Preface*

'Really? You're writing *another* book about men?

My friend's response to my announcement that I was embarked upon *Performance anxieties: Re-producing masculinity* did not appear to include delight. Or even excitement, for that matter. Rather, the implication was either that I had said everything that there was to say about men in *Masculinities and identities*, my earlier book, or, less flatteringly, that I had said everything that *I* was capable of saying about men. My friend, clearly in the grip of some profoundly Keatsian moment, went on to snap: 'All men are bastards; all bastards are men—that is all ye know on earth, and all ye need to know.'

This story conveniently allows me to explain and explore the title of the present work. The statement 'All men are bastards' is, regardless of whatever experience may have induced or compelled my friend to utter that deathless line, a form of representation of men and thence also of masculinity. Indeed, the culture is filled with such representations, though of course we may not always see them that way. In fact, we may go so far as to say that the culture often works to *prevent* us from seeing them as *representations*, so that we take them instead for reality, for truth. Alternatively, we may understand *formally* representational material (literary works, films, paintings, and so on) as somehow offering an authentic snapshot of some social reality or truth. In this book, I begin from the premise that this position is not only naive but even potentially dangerous, for representations are encoded in and through ideological discourses abroad in the culture, and therefore will inevitably articulate the viewpoint and the advantage of *some* group in the culture. The uncritical acceptance of a particular representation thus tacitly and unthinkingly affirms a particular ideological structure and its material consequences in society—for how people *are*, as social beings characterised by both differences and similarities in sex, gender, class and age; and for how they behave socially. Thus, representations of men and their activities not only often reproduce dominant notions of masculinity— in the sense that a painting may be reproduced— but also re-produce those notions, inviting men to 'recognise' themselves and other men in such representations.

*Performance anxieties: Re-producing masculinity* focuses specifically on how men and various masculinities are represented—re-produced—and what those representations have to say about men and masculinity; but also—and importantly—on what such representations try *not* to say or what they might ignore. I have marshalled various theories to assist me in this, explaining the theoretical arguments as they arise. Where I have employed technical terms, I have sought to ensure that their sense is clear from the context, or else I have defined them in passing.

The book's title, *Performance anxieties*, is intended, through its play on the notion of sexual performance anxiety, to foreground first the idea of gender, masculinity included, as a performance undertaken in order to be identified by others as belonging to one or the other sex (a theme which I take up in more detail in Chapters 6 and 7). It is, however, a performance in which people must engage continuously, lest they be (mis)taken as belonging to the 'wrong' gender. This imposed need continually to announce one's gender inevitably, therefore, will be signalled by the anxiety it occasions.

There is, however, another anxiety which we might think of as particular to men in a patriarchal culture, namely, the individual male's need to perform masculinity as flawlessly as possible, lest he suffer the withdrawal of power available (notionally, anyway) to all men in the culture, and the consequence of the displeasure, and possibly ridicule, of other men. This is bound up with the need for the individual man to find his place within the patriarchal order, a theme which is explored in Chapter 3 through a reading of the Australian film *Strictly ballroom*, and in Chapter 4, which considers the case, first, of the man who fails to meet the required (but usually formally unstated) criteria for 'being a man' (Shakespeare's Antony is one example) and, second, of the man who exceeds those criteria (for example, Stoker's Dracula).

Sexual matters often bring out a variety of anxieties regarding performance. Chapter 5 discusses some of these through an exploration of pornography as a genre, focusing on the ways that men consuming porn also engage in a form of homosocial bonding that always carries the risk of shading into the homoerotic. The pornographic text, then, actually functions to *produce* certain anxieties at the same time as it seeks, ostensibly, to allay them by exposing the secrets of the sexes as well as the techniques of sex, together with representations of sexual responsiveness.

Chapter 1 commences from the premise that gender, rather than being innate, is socially and culturally constructed, and therefore is both ideological—with a particular politics—and discursive—constituting a relay of power in society. Chapters 2 and 7 may be read as a consideration of two sorts of response to such a position. In Chapter 2, I examine Robert Bly's popular book *Iron John*, showing that, in its nostalgic yearning for the return of a mythical masculine past, it asserts gender as essential rather than as culturally constructed, a comforting strategy for men unsettled by socioeconomic conditions, including the economic and political ascendancy of women, in the latter half of the twentieth century. However, Bly's desire for the restoration of a kind of tribalised masculinity, together with formal rites of passage and other rituals, signifies not merely a conservative attitude to gender (and especially masculinity) but also the romanticisation of an imperfectly understood or analysed past.

In Chapter 7, I turn to the recently emerged phenomenon of queer theory and criticism, which, in contradistinction to Bly's book, deconstructs traditional sex/gender divisions, and asserts, rather, the provisionality and contingency of these. In its inclusive catholicity (for heterosexuals as well as non-heterosexuals may be embraced by 'queer'), queer theory and the politics attendant upon it enable us to conceive 'other-wise' of issues to do with sex, gender and sexuality (and, as queer theorists continue to explore the culture, also with race, class and ethnicity). Yet 'queer' may itself be a source of anxiety to many men reluctant to let go of the male/female, masculine/feminine, heterosexual/homosexual binaries which have traditionally supported and structured so much of our thinking and behaviour; and who may find the very word 'queer' repellent because of its history as a derisive, ghettoising term.

In selecting textual examples ranging from the literary classics through popular culture to the very margins of the officially sanctioned and legally authorised, I wanted to explore the ways in which the patriarchal masculine, which is not defined the same way at all times and in all textual genres and modes, nonetheless seeks always to repress and silence the terms on which it relies and which it employs in order to construct itself, chief among these the feminine and the homosexual. In this way, texts seek to reproduce the dominant masculine as both a reflection of a particular social reality and as a model on which men in the culture may pattern themselves. Insofar as the latter aim is successful, masculinity is re-produced.

But the representation of gender, and specifically of masculinity, is not limited to the way producers of texts construct their works. It includes also the way the consumers of texts position themselves in reading and making sense of them. The astute reader of *this* text will have noticed that I omitted to attribute a gender to the anonymous friend cited above. I did so deliberately, taking my cue from Jeanette Winterson's novel *Written on the body*, for in providing a definite gender I would have invited you, the reader, to summon up around the anecdote a whole set of assumptions, even perhaps a fully developed scenario. Depending on your own sex identification, gender affiliation and sexual orientation, as well as (gender-)political stance, these might have included: a wholehearted endorsement of the tenet that all men are bastards; a rejection of the concept as political ranting or the result of personal disappointment; and a suspicion that its speaker might be being ironical and self-parodying. In this way, you would have assisted in constructing a particular representation, and thus have been complicit in affirming particular ideological positions.

The lesson to draw from this is not that we should seek to produce texts *without* ideological colourings: given the pervasive nature and function of the ideological, this would be an impossible task. We should, rather, try to remain conscious of the presence of ideology in representations of all kinds, and to read texts with this in mind, asking not only such questions as 'What does this mean? and 'Do I recognise myself and my experience here?', but also 'What is *not* being said here?', 'Whose interests are being served and whose denied?', and 'Who and what are being represented, and who and what silenced and made invisible?'.

Though this book may bear my name on its title page as sole author, it is in fact the end-product of a sort of cooperative venture undertaken over the course of several years, and with the good will of a number of people; and I wish here to acknowledge this. First, I want to thank John Iremonger, of Allen & Unwin, and his staff: John invited me to submit the idea that became this book, and has supported it throughout. He generously gave me much-needed time to work on the manuscript; and his assistants, especially Jennifer Watson, have been patient with my various requests, anxieties and queries.

The helpfulness and generosity of David Stevenson and Elaine Jones of Holeproof in Melbourne, and Randal Glennon and Alex Fyfe of The Campaign Palace, likewise in Melbourne, must also be acknowledged. Apprised of the fact that I intended to make their commercials for Underdaks men's underpants a text to analyse in this book, Mr Stevenson and Mr Glennon provided me with copies of the commercials on videotape, while Ms Fyfe hunted down the stills which are reproduced here with the permission of both companies. Mr Stevenson additionally made available to me an audiotape copy as well as transcripts of the messages left by callers Australia-wide who took advantage of the toll-free number that Holeproof set up for the public to make known its opinions about the advertising campaign. Mr Glennon, Mr Stevenson and their colleagues remained interested in the work I was doing on the commercials, Ms Jones helpfully correcting some errors in my transcription of dialogue from the videotape of the commercials. Throughout our dealings with one another all these people were courteous, patient and helpful—a scholar could not have hoped for greater cooperation in his research.

Likewise, Mr Al Clark, producer of the film *The adventures of Priscilla, queen of the desert*, proved helpful and expressed interest in my treatment of the film.

Parts of Chapter 5 were adapted from an article of mine published in *Social semiotics: a transdisciplinary journal in functional linguistics, semiotics and critical theory*. The journal's editor, Professor David Birch, of the School of Literary and Communication Studies in the Faculty of Arts, Central Queensland University, has kindly given me permission to rework the material for this book.

Two conference papers, likewise reworked, provided the material for Chapter 6. The first of these, 'Straight acting: masculinity, subjectivity and (same-sex) desire', was presented at the Forces of Desire conference, held at the Humanities Research Centre of the Australian National University, Canberra, in August 1993. The second, which also furnished the title for the chapter, was presented at the Crossroads in Cultural Studies conference in Tampere, Finland, in July 1996.

When it comes to acknowledging my friends and colleagues for their support, patience and willingness to discuss various aspects of the book-in-the-making with me, as well as reading versions of the manuscript and offering advice and suggestions, I feel rather like Captain Louis Renault, who at the end of the film *Casablanca* orders, 'Round up the usual suspects'. The suspects in this case include Ron Blaber, Robert Curry, Dean Kiley, Jene Lloyd Myles, Sarah Schladow, Steve Singer and Leighton Skinner, many of whom have performed the same service for me in other projects of my devising.

I particularly want to thank my very dear friends and colleagues Brian Dibble, Ann McGuire, Margaret Macintyre and Barbara Milech, who have ever been staunch supporters and have made room in their own extremely busy schedules to read my material carefully, annotating it closely with corrections of faulty typography or style, suggested revisions or improvements in argument, and proposed further ideas. Their help—as well as the lively arguments I have sometimes had with them over the material—has been inestimable.

Last, but by no means least, I wish to thank my 1996 third-year undergraduate class in studies in masculinities, in the School of Communication and Cultural Studies at Curtin University of Technology. I tried out some of my material on them and they rose gallantly to the challenge, arguing many of my contentions, finding examples both *pro* and *contra*, and stimulating discussion in the class as well as further ideas in my head.

Some notes on referencing and scholarly practice in this book are necessary. First, in order to avoid any errors in quoting from the films discussed, I have cited dialogue from the published screenplays. Details about the films themselves will be found in the filmography at the end of the book.

Second, with an eye to keeping the endnotes and bibliography simple and accessible, and bearing in mind that readers may not easily find certain journals or specific issues of these in their local libraries (particularly these days, when many librarians are faced with problems of storage space and the cost of continuing the funding of serials collections), I have omitted original publication information of some works in the bibliography, preferring to list collections in which this material has been reprinted. Likewise, with translated or reissued monographs, I have given the more readily available publication. This practice, I am aware, has the effect of telescoping the historical dimensions of the theoretical dialogue and the debates around the material referred to, but I have accepted this as a reasonable cost for providing a bibliography relatively unencumbered with detail that many readers may not find helpful.

Finally, where there are repeated references to a single work, I have provided an endnote referencing the work when it is first introduced in each chapter, and then have cited page numbers parenthetically in the text. In the case of the Shakespeare plays cited, I have provided parenthetical references to act, scene and line number.

*Performance anxieties: Re-producing masculinity* is not intended to be an exhaustive coverage of all aspects of representation, its techniques and technologies, its theorisation and its effects. Nor do I wish the book to be understood, *à la* the work of Morris Zapp (the academic in David Lodge's novel *Changing places* who wishes to put paid once and for all to the Jane Austen scholarship industry), as *the* definitive statement about men and their several masculinities. Rather, I hope that it serves as a model and a starting point for the reader's own explorations and deconstructions of theories of representation, and of ideologies, discourses and politics of gender. I certainly trust that *Performance anxieties: Re-producing masculinity* is not merely—as M. H. Abrams says of deconstruction in his celebrated attack—'a sealed echo-chamber in which meanings are reduced to a ceaseless echolalia, a vertical and lateral reverberation from sign to sign of ghostly non-presences emanating from no voice, intended by no one, referring to nothing, bombinating in a void'.[1]

# 1

# *Fabulous monsters*

At the end of the battle with the Lion for the White King's crown in Lewis Carroll's *Through the looking-glass*, the Unicorn catches sight of Alice:

> . . . he turned round instantly, and stood for some time looking at her with an air of the deepest disgust.
>
> 'What—is—this?' he said at last.
>
> 'This is a child!' Haigha replied eagerly, coming in front of Alice to introduce her, and spreading out both his hands towards her in an Anglo-Saxon attitude. 'We only found it to-day. It's as large as life, and twice as natural!'
>
> 'I always thought they were fabulous monsters!' said the Unicorn. 'Is it alive?'
>
> 'It can talk,' said Haigha solemnly.[1]

This passage provides an interesting introduction to a discussion of the representation of people and gender. It is, after all, the task of representation to make what is represented seem, to the viewer, reader or onlooker, 'as large as life, and twice as natural'. And while the object represented may well, like Alice, be able to talk, the representation itself often speaks more powerfully, if not always so overtly.

The Unicorn's epithet, 'fabulous monsters', is also particularly apposite in discussing the representation, across a wide spectrum of cultural texts, of people as social beings. 'Fabulous', in current parlance, indicates something wonderful, glamorous and attractive, while 'monster' signifies rather something grotesque, terrifying and repellent. Taken thus, the phrase is an oxymoron, its parts appearing to contradict one another.

Etymologically, however, the phrase 'fabulous monster' yields other senses that enable us to explore further the ways that representation contributes to the construction of gender and identity in our culture, as well as their representations. 'Fabulous' derives from the Latin *fabula*, a story or a fable, a narrative frequently characterised by astounding or barely credible themes or details, such as magical objects or powers, or speech by creatures or objects that normally do not speak to humans. The fable might also rework a legend, if by 'legend' we understand a narrative with a kernel of historical fact that custom and retelling have concealed beneath a web of marvellous incident and narrative invention. Fables usually have a point to make: some, like the classical *Aesop's fables*, or those written in the seventeenth century by Jean de la Fontaine, offer a wise proverb or observation about the world and human society; others, like the fables that grew up around the classical myth of Heracles (Hercules, in his Roman manifestation), hold up examples of physical strength and courage and/or moral fortitude for others to admire and emulate.

'Monster', from the Latin *monstrum*, originally meant something that served as a portent or a warning (*monere*: to warn), but later it also came to mean (perhaps by contamination from *monstrare*: to show) something to be put on display and viewed. Shakespeare appears to have both meanings of 'monster' in mind in *Macbeth*, when Macduff jeers at the defeated Macbeth, who refuses to fight:

> Then yield thee, coward,
> And live to be the show and gaze o' th' time:
> We'll have thee, as our rarer monsters are,
> Painted upon a pole, and underwrit,
> 'Here may you see the tyrant.' (V.viii.23–7)[2]

Similarly, in *The Tempest* Trinculo says of Caliban:

> What have we here? a man or a fish? dead or alive? A fish: he smells like a fish; a very ancient and fish-like smell; a kind of, not of the newest Poor-John [dried hake]. A strange fish! Were I in England now, as once I was, and had but this fish painted [as on a board at a fair], not a holiday fool there but would give a piece of silver: there would this monster make a man [i.e. make a man's fortune]; any strange beast there makes a man . . . (II.ii.24–31)[3]

A fabulous monster, then, would seem to be a creature whose very existence is on show, whether as a moral lesson or an admirable model. We might say that representation, insofar as it offers fabulous monsters to our gaze, constructs models of being-in-society that, on the one hand, invite us to desire and imitate those models which society and ideology approve and, on the other, warn us against other possibilities. And it is here that gender and representation intersect in interesting ways, for if representation shows us ourselves, it also serves the important function of telling us how to be ourselves—as men and women in the culture—which in turn implies a warning: how *not* to be.

Commonsense ideas about representation are often fairly naive in that they assume a close correspondence between the representation and the thing or things represented—hence criticisms of films or novels as not being 'true to life', for example; or of fantasy texts as 'unrealistic' precisely because of their fantasy content. However, representation in fact goes beyond the life-likeness or otherwise of texts: it extends also to social institutions and practices, and the ways that these not only organise our lives but enable us to 'recognise' particular versions of ourselves—as law-abiding citizens, felons, parents, children, teachers, students and so on. Thus, even an 'unrealistic' fantasy tale may represent a moral framework that the reader or viewer recognises (and, in all likelihood, approves of also). J. R. R. Tolkien's epic fantasy novel, *The Lord of the Rings*, operates precisely in this manner: behind the imaginary settings and the cast of hobbits, wizards, elves, orcs and the rest, we can discern certain values familiar to us, values to do with love, trust, loyalty, conservation of ways of life and the sustaining of tradition on the one hand, and on the other, hatred, suspicion, treachery, and the destruction of all familiar traditional beliefs and practices.

Representation, then, is bound up with the culture's ideology. 'Ideology' is a critical concept developed notably by Marxist social theorists to describe the power relationship among social classes; however, the term has been frequently misunderstood in popular speech as signifying an obvious, programmatic system of (someone else's) political beliefs imposed on a population or a fraction of it. Thus, at least until fairly recently, communism was held, in the capitalist West, to be 'ideological', and entire nations—the former Soviet Union, China and others—were believed to be held captive and to ransom by this 'ideology'.

However, this was to miss the point about ideology, namely that *it is ideology's task to make itself invisible* in order that it continue undisturbed to sustain the existing class structure and the consequent power relations among social groups. It is therefore in the interests of the dominant class to preserve the ideology that enables its dominance; and this is done by establishing and maintaining a system of beliefs and practices that seem natural and inevitable. We should note though that this is often accomplished unconsciously and without deliberate intent by those with a stake in the existing social order. After all, if ideology were really self-evident, it would be easily resisted by those who, though privileged by it, reject its inequities, as well as by those who suffer its oppression.

So in the example of the criticism of communist 'ideology', what was overlooked—because being thought natural it became invisible—was the possibility that neither capitalism nor democracy is to be found in nature. Rather, both capitalism and democracy are themselves as ideological as communism.

The products of culture, whether in the form of works of art or of social institutions (both of which, for brevity's sake, we will include under the rubric of 'text'), are produced within and by ideology. Indeed, their task, is to articulate the culture's ideology to us and to affirm its validity. If they do so successfully, we readily accept the rightness of the ideology presented. Alan Sinfield remarks:

> The strength of ideology derives from the way it gets to be common sense; it 'goes without saying'. For its production is not an external process, stories are not outside ourselves, something we just hear or read about. Ideology makes sense for us—of us—because it is already proceeding when we arrive in the world, and we come to consciousness in its terms. As the world shapes itself around and through us, certain interpretations of experience strike us as plausible: they fit with what we have experienced already, and are confirmed by others around us.

He goes on to observe that

> The conditions of plausibility which determine what we will believe and accept in what is told or represented to us are therefore crucial. They govern our understandings of the world and how to live in it, thereby seeming to define the scope of feasible political change.[4]

However, something else happens in the processes by which ideology is disseminated and assimilated. It is not simply that the currently dominant social organisation of people is perpetuated and protected, and a particular construction of the world preserved, but also that we are given identity within ideology, and hence enabled to 'find' a place in the social structure—we develop a sense of self, of ourselves as individuals, and of the rightness and inevitability of who we are. To use the terminology of Louis Althusser, we become ideological *subjects*. In a famous passage in his essay 'Ideology and ideological state apparatuses (notes towards an investigation)', Althusser provides a striking metaphor for the way in which ideology interpellates or hails the individual as a subject:

> . . . ideology 'acts' or 'functions' in such a way that it 'recruits' subjects among the individuals (it recruits them all), or 'transforms' the individuals into subjects (it transforms them all) by that very precise operation which I have called *interpellation* or hailing, and which can be imagined along the lines of the most commonplace everyday police (or other) hailing: 'Hey, you there!'
>
> Assuming that the theoretical scene I have imagined takes place in the street, the hailed individual will turn around. By this mere one-hundred-and-eighty-degree physical conversion, he becomes a *subject*. Why? Because he has recognized that the hail was 'really' addressed to him, and that 'it was *really him* who was hailed' (and not someone else). Experience shows that the practical telecommunication of hailings is such that they hardly ever miss their man: verbal call or whistle, the one hailed always recognizes that it is really him who is being hailed . . .
>
> . . . The existence of ideology and the hailing or interpellation of individuals as subjects are one and the same thing.[5]

This being the case, argues Althusser, we are always-already in ideology, since it precedes us and will always interpellate us. Thus, we are always-already ideological subjects.

A number of comments should be made about this theorisation of ideology and how it works. The first of these is a clarification: while it may be true that ideology is always-already there, and always-already interpellating us as subjects, it is also true that ideology is not always the same. That is, ideologies may arise, flourish and decay because of differences in historical and cultural conjuncture. The 'Hey, you there!' addressed to women in a traditional Islamic society, for example, necessarily interpellates them differently from the hailing of women in a secular, Western society, especially where feminism may have made significant changes in how women behave and, in turn, how men behave toward them. Likewise, the interpellation of women even in a given Western society, looked at historically, will also show signs of ideological difference as well as similarity.

Such ideological change suggests that, at any given moment

in a society's history, there is a *dominant* ideology which struggles to maintain its ascendancy over a range of *subordinated* ideologies, not all of which of course are necessarily compliant with it. Here, Raymond Williams' three-part distinction among the dominant, the residual and the emergent elements in a culture is a useful way to conceive of the relations between dominant and subordinated ideologies. Williams suggests that the residual, consisting of remnants of the past, both archaic and relatively recent, may be partly appropriated by the dominant in order both to authorise itself (it thus is seen to have a tradition) and to solicit the support of conservatively inclined groups in the culture. The emergent, by contrast, is generated by significant new social processes and movements, and is not merely novel.[6]

Williams' analysis points up an important difficulty with Althusser's formulation, useful as it is for an analysis of the way ideology saturates all social levels: that is, its implication of a monolithic ideology running uniformly if secretively throughout the social structure. This, in turn, suggests that resistance to such ideological coercion is useless, not only because so much of it is covert but also because, being monolithic, ideology is immovable. Althusserian theory therefore has difficulty explaining ideological change in a culture, short of positing social cataclysm through revolution or some other form of wholesale and presumably conscious process of ideological substitution. However, not all societies have been politically so unstable, yet their dominant ideologies have changed.

Texts thus cannot, in general, encode only one ideological perspective, namely the dominant ideology, because that already implies other subordinated and potentially (if not actually) subversive ideologies. Textual representation, therefore, may be thought of as *ideologically overloaded*, and it is therefore of concern to those social institutions which serve the dominant ideology that the overload be controlled by preferring and privileging certain facets of it, and ignoring, silencing or disparaging others. This is, as Sinfield argues, one of the tasks, if not indeed the chief task, of normative criticism: to foreground the understanding of a text which shores up the dominant ideology and the social structure which stands behind it (see Sinfield, 1992, pp. 1–28).

Therefore, when we read a text of whatever kind, we must bear in mind that the ideology in which its creator lived and wrote, and which is articulated in and by the text, may have changed. It may therefore differ significantly in a number of respects from the ideology with which we are familiar and which makes the social world familiar to us. This does not mean that in order to read Shakespeare, we must first become scholars of English Renaissance culture—though that would doubtless enrich our understanding of the text's meaning. Still less does it mean that we are absolutely forbidden to read a Shakespeare play in terms of our own ideological assumptions—indeed, we cannot help but do this. But it does mean that we should be sensitive to possible ideological anachronisms of our own imposition as we make our way through the text.

Althusser's theory of ideology is not invulnerable to other criticisms. His idea of interpellation is embedded in a larger hypothesis about state apparatuses, specifically: ideological state apparatuses (ISAs) and repressive state apparatuses (RSAs). ISAs include social institutions, such as the family, religion, education and the law (as a complex code of permissible social behaviours and practices); while RSAs include modes of enforcement, such as the police, the military and the law (as a means of coercion and punishment for infractions of the legal codes). Each kind of state apparatus is implicated in the other in both subtle and not-so-subtle ways. It is important to understand, however, that the imposition of these apparatuses is not accomplished in serial fashion; that is, the RSAs are not invoked only when the ISAs fail. Rather, as we can see in the case of the law, which straddles both kinds of apparatuses, the ISAs lend legitimacy to the RSAs, while the latter guarantee compliance by subjects with the former. Thus, the legal codes have force only insofar as they are backed up by a large and forbidding machinery of law courts and officers of the law, together with disciplinary institutions such as reformatories and prisons. And these have propriety of status only insofar as they are seen as serving the judiciary and other ISAs.

This formulation in effect denies political agency to social subjects. That is, Althusser's theory suggests not only that we are irresistibly and unknowingly coerced into acceptance of a dominant ideology, but also that we are actually complicit in that coercion—we acquiesce in our own *subjection* (reduction to subordinate status) as well as our own *subjectivation* (attainment of subjectivity within and through ideology). The implications of this for the reading of culture and of cultural texts are important, for it would seem to indicate—just as in older and cruder versions of Marxist criticism (what Terry Eagleton calls 'vulgar Marxist' readings[7])—that all texts may finally be reduced to the same meaning: the oppression of other classes by one dominant class, and hence the subjection of the individual through the process of subjectivation. If this were the case, then we read the same story over and over again; only the superficial plot situations, the settings and the characters are different. However, literary and cultural critics have produced such multifarious interpretations of texts as to suggest that ideology does not work so simply, forcefully and irresistibly as Althusser's framing of the issue might be taken to indicate.

Michel Foucault offers an alternative way of thinking about this matter in his notion of discourse, which also allows us to avoid the cumbersome phrases 'dominant ideology' and 'subordinate ideologies'. It is important, however, to bear in mind that Foucault's work does not quite run on all fours with Marxist theories of ideology, chiefly because Foucault's is an epistemological investigation (i.e. to do with knowledge), rather than a purely sociological or historical one.

Though 'discourse' is derived from a word meaning 'speech (about something)', in the terminology of much current theory, and especially that of Foucault, the term has come to signify the network of social, political and cultural relationships, including those created by language, which provide the relays for the circulation and dispersal of power across and throughout the social structure. To speak, therefore, of a discourse of gender is not merely to identify gender as a cultural topic, as it were; it is also to signal that gender is implicated in power relationships that go beyond the fundamental distinctions of male/female or masculine/feminine and take in social as well as historical formations of the concept. Foucault's work is dedicated to identifying such formations and to tracing the trajectories which power relationships have taken across them, as well as how power has been central in *constituting* those realities.

A discourse, then, develops both out of and within the historical experience of a culture. Thus, though we may think that a particular discourse—say, that of sexuality—appears to be constant throughout a culture's history, if we pay attention to the terms of the discourse at given historical points, we will find that the social and cultural meanings attached to particular aspects of the discourse have varied. This, in turn, implies something about the ways power is distributed along and through the discourses that intersect with or converge upon that of sexuality. Think, for instance, how in our culture heterosexuality is the dominant sexuality, and what that means *socially, legally and politically* for homosexuals and bisexuals, both male and female. The dominance of heterosexuality also has implications regarding the relative empowerment or disempowerment of men and women generally in the culture, since—especially in a patriarchal culture—heterosexuality may be thought of not only as a sexual desire for the other sex, but also as a matter of who penetrates whom, and what that might mean in social and ideological terms. This issue becomes still more complex in the presence of technologies which can alter the original sex of the subject (or, as many gender dysphorics assert, which can restore the sex felt by the subject to be the 'right' or 'appropriate' one).

These differences in meaning are the result of differences in what Foucault calls the *episteme* on which a particular discourse is centred, and which actually helps to shape the discourse. Foucault describes his project thus:

> . . . what I am attempting to bring to light is the epistemological field, the *episteme* in which knowledge, envisaged apart from all criteria having reference to its rational value or to its objective forms, grounds its positivity and thereby manifests a history which is not that of its growing perfection, but rather that of its conditions of possibility . . .[8]

Briefly to explain this perhaps not very transparent passage: Foucault proposes to trace the conditions by and within which we, as members of a culture at a particular historical moment, 'know' about the world; he is not concerned to assess the truth or validity of that knowledge. The episteme, then, differs from what another theoretical and critical tradition has called a culture's world view, that is, a system of knowledges and beliefs which makes sense of the world to the members of that culture. (With chapter titles like 'Order', 'Sin', 'The chain of being', 'The cosmic dance', E. M. W. Tillyard's 1943 *The Elizabethan world picture*, a staple for many generations of students of Renaissance literature, provides an exemplary case.)[9] Rather, the episteme is that which actually shapes that world view and makes it possible. Thus, an epistemic analysis seeks to identify, first, the *categories of thought* pervading a culture at a given historical point; and, second, *their configuration or constellation* (including their relationship to one another) as typical of or central to the culture at that time.

We can understand this better by way of an example of the sort which Foucault himself discusses in the second chapter of

*The order of things.* In our epistemic world, the things of nature, whether animate or inanimate, can be classified by genus and species. Thus, when we see, say, a snake, we identify it as belonging to a particular class of animal (reptiles), and we categorise it as different not only from other animal classes (mammals, birds), but also from inanimates like stones or trees. We might also identify it in terms of whether it is a domestic or a non-domestic animal. Our system of classification and identification would, moreover, be considerably sharpened if we had a good working knowledge of biology or zoology—we would then be able to invoke classes like vertebrate/invertebrate, and so on.

However, what if we lived in an epistemic world in which snakes, along with other animals and objects, were given other, perhaps more mystical meanings? This was precisely the case in the Middle Ages. For instance, a twelfth-century bestiary (book of beasts) introduces the topic of the snake thus:

> Believe it, SNAKES have three odd things about them. The first odd thing is that when they are getting old their eyes grow blind, and if they want to renovate themselves, they go away somewhere and fast for a long time until their skins are loose. Then they look for a tight crack in the rocks, and go in, and lay aside the old skin by scraping it off. Thus we, through much tribulation and abstinence for the sake of Christ, put off the old man and his garment. In this way we may seek the spiritual rock, Jesus, and the tight crack, i.e. the Strait Gate.[10]

To dismiss this and the rest of the account in the bestiary as the erroneous ramblings of a pre-modern, pre-scientific culture whose individuals failed to observe accurately would be mistaken. As Foucault argues, the cultural episteme shapes not only the discourse, but the way in which knowledge can be gained and 'thought'. In a world which was understood to be a system of interlocking similarities and allusions, all governed ultimately by reference to God, the simple natural (that is, biological) fact of a snake, as we understand it, was not available. Instead, nature was perceived to provide humanity, first, with lessons about the way in which God had made the world; and, second, with instruction in Christian morality and ethics. Questions about the species or genus into which a snake might be classified were therefore minor—if not, indeed, entirely irrelevant—compared with the issue of deciding what lesson about good or evil we might learn from the snake.

Thomas Laqueur's Foucaultian study of the discourses of body and gender, *Making sex: body and gender from the Greeks to Freud*, provides another helpful and fascinating example.[11] His research indicates that prior to the eighteenth century it was commonly held that, though there were two *genders* (masculine and feminine), there was, biologically, only one *sex*. This was because, from the time of the Greeks until the late Renaissance, the female genitalia were understood to be simply the (inferior) inverse of the male. As Laqueur observes, it is not that empirical experience through autopsies and anatomy lessons failed to teach people anything different, but rather that the way in which people *thought* caused them to *see* (to 'know') in certain ways—ways which we today no doubt find utterly foreign, because our own epistemic view of things is so different.

A discourse, then, shapes the way in which the experience of individuals is perceived and given meaning. Indeed, we might say that a discourse, given the episteme on which it is based and by which it is informed, allows us to see in certain ways and not in others. We then operate within the field of a particular *discursive practice*, in that the cultural discourses available to us—and they are many—prompt us to accept and emulate or to reject and condemn certain behaviours or attitudes; these discourses also blind us to other behaviours and practices, so that to all intents and purposes these latter may not even exist for us.

Social or cultural discourse, then, determines *what* can be spoken about, and in what terms and with what sorts of values. It also determines *who* has the authority to speak about and to whom, and who can only be spoken to. Thus, the opinions of congregants or patients are not usually welcomed or treated with the same seriousness as those—such as divines or doctors—who are authorised to speak and empowered by the relevant discourses. In addition, it determines *where* and *when* the topic can be addressed (always and everywhere or only in certain situations and under particular conditions). In this way, sites of power and authority are established within any individual discourse.

It is here that Foucault's theory allows some overlap with theories of ideology. We may understand discursive practices to be ideological, insofar as they tend to reflect and support the discourses of the dominant social class or group. Indeed, several ideologies may be encoded in a particular discourse: the discourse of gender, for instance, embraces both patriarchal ideology, which assumes the physical, sexual, social and political supremacy of men over women, and ideologies that resist that dominance—

feminist, gay/queer, anti-sexist and so on—as well as ideologies governing social position and power.

At the same time, however, the coalescence of multiple ideologies within a single discursive practice allows not only for variety (which is why we don't all think exactly alike within a given discourse) but also for contradiction and conflict. This, in turn, indicates that power is distributed unequally (and inequitably) through the culture. Therefore Foucault, unlike Althusser, acknowledges the emergence and presence of dissenting or resistant discourses, and indeed argues that any dominant discourse necessarily produces a resistant discourse.

For when Foucault speaks about power and power relationships, he does not mean simply the overt exercise of strength or will by an individual or a group upon another individual or group. Rather, *power is part of the way that social relationships and configurations are actually structured*: 'power is exercised from innumerable points'.[12] The very way the family, the smaller and larger social groups, and social and political institutions are structured and function produces nodes or sites of power which influence the way in which we behave, think and 'know'.

However, as Foucault so elegantly points out, power is power only where it can be exercised over sites of dissent and/or resistance:

> Where there is power, there is resistance . . . [The] existence of [power relationships] depends on a multiplicity of points of resistance: these play the role of adversary, target, support, or handle in power relations. These points of resistance are present everywhere in the power network. Hence there is no single locus of great Refusal, no soul of revolt, source of all rebellions, or pure law of the revolutionary. Instead there is a plurality of resistances, each of them a special case: resistances that are possible, necessary, improbable; others that are spontaneous, savage, solitary, concerted, rampant, or violent; still others that are quick to compromise, interested, or sacrificial; by definition, they can only exist in the strategic field of power relations. But this does not mean that they are only a reaction or rebound, forming with respect to the basic domination an underside that is in the end always passive, doomed to perpetual defeat . . . They are the odd term in relations of power; they are inscribed in the latter as an irreducible opposite. (1978, pp. 95–6)

Such resistance in turn creates counter-discourses which often function to subvert the dominant discourse, and thus themselves acquire a different, oppositional power, through the threat posed to the dominant discourse in question and to the group or groups which it privileges. Feminism and the women's movements may thus be said to have constituted a counter-discourse to resist the dominant discourses of masculinity and patriarchy in the culture; likewise, homosexuality and bisexuality, both male and female, constitute a site of resistance which subverts the dominant discourse of pure heterosexuality by revealing an alternative sexuality and sense of the erotic, as well, often, as a different lifestyle. As counter-discourses, they persistently show, by challenging the dominant discourses, the ideological illogicalities, gaps and injustices in those discourses which, of course, try to operate as if natural, inevitable, equitable and normal.

The discursive frames generally deemed powerfully influential in the construction of subjectivity are those of race, class, age and gender (this last term often being made to include issues of sexuality, which, however, arguably form a separate yet equally significant category). The dominant group—whether Caucasians in Australia or the middle class in capitalist societies, or the younger, more affluent age groups targeted by producers in consumerist societies, or men generally in Western culture—develops discourses which confer authority on some, but not on all, members of the society. Those deprived of that authority become social Others, as opposed to the 'I' of the subject, who has a sense of the significance of self through an authorised and empowered social identity and position. The sense of self of those Others—Aborigines, Asians or other non-Anglo ethnicities, working-class people, the elderly, women—is correspondingly unauthorised and disempowered. In Althusserian terms, those Others are also ideological subjects, but they have been interpellated in ways which generally coerce them to accept the status of *inferior* subjects.

Shakespeare again offers an insightful example of this in his tragedy *Othello*. Othello's elopement with Desdemona, the daughter of the Venetian senator Brabantio, becomes the occasion of scandal and gossip, and of intervention by the state in the person of the Doge of Venice. It is important to note here that there are *two* reasons for the disturbance, and both of these, though couched in terms of love/non-love, respect/non-respect and so on, really have to do with social identity and subjectivity. Those reasons are, first, Desdemona's disobedience as a daughter in running away with the man she loves: this act redraws the social relationship between Brabantio and Desdemona, and in effect puts the daughter beyond the father's control (though it also—and with tragic consequences—puts Desdemona within her husband's power).

Second, the fact that Othello is black is not merely coincidental detail. To be a stranger in a particular society positions one in certain ways, while to be visibly different has further implications of an ideological kind. Othello first appears as a social alien who, *despite his difference*, has secured a socially central position commanding respect and honour. As a former slave (I.iii.138), he has had to work much harder for that position than a Venetian might have had to. However, the extreme precariousness of this prominence—which, in a racist discourse, might be viewed as improper, untenable and/or undeserved—is demonstrated in the unfolding of the play's action. Though in the eyes of Venice, Othello may remain a commander—indeed, Lodovico and the other envoys to Cyprus are both puzzled and perturbed by Othello's apparent distemper (IV.i)—in the audience's view (for we have seen Iago working upon the Moor's peace of mind), Othello shifts from the social centre to the margins. This is an exile engineered by Iago, whose machinations create out of Othello (read: strip the veneer of civilisation from the Moor to reveal) a savage (non-European) driven by jealousy to murder his wife.[13]

Desdemona, when challenged by her father, unequivocally states, 'I saw Othello's visage in his mind' (I.iii.252); that is, the colour of his skin was of no account to her in comparison with his other virtues. Yet later, on Cyprus, Iago's rhetoric about miscegenation (racial intermarriage) is sufficiently persuasive that the perplexed Othello himself advances as one reason for his wife's supposed infidelity to him the fact of his own racial inferiority: 'Haply [perhaps], for [because] I am black . . . ,' he sadly reflects (III.iii.267). This example allows us to see how cultural discourses are also ideological, for Iago, in voicing a particular discourse of race, acts as agent for the interpellation of Othello as the inferior Other—inferior, that is, to the white Venetians who have honoured the Moor.

The constellation of the discourses of race, class and gender as central to the fashioning of subjectivity shows how discourses may, and often do, intersect with others, or run alongside one another. The individual's sense of the integrated self—of one's sense of unity as a subject—is thus actually made up of the intersection of many discourses, some of which may exist in contradictory relation to one another. These pre-exist us in the culture, and in order to function and survive in that culture, we must learn them, whether through formal or informal processes (the instruction of children by parents by their behaviour, or of students by teachers in terms of a formally taught ethics—for instance, about how to behave towards people of another race, religion or sexuality); through dominant social practices and behaviours (including what the law of the society defines as licit or illicit); or through language itself, for language encodes many of these discourses for us. And all of these, in turn, are part of the ideology of the culture.

Another way of putting this is to say that as subjects—that is, as individuals with a sense of self—we are constituted through language, through what the culture enables and allows us to 'think' epistemically, and through our positions in the social structure. These factors necessarily, therefore, involve sex difference, gender behaviour, differences in social class, intellectual difference, political allegiances, even philosophical affiliations, sexual preference and practice, and so on. All these aspects of our identities develop through our interaction in the various groups through and within which we move, and with which or against which we identify ourselves.

A series of three commercials aired on Australian television in 1994 and 1995 show how ideological discourses not only converge in particular texts, but may also exist in a contradictory relation to one another. The product advertised was Underdaks, a label for men's underpants manufactured by the Holeproof company. The 'narrative' in each of the three commercials is identical: the scene is set in an airport—at the scanning device through which passengers must pass to check they do not carry any dangerous devices. The scanner is supervised in the commercials by a woman security officer who stands with one hand in the pocket of her uniform trousers (this turns out to be significant in the unfolding of the text's narrative). A handsome, well-built young man walks through the scanner's gateway and a buzzer sounds. The officer orders him to remove his shirt, which he does; but when he proceeds once more through the gateway, the buzzer sounds again. The officer now requires him to remove his pants: he looks at her in exasperated disbelief, but complies, striding through the gateway, this time without further incident. As he passes by the officer, he looks down at her with an expression combining smug triumph and challenging insolence. The entire episode has been watched by another female security officer operating a different scanner; she comes over to the first officer, reaches into her pocket and removes an electronic device which, we now learn, can be made to set off the scanner's alarm. 'One day you're gonna get caught', she tells the first officer. (This is an allusion to the slogan used to sell this product in the 1980s, when the commercials showed various young men who, dressed only in their underpants, were inadvertently exposed to the public gaze, because they had become accidentally locked out of their rooms, or mistaken a department store window for a changing room. The denouement was accompanied by a male chorus warning, 'One day you're gonna get caught . . . with your pants down'.)

The camera next switches to a view of the young man, still clad only in his underpants, striding down the corridor to the transit area, carrying his luggage. He pauses just before turning right and out of view of the camera, and looks back briefly—we presume at the two women officers. There is again the impression of triumph and challenge in his gaze. As we watch him disappear from sight, we hear the final line of the commercial, spoken by the first officer, and it is this that differs in each of the versions. In 1994, two versions were, suggestively, 'Nice . . . luggage', and

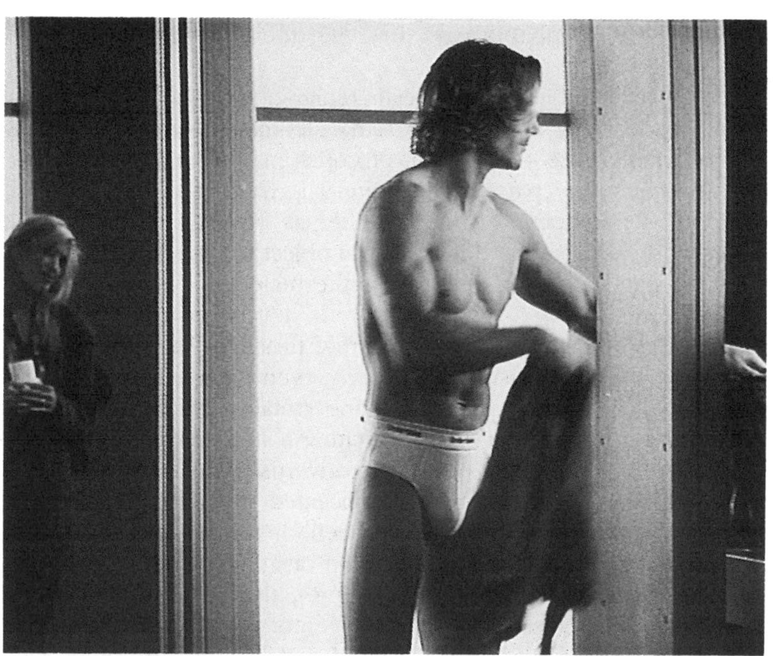

forlornly 'He's probably gay'. In 1995, the closing line was 'One day I'm gonna get lucky'.

What makes these commercials remarkable is the representation of the male body as docile to female command and as available to the female gaze—a reversal, of course, of the traditional power relationship under patriarchy, where it is woman who obeys man, and offers her body to him, whether as object to be looked at, object to be touched and fondled, or object to be entered sexually. That docility, however, also makes the male body available to the *male* viewer.

The advertising industry has rarely flirted in the past with the notion of homoeroticism and scarcely even hinted at the presence of a gay consumer-population. One notable example that suggested there might be a shift to inviting a homoerotic reading was the mid-1980s Sheridan bed linen advertisement. This offered to the Australian viewer a barely concealed nude male body, and though the pretext may have been heterosexual desire (the advertisement was ostensibly aimed at women, the presumed purchasers of bed linen for the home), the advertisement found a particularly enthusiastic audience among gay men. (A similar phenomenon occurred in the United States with the Calvin Klein advertisements for men's underwear, particularly those which used the singer Marky Mark as the model.)

On the whole, however, the gay sector of the population has rarely been directly addressed or presented positively. Much more typical has been the Australian television commercial for Décoré hair products which showed a presumably gay hairdresser becoming almost hysterical because a client had used a Décoré product to colour and highlight her hair herself, instead of relying on his expertise. Thus the familiar stereotype of the homosexual as over-emotional (and hence not to be thought of as masculine) and as engaged in 'artistic' pursuits (in this case, the cutting and colouring of women's hair—likewise not generally thought of as a masculine profession) are re-invoked, and presented as a cause for amusement to the viewing public. In this context, therefore, these three Underdaks commercials courageously broke new ground in cultural representations of gender and sexuality.

This is, however, to look at the commercials from the ideological position privileged and preferred by the texts themselves. Precisely the fact that this position *is* privileged and preferred should alert us to the possibility that other ideological positions may also be present but masked. The stage conjuror provides a

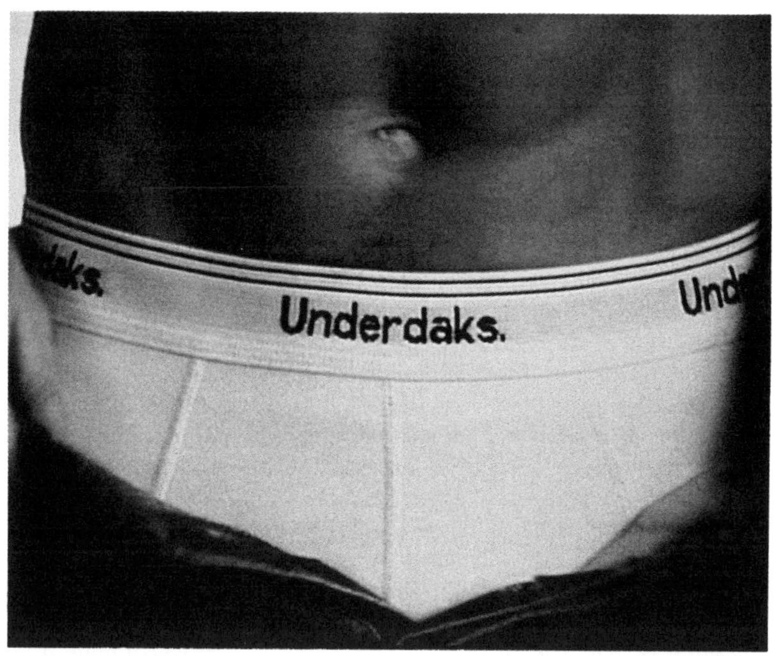
Underdaks.

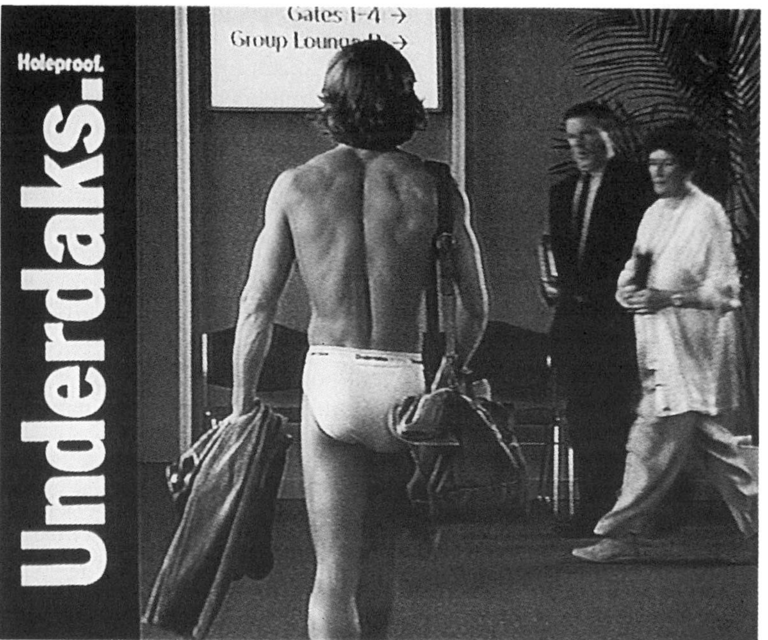
Gates 1-4 →
Holeproof.
Underdaks.

useful comparison with the way ideology often works: we are disposed to take the appearance and disappearance of objects in his hand and on his person as wonderful, inexplicable. But this 'magic' is really trickery, sleight of hand: the conjuror either distracts us by his patter or directs our attention to the hand or part of the body or sector of the stage where nothing is really happening, while elsewhere his hand or hands are busy extracting objects from places of concealment or secreting them there. So also ideology will often direct our attention to an operation or a discourse that may be unremarkable, even quite ordinary or acceptable, or, as in this case, fairly novel and controversial. It thus hides from us another operation or discourse that is the real ideological objective or function.

In the Underdaks commercials, we can discern initially two ideological operations. The first and most obvious we might categorise as the politically correct one, that is, the taking account of developments in feminism and women's increasingly high profile in the culture. These texts thus emphasise female desire for and the feminine gaze upon the male body. This is signalled not only by the events in the 'narrative', but also by the final dialogue of each version: 'Nice . . . luggage' draws our attention to the body of the young man, and specifically to his genital area, which we have earlier seen concealed/revealed by a close-up of his crotch as he removes his pants. Interestingly, the label on the cover of the videotape of the 1994 commercials provided to me by The Campaign Palace, the advertising agency responsible, gives the title as 'Packed lunch—gay/luggage'. While 'packed lunch' usually denotes a meal of sandwiches or the like to be taken to work or school, 'lunch' in Australian gay slang can also refer to the male genitals, as in 'to show one's lunch' or 'to look at someone's lunch'. In the present context, then, a 'packed lunch' signifies a well-filled male crotch. The title thus neatly encapsulates both the final slogans of the two versions of the commercial: 'Nice . . . luggage' and 'He's probably gay'; it may also refer to the way the underpants themselves are designed and cut to make the genitals more prominent.

The line 'Nice . . . luggage' also permits the sort of *double entendre* so beloved in much British comedy: that is, it both articulates female desire—or at any rate the desire of one woman—and denies it. In order to understand the line's erotic signification, we must first understand the coding that surrounds the significant pause before 'luggage' and be prepared to read an erotic sense into 'luggage' itself. Second, we may perceive the young man to be out of earshot of the women, so that the line sounds like the sort of confidence women might exchange privately with one another. However, if the line is taken at face value only, it conceals and refuses the idea of female desire.

'He's probably gay' signals at once the desirability of the male body being surveyed and its inaccessibility to female desire. The line also adverts to what has purportedly been the cry of many women, especially in Sydney, namely, that 'All the good/attractive/sexy men are either married or gay'. The line thus articulates heterosexual female desire but renders it futile or impotent at the same time.

The line 'One day I'm gonna get lucky' suggests a female sexual appetite untrammelled by the constraints normally placed upon female desire under patriarchy; indeed, 'to get lucky' has customarily been used by men to signify success in their sexual pursuits, so its use in this context indicates an appropriation by a female subject of the independence and fabled voraciousness of male sexual desire. Yet the very articulation of female desire in this case also marks that desire as frustrated—and indefinitely so, since 'One day' refers to an indistinct future date which, because of its very lack of certainty, may be infinitely deferred.

Female sexual desire is intricately bound up in discourses not only of gender and sexuality but also of social structure. Much feminist writing—for instance, that of Hélène Cixous and Luce Irigaray—focuses on the differences between male and female sexual desire, and explores the latter in various ways, for instance, through *écriture féminine* (feminine writing).[14] What emerges from the work of these theorists and others is that female sexual desire has often traditionally been a focus of conflicting beliefs, as the dichotomy between woman as either virgin or whore reveals. Jeffrey Weeks shows that in nineteenth-century Britain classifications of female sexuality and desire were often divided along class lines, and underlain by Darwinian notions of evolution. Thus, working-class women were thought of as sexual beings because they were more animal (less civilised, hence less evolved) than their middle-class sisters—and it was working-class women who made up most, if not all, of the population of prostitutes in London and the larger cities.[15] It was amongst these that middle-class men tended to 'sow their wild oats' (an interestingly agrarian and hence 'primitive' metaphor); and it was these women who figured prominently in the pornographic literature of the nineteenth century. Middle-class women, by contrast, were ideologically conceived as virtually asexual, because they were more highly evolved. Indeed, the physician William Acton believed that 'The best mothers, wives and managers of households know little or nothing of sexual indulgence.'[16] Such women's real desire, then, was for maternity—sex was merely the means to that end. (Bram Dijkstra's *Idols of perversity: fantasies of feminine evil in fin-de-siècle culture*, an exploration of the art and literature of the late nineteenth century in Europe, provides interesting examples of the fascination with and fear of female sexuality.)

Female desire in a patriarchal culture is constructed as dependent on male desire, much as a satellite is dependent for its orbit upon the gravitational force of a larger planetary body. The possibility that female desire may be independent of male desire is threatening to contemplate for men in such a culture, for if female desire resists the dominance of male desire, it also resists, both implicitly and explicitly, the patriarchal structure and the way in which this locates woman as subordinate to man.

The full meaning of the Underdaks commercials depends on such a discursive and ideological context. While these texts may invoke in an overt and obvious manner the presence of a feminist discourse and recent cultural history which has seen women take an unusual ascendancy through that discourse, the commercials, as we have seen, present female desire ambiguously, offering it to the viewer but at the same time withholding, concealing or nullifying it. Thus, the commercials both construct and deconstruct female sexual desire, and by simultaneously foregrounding and neutralising the danger it represents to patriarchy, make it comic and 'safe'. Woman may experience sexual desire, but ultimately—so the commercials suggest—it is impotent, and so is she. The sacrifice required (of men) by political correctness—by the recognition of feminist politics—is thus in fact countermanded and redeemed by a different dynamic which restores the traditional ideological and social balance (or inequity).

The second ideological operation in the series of commercials is similarly ambiguous and for similar reasons, here centring on issues of power rather than desire. Within the diegetic (narrative) frame, the first woman officer both represents power and exercises it. Her uniform *symbolises* the power—directly that of the airport authority, but more generally and diffusely also that of the state—which invests her with power and authorises her actions. And in her function as supervisor and observer of the licitness or otherwise of passengers, she *exercises* power—even, it would seem, to the extent of being able to require a passenger progressively to remove his clothing. At one level, therefore, woman is represented as empowered and authoritative; and in this respect we are in the presence once more of an overt ideology of feminist politics. We should note, too, that in the officer's assumption of the authority to demand that the young man strip, the discourse of overt, authorised power converges with that of sexual desire.

However, the second security officer confirms for us that the first officer's requirement of the young man is *not* in fact authorised by the power symbolised by the uniform ('One day you're gonna get caught'). This disclosure has the effect of diminishing still further the officer's apparent authority: she now seems much more a maverick functionary or agent of state power than a wielder of official power in her own right.

Moreover, though the overt objective of having the young man strip is to make him vulnerable by opening up his near-naked body to the female gaze, the narrative instead substitutes a different effect, namely, rendering that body resistant to that gaze, so that it both challenges and triumphs over it and implicitly also over female desire. The man's body is taut and muscular, signifying physical strength and power; the close-up of his crotch suggests that he has large genitals, symbolising sexual dominance and potency; and his return of the officer's gaze may be described as proud, confident, even insolent, suggesting that while he may comply with her order, because of the authority with which she is apparently invested, he remains indomitable: he cannot be cowed by her. That he remains intrinsically independent of her authority, as well as implicitly rejecting it, is shown by his strolling, still in his underwear, in leisurely fashion away from her, rather than hurriedly climbing back into his clothes: he thus converts an ostensible humiliation into his own victory and, at the same time, continues to flaunt his body, inaccessible to the officer, to her desiring gaze. His backward look, as he turns down the corridor, suggests that he is aware that she and possibly also her fellow officer continue to look at him as he distances himself from the site of his intended humiliation.

Read in the ways suggested above, this text in its three variants may be seen to invert the dominant/subordinate relationship between ideologies. It subscribes overtly to an ideologically subordinate position—that of the feminist—which it then presents as acceptable, because politically correct and because it is intended to appeal to women viewers and—presumably—to men who sympathise with feminist politics. Yet that position is really still dissident within patriarchy. The fact of its dissidence is made clear when we understand that underlying the commercial is a further, more covert ideological position which is really traditional and patriarchal: in the end, the commercial seems to suggest, it is still men who control the world and its women.

The commercial thus serves usefully to show how a single text may encode at least two mutually contradictory, even antagonistic ideological positions within a single discourse—here, that of gender relations (we will see later that other ideological and discursive positions are also present). It is not necessary to deduce from this a sort of conspiracy between the manufacturer and the advertising agency that ran the campaign—to suppose that in some smoke-filled back-room somewhere in Melbourne a plot was cynically hatched by powerful businessmen to dupe Australian women into the delusion that the end of patriarchy is at hand, while at the same time secretively signalling to men that business will continue as usual—though our analysis of the commercials might seem to suggest exactly that. Cynicism of some sort there no doubt is, if only because the business of persuading people to buy products is itself a cynical one; moreover, since it seems that women are the more frequent purchasers of men's underwear—for their menfolk, one supposes—there is also a measure at least of irony, if not also of cynicism, in addressing this sector of the buying public in the terms of feminist politics. But the important point is that ideological operations are shifty and complex, and they are all the more powerful in the ways that they may be layered over and under one another, in order to sustain and control the dominant order of things in society. Textual representations both reflect and articulate this; and are powerful agents in the discursive dissemination of ideology in the workaday lives of people.

This is exemplified in the responses to the commercials received by Holeproof. In 1994, the company set up a toll-free telephone number for members of the public to register their comments on the first of the commercials. Those comments mostly fell into the following categories:

- approval of a feminist position which recognises that women and female desire have been traditionally repressed by patriarchal social practices (this category includes those responses from anti-sexist and New Age men);

- hostility towards the use of the male body as object of the gaze (this category contains two principal subcategories: responses from women who criticise the commercial for applying to men the same technique that has abased women for centuries, and responses from men who resent the feminisation of the male body through this technique);
- amusement occasioned by the reversal of the gendered subject–object relationship with regard to the gaze; approval of the suggestion that gay men are attractive objects of the gaze, even to women; and
- open—indeed, on occasion, violent—homophobia, caused apparently by the mere mention of the word 'gay'.

This variety of responses suggests that, ideologically, the commercials were very successful, for even the negative rejecting responses to elements in the text are themselves indications of the reinforcement of the viewers'/callers' own ideological positions, challenged by the apparent progressiveness of the overt ideological message. Thus, whether the Holeproof company successfully sells its product mainly to women who feel that they have been positively interpellated by the commercials, or to men who, though perhaps initially alarmed at the ideological trend of the commercials' narrative line, in the end feel interpellated in familiar and comforting ways, the advertising campaign nonetheless managed to confirm the ideological position (whether we would describe it as progressive, politically correct, traditional or reactionary) of each viewer.

To sum up: subjectivity—that is, the sense of self—is bound up in social and cultural discourses which allocate to individuals the authority to 'speak' certain topics in particular ways. Such discourses necessarily therefore privilege certain kinds of subjectivity—for instance, white, male, Christian, heterosexual—while deprivileging others, so that people in the subordinated category are pressed to acquiesce in their own disempowerment. The point to note here is that dominant discourses of a culture seek to present themselves as inevitable, normal, natural, even universal.

Hence, whenever we read a novel or a newspaper, watch a television sitcom or a dramatic film, listen to the radio or to our teachers, interact with our parents or our friends, a number of cultural discourses are being marshalled and combined in complex and subtle ways. Subjectivity is created or, as it were, un-created; power shifts from individual subject to individual subject, or from group to group, and the culture's dominant (or privileged) ideologies are articulated and reinforced. The representation of subjectivities, therefore, in whatever medium—the media of print, radio, television and film are particularly powerful, because popular—will inevitably draw on the available cultural discourses of gender, race, class, age and the like—in short, on those discursive elements which make up our sense of self, and which therefore contribute to our sense that we are unique.

This works, first, to naturalise the discourses, subjectivities and ideologies of the culture, so that the individual person comes to think in a particular range of ways, and to think a range of particular things—*and believes that the way s/he perceives things to be is normal, natural and universal.* As members of the culture, therefore, we are always subject to a bombardment which is the more subtle because largely invisible and apparently silent, a bombardment which continually invites us or orders us to behave in certain ways or take the consequences. And the consequences can range from the relatively insignificant—think, for example, of the flood of jokes about feminist women or homosexual men—to the physically threatening and dangerous: socially, legally and industrially prejudicial action against citizens, or actual physical violence inflicted on the bodies of individuals.

Second, the articulation and reiteration of certain discourses which both produce and are produced by cultural representations of subjectivity function as a mirror by which we may confirm our own subjectivity in the culture, and hence our power (or lack of it), our sense of identity, and our place in the social structure. In this respect, such representation helps us to imagine ourselves as *self*-fashioned and -fashioning through our identification of a particular set of traits or behaviours, the modelling of ourselves on an individual or group who seem to embody this trait, or through our sense of feeling 'authenticated' when we are successfully interpellated by a particular (and especially ideologically approved) representation. Representations of subjectivity, which must, of course, include representations of sexual and gender behaviour, are thus very powerful and important factors in our day-to-day living in the culture, and contribute significantly to the ways in which we get on—or not—with our fellow beings.

Representation, however, is not always a straightforward articulation of the ideologies and discourses of a culture. Because, as we have seen, these are multiple, and are constellated in many different ways, cultural products often become sites of contesting ideologies and discourses, though the dominant ideological configuration of course will prefer and privilege certain understandings and readings over others. Nonetheless, read against the grain, cultural products can frequently be shown to encode an ideological excess, a mass of contradictory ideological impulses and imperatives: hence the richness, whether actual or only potential, of interpretation of cultural texts.

For this reason Sinfield observes that:

> . . . the texts we call 'literary' characteristically address contested aspects of our ideological formation. When a part of our worldview threatens disruption by manifestly failing to cohere with the rest, then we reorganize and retell its story, trying to get it into shape—back into the old shape if we are conservative-minded, or into a new shape if we are more adventurous. These I call 'faultline' stories. They address the awkward, unresolved issues; they require most assiduous and continuous reworking; they hinge upon a fundamental, unresolved ideological complication that finds its way, willy-nilly, into texts. Through diverse literary genres and institutions, people write about faultlines, in order to address aspects of their life that they find hard to handle.[17]

Though Sinfield appears here to limit himself to literature, what he has to say applies just as much to last night's TV news or last weekend's football match as it does to Shakespeare and the rest of the canon of classical and contemporary writing. (In fact, Sinfield traverses a wide cultural field in his own work.)

When a fabulous monster speaks, therefore, it does so in several voices, but not all of these may be heard or sanctioned or singled out for attention; nor are all these voices necessarily in harmony with one another. Where men and masculinity are concerned, issues of fabulousness and monstrosity may be particularly emphasised in a patriarchal culture's many texts—men and their behaviours may be characterised as heroic or villainous, constructive or destructive, supportive or annihilating, and so on. Yet these multiple facets are also involved in the cultural enterprise of presenting an ideologically unitary model of the masculine, which I have elsewhere called the dominant model of masculinity,[18] and which Robert Connell calls hegemonic masculinity.[19] However, the mere fact that there is cultural pressure to force notions of masculinity into neat representational configurations suggests, first, that actualisations of the masculine tend to stray, refusing to recognise such borders; and, second, that this is the cause of some considerable anxiety in the culture. This seems especially so now that one of the effects of the feminist critique of masculinity has been to re-characterise certain traditionally admired traits among men as reprehensible in some way. Thus, for instance, stoicism has been redefined as emotional blankness or illiteracy; the engagement in the public world (as a worker, say), once viewed as the sphere most appropriate to men and which enabled men to measure themselves against one another as go-getters, pillars of the community and so on, has been seen rather as a flight from personal, emotional commitment, an abdication from the responsibilities of child rearing and education, and the gravitation to an 'all boys' society, which is both exclusive of women and committed to destructive games of power and one-upmanship.

# 2

# *A man among men*

If the premise of the preceding chapter is correct—that representation not only takes place within ideology, but also articulates and disseminates that ideology—then we may infer that the representation of men and masculinity in the culture is not merely accidental or undertaken simply in the spirit of a sort of photographic fidelity and realism. Rather, it is more likely that such representation works to enable men to 'recognise' themselves and each other within the relevant culture and social class, and hence to approve male behaviour in terms of ideological correctness. In such a recognition, therefore, is encoded a system of *prescriptions* ('Men shall be thus and thus') and *proscriptions* ('Men shall not be thus and thus').

The process of recognition begins with the body, for what all boys and men apparently have in common, transcending differences of race, culture and class, traversing the distinctions of occupation, and crossing the limits even of time and history, is of course the penis. It is for this small anatomical difference between male and female at birth that the doctor or midwife looks to the mother and says—not 'Congratulations! It's a baby!'—but 'Congratulations! It's a boy/girl!'. In other words, from the moment we come into the world, we are sexed; and if we are sexed male the mere fact that we possess a penis will provide us with an access to privilege and power in our society.

The ideological connection between anatomical sex and social destiny seems commonsensical. It also underlies one of the older sociological and psychological notions about gender, namely, the theory of sex-linked roles. Developing the idea in the 1940s, the US sociologist Talcott Parsons defined male sex roles as 'instrumental'—that is, aggressive, competitive, rational—and female ones as 'expressive'—that is, nurturing, gentle, emotional, and non-ambitious, even fearful of success.[1] He saw these distinctions between male and female sex roles as complementary rather than as identifying a differential relationship of power. Other role theorists since Parsons have modified and re-interpreted the idea of sex roles for individuals; and some feminists have found the notion useful in identifying the male sex role as dominant and oppressive.

There are, however, a number of problems with sex role theory, particularly in relation to its application to men and to masculinity. Aggressive and/or violent behaviours in males, for instance, have been analysed as *both* the result of the individual man's internalisation of his sex role, as defined by the culture, *and* his attempt to deny or defy it. Of course, theorists have made adjustments and offered explanations for such contradictory results of sex-role theory; and a number of these inflect sex role theory in interesting and subtle ways.

A more radical and intrinsic difficulty with sex-role theory is its implication that there is or can be a 'self' for the individual *outside* the sex role. This is present in the assumption that we, as individuals, acquire or learn the sex role on top, as it were, of our own identities or senses of self. Theories which recommend changes in sex roles thus also imply that these roles can be removed to release the 'real' self underneath, so that it can grow and become functional in the culture independently of the sex role. (Without positing an underlying self these theories must recommend that certain sex roles be supplanted by others in order that the individual function 'correctly' in society. This begins to look very like social engineering, an idea that has a number of political and social, not to mention ethical and philosophical, difficulties.)

Though sex-role theory has lost much of the influence it once had on the theorising of gender, particularly in sociology and psychology, it remains a factor in some of the popular writing on gender. We can discern its presence, for instance, in the work of Robert Bly, who is credited with being the father (in the senses both of 'originator' and 'father-figure') of the so-called 'mythopoetic' men's movement. *Iron John: a book about men* belongs to the comparatively recent genre of men's self-help literature, which constitutes a powerful, because strongly influential, representation of the masculine.[2] It invites its male readers to 'recognise' or refashion themselves in accord with a notion of masculinity whose authenticity is simultaneously constructed and guaranteed by reference to an archaic model of gender and the roles appropriate to males and females which has more in common with myth than with history. That model thus serves to create the illusion of being universally true, and hence more deserving of dominance than the current (and, in Bly's view, severely weakened) model of masculinity, especially in representations which, like the Underdaks commercials, show men as obedient (at least ostensibly) to the demands and commands of women. Much of this kind of men's self-help literature is strongly affiliated with mythological approaches and particularly with Jungian psychology. Even its titles suggest this, for instance, John Rowan's *The horned god* or Sam Keen's *Fire in the belly.*

*Iron John* is an extraordinary pot-pourri of myth, folk- and fairytale, literature (especially poetry—Bly is himself a well known US poet), as well as anthropological practices and rituals gleaned from various cultures, popular psychology and psychoanalysis, personal accounts and anecdote, together with an admixture of the sort of myth or archetypal literary criticism popular in the late 1960s and early 1970s. (One influential text of this school of thought was Northrop Frye's *Anatomy of criticism: four essays*, which attempted to regularise various literary genres into categories relating to myths of birth, growth, union, and death and renewal, associated with various seasonal myths and rituals.) The apparently wide range of reading undertaken by Bly is not matched, however, by evidence of careful and thorough scholarship, despite the scholarly apparatus of endnotes. Thus, we are told about the tale from which the book takes its title:

> One of the fairy tales that speak of a third possibility for men, a third mode, is a story called 'Iron John' or 'Iron Hans'. Though it was first set down by the Grimm brothers around 1820, this story could be ten or twenty thousand years old. (Bly, p. 5)

The dating of the tale at between ten and twenty *millennia* is, surely, rather vague. Moreover, even if the story really has so venerable an ancestry, it is unlikely that it 'was first set down by the Grimm brothers' in its original form. Iona and Peter Opie, for instance, remark:

> The Grimms were the first substantial collectors to like folktales for their own sake; the first to write the tales down in the way ordinary

> people told them, and not attempt to improve them; and they were the first to realize that everything about the tales was of interest, including the identity of the person who told the tale. *Thus, although they put forward ideas about the antiquity and significance of the tales which subsequent research has not confirmed; and although they did not always adhere to the high standards they set themselves, and were willing to mend some of their tales, fitting two and more variants together to make what they believed to be the full story,* their collection (which Wilhelm continued enlarging to the end of his life) stands as the pre-eminent commendation of the traditional tale . . . [Emphasis added][3]

The italicised passage above indicates, not that the Grimms were charlatans as scholars, but rather that, like many other nineteenth-century historians, *littérateurs* and gentlemen scholars, they did not observe the rules which govern modern scholarship regarding the researcher's assumed objectivity toward and non-intervention in the evidence. This in turn suggests that, Bly's optimism about the longevity and authenticity of the tale apart, we cannot know for sure that 'Iron John' has come down to us in either an archaic or an uncontaminated form. This necessarily raises questions about the book's claims for the antiquity and hence the mythic authority of the story.

There are numerous inconsistencies, contradictions and gaps of logic in *Iron John*. For example, the preface states:

> There is male initiation, female initiation, and human initiation. In this book I am talking about male initiation only. I want to make clear that this book does not seek to turn men against women, nor to return men to the domineering mode that has led to repression of women and their values for centuries. The thought in this book does not constitute a challenge to the women's movement. (Bly, p. x)

Yet throughout the book there are references, some of which might be thought jeering in tone, to feminism, women's separatism, their 'feminisation' of men, their wounding of men and so on; for instance, 'In recent decades, the separatist wing of the feminist movement, in a justified fear of brutality, has laboured to breed fierceness out of men' (Bly, p. 46)—fierceness evidently being both a natural and a desirable quality in men. (The connection here between the book's hypothesis and the behaviourist theory—for example, as expressed in Lionel Tiger's *Men in groups*—that modern human behaviours are simply a veneer over more archaic, primitive, even reflexive ones is fairly clear.)

*Iron John*'s attitude toward male homosexuals, again in the preface, is similarly questionable:

> Most of the language in this book speaks to heterosexual men but does not exclude homosexual men. It wasn't until the eighteenth century that people ever used the term homosexual; before that time gay men were understood simply as a part of the large community of men. The mythology as I see it does not make a big distinction between homosexual and heterosexual men. (Bly, p. x)

Since the *experience* of homosexual men is very different from that of their heterosexual counterparts—not merely in terms of the erotics of each, but rather also in terms of society's general acceptance or otherwise of homosexuality, the individual homosexual's sense of belonging or of being persecuted as an alien—it is idealistic, at best, to imagine that a book which 'speaks to heterosexual men' also speaks to homosexual ones in exactly the same way.

The book is also wrong about history: the term 'homosexuality' was not coined until 1869 in German, by a doctor, Karóly Mária Benkert (also known as Kertbeny), and did not enter the English language until the 1890s, through the work of Havelock Ellis.[4] Bly's work errs further in its claim that, prior to the eighteenth century, 'gay men were understood simply as a part of the large community of men': to begin with, 'gay men', both as term and as identity, politics and lifestyle, are a product of the later twentieth century. Placing these before the eighteenth century is thus clearly an anachronism.

In addition, as Foucault is at pains to point out, 'the homosexual', both as pathology and as identity, is the product of a number of nineteenth-century discourses, primary among them that of medicine.[5] Prior to this, the term for a man who engaged in sex with another man was 'sodomite', and it signified one who committed a prohibited act rather than a social identity or a psychology.[6] Bly's remark, therefore, is misleading, for indeed the sodomite *was* seen as part of the large community of men, but the *act* of sodomy could attract both ecclesiastical and civil penalties.[7] It was not usual to identify the man with the act, however; whereas the term 'homosexual' or even 'gay man' does suggest an immersion of the subjectivity of the individual in a particular erotics and sexuality as well as a specific subculture (the 'gay community') and a set of experiences (for instance, the process of 'coming out' to one's family, friends and colleagues).

If it is true that 'The mythology . . . does not make a big

distinction between homosexual and heterosexual men', then homophobia through the ages and in various cultures (though by no means all) becomes exceedingly hard to explain. Equally puzzling is the book's failure to mention, in its citations of initiation myths and rites from a multitude of cultures, rituals of the insemination of boys about to become men, whether through male–male fellatio (oral sex) or the sodomisation of the boys by older men. The omission is all the more significant since Bly cites (p. 262) as one of his sources the work of Gilbert Herdt, an anthropologist who highlighted such practices amongst some of the peoples of New Guinea. It would seem that maybe mythology *does*, after all, make some distinction between straight and gay men; or, to put it a little more precisely, the book screens out those elements that might cause discomfort and anxiety to Bly's (heterosexual) male readers. This is, then, on the one hand an instance of ideologically driven censorship, and on the other an interpellation of a specific sector, even if the largest, of the male readership.

Indeed, *Iron John* generally displays a tendency to trivialise the myths, tales and rituals so assiduously quoted as justification for what proponents of the mythopoetic approach to masculinity are inclined to call a 'deep masculine'. This latter must be sought and invoked in order to avoid the fate of the 'soft male' (the metaphors suggesting bodily penetration of the male and the loss of penile erection are interesting in this connection). For instance, within the space of less than half a page, the book juxtaposes the Greek myths of Apollo and Dionysus, Bhutanese and Hindu myths, and the Christian mythology of Jesus, apparently in order to demonstrate a transcultural (and transhistorical) anthropological 'fact' about masculinity (Bly, pp. 25–6). That a certain figure or event or even narrative structure appears in several mythologies may indeed mean no more than that human experience, for all its variety, is nonetheless limited: the *meaning*, however, of these apparently universal motifs, characters or narratives more often than not depends on the immediate cultural context, and ought not to be so lightly transferred from culture to culture, as Bly seems to do. To take only a simple example, the rising of Christ from the tomb three days after the Crucifixion is understood, in our culture, to signify a number of things, not least among them Christ's divinity rather than his humanity, and a promise to people that they will be resurrected and, if among the saved, will enjoy life after death in the presence of God. However, another culture might choose to understand the story of Christ's resurrection as a simple ghost story, about life *in* death, not *after* it. Thus, a mythic event that offers hope and comfort in one culture might serve instead to frighten in another by emphasising mortality as the end and goal of human life.

Another, more egregious instance of the trivialisation of the meanings of rituals and myths of other cultures may be seen in the following passage:

> We recall that most cultures describe the first stage of initiation as a sharp and clean break with the mother. Old men simply go into the women's compounds with spears one day when the boys are between eight and twelve and take the boys away. Up to that point, the boys have lived exclusively with the women. In New Guinea, to take one example, the initiated men live together in houses at the edge of the village. Mothers in New Guinea carefully refrain from telling the boys anything about the impending events, retaining the element of surprise. As the men lead them away, the boys may be crying out, 'Save me, Mamma, save me!' The mother's world looks wonderful all at once. The women put up a resistance, but it does no good. The old men start to take the boys to, say, an island where the initiator's hut has been built. The mothers of the boys being abducted appear on the bridge with spears. 'Here I am, Mamma! Save me!' the boys say, but the old men drive the mothers back. The mothers go home, have coffee, meet the other women and say things like, 'How did I do? Did I look fierce enough?' 'You were great'. (Bly, p. 86)

It is hard to know where to begin a critique of this account. There is, of course, the tendency to universalise from specific practices, so that what happens in New Guinea (apparently in all the various ethnic and tribal groups) is read back into a sort of world myth about initiation rites. But more astounding than this is the rendering of the event as an empty form which, it would seem, is recognised as a mere anthropological curiosity *even by the people most affected by it.*

Completely absent from this account is any sense that the mothers' silence about what is to happen to their sons may in fact be governed by particular beliefs, practices and taboos, and not by some intent to create dramatic suspense, followed by a theatrical climax; nor does the book appear to be sensitive to any notion that, given some sorts of initiation rites—we have mentioned sodomisation and fellatio, but there are others, such as circumcision of the penis, blood-letting, wounding and scarification of the boys' bodies, or pitting the boys against animals capable of killing them—the mothers' anguish at the removal of their sons might not be mere play-acting. Reducing the aftermath to a good gossip over a cup of coffee, while one's cronies congratulate one on the day's performance, is not only to trivialise the whole thing: it is also to assimilate an important event in a different culture to a middle-class, Western (specifically, perhaps, US) lifestyle, and thus to homogenise *all* cultures and *all* cultural events.

Yet, despite these and other deficiencies, *Iron John* continues to sell to men, which suggests that the book successfully interpellates many men by representing them in particular ways. This, in turn, implies that *Iron John* tells men a faultline story about themselves. A key factor here is the historical conjuncture in which it was published, for Bly addresses a (male) readership disoriented by a number of changes in social structures and practices. These include the increasing female presence in the public sphere, which used to be exclusively a male domain. This has come about partly through feminist politics and the various women's movements, which have resulted in, among other things, legislation for equal employment opportunities for women, as well as legislation against sexism (in language, for instance); a developing social independence among women, for many of whom a monogamous union with a man is no longer either compulsory or expected; and a parallel developing sexual independence, together with an emphasis on exploring the forms and pleasures of female sexuality and eroticism, rather than serving chiefly the sexual needs of men.

In addition, economic conditions have, in the latter part of the twentieth century, made it impossible for men to assume that they will be successful in finding employment, or even in keeping their jobs, and this, in turn, has resulted in a changing perception of men as the breadwinners of society—especially given the movement of women into the workforce after World War Two. As so often in the past, members of the working class have been affected—through 'downsizing', 'rationalisation' and the other euphemisms for sacking workers; but now such dismissals, redundancies and so on have also touched middle management, whose population has traditionally been drawn from the middle class.

One might add to these factors the challenge issued by a more and more vocal and critical gay and lesbian politics to male heterosexuality as an assumed normality among men. We might note, too, that this politics has in recent years also voiced support of bisexuality, hitherto often ignored or assumed to be a way for homosexuals to 'pass' as heterosexual. Bisexuality thus interrogates the cultural assumption that one is *either* heterosexual *or* homosexual. Initiated by a liberationist politics which also saw the rise of feminism in the 1960s, the homosexual/bisexual presence has been accentuated and given higher prominence through the advent of the HIV/AIDS epidemic, initially affecting the gay population in Western cultures most severely. This epidemic has brought many otherwise ignorant people to a better understanding of homosexuality as a social, lived experience as well as an erotic practice, even if they did not approve of it. And, of course, it has also been the gay community which has led the way in finding practices, social as well as sexual, to contain the disease—for instance, advertising safe sex to the general community—and to provide care through hospices for people living with AIDS. In addition, this community has lobbied for funding for AIDS research, and has demonstrated for all AIDS sufferers a humanity and compassion apparently lacking in the general community and the media, the latter especially contenting themselves with blaming the victims. Now, as gay and bisexual men feel less inclined to remain in the closet and as they occupy more public positions, becoming correspondingly more assertive, they subvert not only traditional, comfortable assumptions about homosexuals as a very small and insignificant minority, but also those which characterise homosexual men as effeminate, incompetent cowards skulking in the shadow of the 'real' men of this world. What, for instance, could be braver than a drag queen parading in full fig down a main street, attracting the attention and, all too often, the hostility and derision of those around her—and what could be more challenging to a conservative heterosexual man?

This is, to be sure, an incomplete picture—a mere sketch, in fact—of the historical, social and economic conditions which make up the context of the publication of Bly's book and of the book's readership. Bly's version of this context, however, transforms a very complex situation and background, full of nuances and involutions, into a simplified and flattened-out world of clear shapes and primary colours: men have become 'soft' because they are no longer in touch with the 'deep masculine' within them; women have, however unknowingly, encouraged (or caused) this softening; the Industrial Revolution must also take responsibility since it deprived men of the opportunity to work alongside other men and instead put them in soulless factories and indistinguishable office buildings; and so on. (Incidentally, Bly's notion of social conditions before the Industrial Revolution is astonishingly naive: he appears to suppose that all sons worked cooperatively and productively alongside their fathers, unproblematically imbibing not only traditional skills but also some intangible current of the 'true' masculine [Bly, pp. 94–7]. There is little recognition that many societies in Europe—and in America too, if it comes to that—were stratified by class, nor that there were inter- and intra-class conflicts which must have affected relations between fathers and sons, among others. It is doubtful that many members of the urban working class or the agrarian classes would have recognised the pastoral Golden Age that Bly figures as having been eroded and destroyed by the Industrial Revolution.)

Bly's book offers his male readers a way out of the impasse that has been created around them by 'history' and 'society'—forces over which they have no apparent control. The solution is twofold. The first strategy is to find that which history and society have apparently failed to affect and change—namely, a profound, innate and archaic sense of what it is to be a man; and this the book locates in the male body. That is, a person born with a penis has deep within him a knowledge of masculinity which is transhistorical and transcultural, and which apparently he shares with all other males, regardless of historical or cultural conjuncture. It has merely been distorted, disguised or covered over by historical and cultural events on the large scale and those of the individual's life on the smaller scale. All he needs to restore the balance of things is to look within himself and, with the aid of the knowledge of ancient and exotic myths and rituals, help this deep masculine to come forth. According to the tenor of Bly's book, not only will this free the individual man and make him happier, but it will also bring a greater harmony to the social world around him.

It may well be true that men require more introspection, self-examination and self-criticism than they have traditionally been encouraged to undertake. Moreover, we may understand the present constellation of historical, economic and social conditions as providing that impetus; hence the wealth of books—including the present volume—and articles, not to mention journals, devoted in different ways to studying men and masculinity, or offering men ways of helping themselves. However, Bly's advice in a sense predetermines what that process of self-examination will find: the Wild Man within the male consciousness, figured as Iron John caged and seeking liberation. Iron John and whatever he represents (and it is worth noting in passing that Bly's handling of the various myths which appear in his book tends to vacillate between seeing these on the one hand as metaphors for particular conditions of existence or states of consciousness, and on the other as real beings and situations) become hypostatised as stable realities which underlie all social conditions—it is the latter which become, implicitly at least, redefined as unreal, provisional, temporary.

There is little sense in *Iron John*, therefore, that male behaviours may vary from culture to culture, and between historical periods within a culture: such a recognition must acknowledge also that gender is *culturally constructed*, which would in turn reinstate history as the governing principle, and undo the thrust of Bly's argument that the masculine can be found in more or less identical form across a variety of discrete and different cultures. Instead, using as its premise the biological fact of maleness inscribed upon particular bodies, *Iron John* proposes that masculinity is innate, an essence which all men house within their physical selves.

This collapses the notion of gender into that of sex, blurring the distinction between the social and the biological. Owing much to the work of Robert Stoller and Ann Oakley,[8] the current theoretical distinction between sex and gender differentiates between biological, anatomical givens on the one hand, and social or cultural norms of behaviour and attitude on the other. Born with the primary sexual characteristics of maleness or femaleness, we must *learn* to be boys or girls, men or women. In other words, the categories *boy/girl* and *man/woman*, together with the further categories *masculine/feminine*, have attributes, norms of behaviour and sets of assumptions that must be acquired by individuals living in the culture. It is important to note too, at this juncture, that the categories *boy/girl*, *man/woman*, *masculine/feminine* will tend to make different requirements on individuals in other cultures, depending on how those categories are constructed. It is this difference between sex and gender that produces what Gayle Rubin has called the *sex-gender system*.[9]

This is a useful and important notion, linking biological sex to sociocultural constructions of identity in dynamic ways. First, it disengages the individual's social identity from her or his sex, so that while the latter may be a given, the former may vary from culture to culture and from historical moment to moment. Second, it does away with the idea that biology is destiny—that, for instance, the lot of woman is to bear children, which in turn implies a social structure that positions woman as man's wife, dependent on him for security and social identity, and in turn functioning as his emotional and domestic support system, and limited to the tasks of mothering his children and tending his home. Bly's hypothesis, in contrast, not only confuses sex with gender, together with the attendant distortions of history and culture that we have already noted; it recreates the link between biology and destiny. This is almost explicit in the several metaphors he uses to indicate that each sex has a particular path that it must travel.

In effect, what his book proposes is that 'soft' masculinity is a sex role which men have learned, whether at the behest of women, in the desire to grow close to women, in men's oppression by the anti-male fierceness 'separatist wing of the feminist movement' or simply as a result of large, impersonal forces. Seeking the true path of the 'deep masculine' is therefore merely to uncover an already existing, stable, 'true' male self. Bly seems ironically to be unaware that his exposition of this true male self is also a form of sex role model which he proffers for our attention: a model which appears to encourage a separatism on the part of men, who are invited to turn inward to seek the masculine within themselves and to turn toward each other for confirmation of that masculine.

That Bly's book speaks directly and comfortingly to many men is attested by the growth of the mythopoetic men's movement, particularly in its practical manifestations as groups of men spending time in the wild bonding with each other, exploring their own and one another's life histories, seeing parallels and connections in terms of an overarching mythology, and (re)defining the masculine. These goals are accomplished through the telling of tales, accounts and myths, through the undergoing of rituals, many borrowed from Amerindian peoples (the eclecticism and the decontextualisation that such cultural plunderings imply appears to be of little concern), and through activities such as drumming and meditation. For many of the participants, these sessions may open up old psychic or emotional wounds and make them accessible to healing, provide insights and realisations, and offer directions for the future. However, one cannot help but feel some alarm at the strong conservatism implied by this turning back to 'traditional' notions of the masculine.

For if it is true that everything old becomes new again, then what Bly, in his second main strategy, appears to advocate is in effect the return of what we might call an *ur*-patriarchy, the German prefix signifying 'primitive', 'ancestral'. He accomplishes this through his exhortations to men to seek Iron John and the deep masculine within themselves and one another, and to restore traditions like initiation rites (their disappearance from our own culture, in this account, smacking of a sort of conspiracy against men).

What Bly describes, if only by implication, as a desirable state of affairs—namely a return to an imagined past of male bonding and archaic initiation rituals—is, however, historically and anthropologically unlikely in our culture. In the first place, it figures men as existing in a mutually cooperative, symbiotic relationship with one another, the older initiating and assisting the young directly or through ritual and myth; these transitions taking place smoothly, without any conflict, anxiety or failure. In the second place, Bly's schema intimates a sexual separatism that nonetheless lays claim to establishing an equality between the sexes, so that men do men's stuff, women women's, and these are two distinct but equivalent ways of life. Yet it is precisely against such sex-based divisions of role and function that women have struggled. *Iron John* invokes archaic history and a notion of innate nature to justify the re-establishment of such division between the sexes in its analysis of the Grimm tale, the positive characters being those who 'know' instinctively what to do, what their place is in the scheme of things, and who as well as what the Other is—whether the prince or Iron John himself.

The sort of Arcadian existence that the book imagines, if at all possible, might be viable perhaps in a small, ethnically distinct and perhaps geographically isolated community. It does not seem realistic to imagine such a state of affairs obtaining much purchase on the vast urban populations which dominate most of the Western world today, populations which are interconnected as much by technological means and media as by a now-diffuse and heterogeneous cultural inheritance. Thus, while we may still describe our culture as patriarchal, the *ur*-patriarchy is a nostalgic memory, made—for some men, at any rate—all the more desirable by a back-projected mythology of simplicity and communal harmony, when men were men (and women, presumably, were women, that is, creatures who knew their proper place in relation to men). Or as Bly somewhat disingenuously puts it in an appropriation of an Australian Aboriginal ritual:

> The old men, having brought the young boys away from the community, tell the boys the story of the first man, Darwalla. The boys listen intently to this tale of the original man, their Adam. It turns out that Darwalla is sitting in that tree over there. While the

> boys try to see Darwalla in the tree, an old man comes down the line, and knocks out a tooth from each boy's mouth. The old men then remind the boys that something similar happened to Darwalla. He lost a tooth. Their tongues for the rest of their lives associate the broken tooth with a living connection to Darwalla. *Most of us would give up a tooth for a living connection to Adam.* (Bly, pp. 28–9; emphasis added)

Thus, *Iron John* offers a sort of male-centred, tribal global anthology pieced together from various rites, myths and stories. In the rosy glow of the sort of communal male existence that Bly conjures up for the reader, he seems to forget that such tribal communities were, more often than not, *formal* patriarchies, dominated by a father-figure ('patriarchy' means 'rule by the father') who may at one time have been the literal father of the people (such is the role of Abraham in Genesis), but who often was only symbolically the father and hence the leader of the group. Patriarchies are not by definition egalitarian societies: the patriarch dominates other males in the group not only by virtue of his age, experience, wisdom and precedence, but also, for instance, through his control over the distribution of women amongst the men. The less dominant males are thereby made dependent upon the patriarch for the satisfaction of sexual need and the continuation of their own families. In this respect, then, either Bly is misinformed or naive about how 'primitive' or archaic communities function, or he is disingenuous in presenting a pastoral idyll which contradicts much anthropological and historical research.

For us in any case patriarchy is no longer literally rule by the father in a tribal context. The sense which the term 'patriarchy' has today refers to the fact that men have historically and traditionally dominated the culture, and have been privileged by it. It suggests a diffused control of culture and of the members of that culture by men in positions of power. Patriarchal power may thus be overlooked, especially by men, because it becomes part of the social environment: like the air we breathe, it escapes notice unless we put our minds to searching for evidence of its presence.

Various ideological imperatives help to constitute the system known as patriarchy, and they are in turn supported and ratified by it. Extending across the entire social structure, patriarchy functions rather like a class system. In the first place, it may exclude or marginalise certain individuals and groups—women, for instance, men of certain ethnicities deemed 'effeminate' (a prevailing view of the men of some Southeast Asian groups), or homosexual men. Inferiorised subjectivities, these become Others within the patriarchal structure; but they remain constituent subjects, since they help to define those subjectivities which patriarchy defines as central.

In the second place, patriarchy ranks and thus creates power differentials even among those whom it centralises. In this way, differences among individual men, such as age, physical size and strength, class, wealth, social or political clout, sexual activity or hyperactivity—even penis size—and so on are invested with varying degrees of patriarchal power. It is the aggregation of these elements and their investment of power by patriarchy that we recognise as 'masculinity' or the lack of it.

One implication of this is that the degree of conformity by individual men to the norms established and required by patriarchal ideology will determine the level of 'masculinity' that they are perceived to possess. Yet ironically it is *non*conformity that is often overtly and explicitly offered as the ideologically loaded and valued sign of the masculine. This definition may occur through diffuse familial, peer or social pressure, or through direct challenge, as when a boy is dared by his friends to do something that is socially disobedient, mischievous or subversive. Thus, the outsider, the loner so often represented and celebrated in film, television and literature as masculine because of his stoicism, his independence and his disregard of the outmoded or meaningless laws of the social order, may be seen at another level rather as ultimately *obedient* to the ideology imposed upon men by the patriarchal structure. A further interesting corollary of this is that the *truly* unconventional and disobedient male, such as the 'out' gay man, the flamboyantly effeminate drag queen or the so-called 'New Age' man, is often excluded, proscribed, persecuted or otherwise punished for his sexual or behavioural nonconformity. This inconsistency may be understood as an instance of ideological sleight of hand, wherein an overt imperative—nonconformity—actually masks the true interpellation of the masculine subject as compliant with the dictates of patriarchal ideology.

Though in much feminist writing 'patriarchy' has come to signify the power exercised by all men over women in particular, this sense of the term is problematic for, while all men *potentially* have access to power, not all men achieve it; and many may be deprived of it. Indeed, we might go so far as to say that a person's status in terms of masculinity is defined by whether he—or even she—has a place within patriarchy. Thus, the man who is openly a homosexual may be marginalised and/or rejected by patriarchy (by definition heterosexual) because he is defined as having abdicated, given his sexuality, from the privilege offered him. The gay man who remains secretive ('closeted') about his sexual orientation of course is likely to retain his status as an apparently fully functioning member of the patriarchy. While women have traditionally played a subordinate, disempowered role in the patriarchal structure and its dynamics, those who openly wield power may likewise be perceived as masculine, or at least as masculinised. Thus, remarks and jokes about Margaret Thatcher, the former prime minister of Great Britain, as the 'best man' in government or, as she was dubbed by the press, 'Attila the Hen' identify her, whether fondly or maliciously, as masculine in nature. She becomes an anomaly, and hence potentially dangerous to men.

The man who can attract women and dominate them may become a *representative* patriarch and hence bear a symbolic relationship to the real patriarchs of other cultures. Representative patriarchs would include such types as the powerful executive businessman, as well as the father of a marriageable daughter; and the young stud together with the philandering husband: all of these both derive power from and reflect the dynamic of patriarchal control of women. Nonetheless, the authoritative father figure often remains chiefly a *symbolic* social presence through the existence of uniformed enforcers of the social structure, and hence of its law and order—the police, the military; and, of course, there are father figures who head corporations, institutions and governments, as well as families.

Patriarchy, however, affects not only women but men too. In our culture men are oppressed and isolated by the models of masculinity to which they are expected to conform. To begin with, men struggle with other men competitively for recognition *as men*. Though this rivalry in general may use women to affirm masculinity, the latter is bestowed upon a man by other men. Therefore men have to prove themselves every day to other men. The penalties for not doing so are considerable. These include the stigmatisation of the individual as an unworthy competitor, or even as a non-competitor; his marginalisation within the patriarchal structure; and the diminution of his stake in patriarchal power, or even the withholding from him entirely of the power that goes with being male in our culture. For this reason, fathers incite their sons to be 'men'; boys tease one another about their masculinity and maleness; adult men engage in constant competition with one another, whether in drinking, womanising, sport, or acquiring the business edge: all of these forms of rivalry function to assert one's own claim to masculinity. The effect of this is to produce a male-centred structure which is neither monolithic nor uniformly cooperative. Asymmetries are thereby produced within the patriarchal structure which favour some men over others, and confer more power upon those men than upon the others.

Patriarchy, power and maleness are thus intricately linked in the discourse of masculinity in the culture, and provide a context within which the individual male in the culture learns to define himself and others, and an environment which he must negotiate constantly. One of the ways he does this is by learning the masculine strategies of discipline, which involve acceding to the more powerful until one has accrued sufficient power oneself, and learning to control aspects of oneself which are defined as treacherous.

In other cultures, as Bly is at pains to point out, the process by which a masculine identity emerges in the young individual male requires both a disciplining of the body and the assistance of those who have already undergone the process. Each of these elements is to be found in the rite of passage, the initiation of the boy into manhood, for the rite itself constitutes the discipline and is administered and overseen by those already experienced both in the discipline and in the rite. Bly's account of such rites of passage is nostalgic—such rituals are what contemporary, 'civilised' Western man has lost—and betrays a fascination with the exotic and dramatic—and often literal—inscription of adulthood upon the male body.

Here Bly runs into a problem which he fails to acknowledge explicitly, namely, that formal official rites of initiation marking the passage of the individual male from boyhood to manhood have generally evolved in cultures with relatively small populations. Such cultures form stable, closely knit, homogeneous communities, whose members are able or even required to participate in such rituals since these usually demand witnesses to authenticate the event. Formalised rites of passage of the sort that Bly hankers for are more problematic in modern Western populations of millions, whose members in any case tend to group into population fractions, whether these are defined by social class, age, occupation, sexuality or the myriad other terms by which we may be categorised, but whose specific combinations contribute to our senses of subjectivity, uniqueness and individuality. To stage such rituals for so vast a population would not only present logistical difficulties; it would also be to transform them into mere spectacle, and in all likelihood, therefore, drain the ritual of whatever social, cultural or mythic value that it might once have possessed.

In any case, some rites of passage *are* recognised formally in our culture: the coming of legal age, for instance, entitles the individual to vote, to drink alcoholic beverages, to drive a car, and so on. However, these are not necessarily gender-specific, and such specificity is the main thrust of the argument in *Iron John*. Nevertheless, some population fractions *do* impose or recognise unofficial rites of passage, and may even have rituals for them, though these may not be formally acknowledged or approved by the social authorities—nor, evidently, even considered in Bly's book. For instance, in some subcultures—which include those in schools as well as in the larger social community—a boy's first sexual experience (whether of masturbation or of hetero- or homosexual intercourse) may serve to establish his having undergone some transition into adulthood. In other subcultural groups—as illustrated in Dickens' *Oliver Twist* by the Artful Dodger's tutelage of Oliver as one of Fagin's gang of juvenile delinquents—a boy's first act of petty larceny may be the key to his admission as a member of a community of sorts. Bly's attention to the more exotic rites and rituals of men's initiation suggests that what he laments is the substitution of a boy's *fall* from innocence, orchestrated by history and society and in which women seem to be implicated as responsible, for a *loss* of innocence, managed by older, more experienced men for the younger males of their social group. We might render this more concisely by postulating that in *Iron John* Bly regrets the loss of the tribal masculine in the evolution of industrial, capitalist mass society.

As an example of a popular genre amongst male readers, *Iron John* shows how these men's self-help books interpellate men as maimed or incomplete subjects who may yet attain to a perfect subjectivity. The book proposes that they do so by returning to an idealised—and, in Raymond Williams' now-familiar terms, both dominant *and* residual—notion of 'authentic' masculine subjectivity located either in a past with traditional values or in an alien society which preserves, it would seem, those same values. Nostalgia is always conservative in nature; but here it masks the gender politics that have disenfranchised women (and gay men) in the first place by apparently *disavowing* any political conservatism or desire to disenfranchise. Likewise, while Bly's book proposes a liberation of the 'deep masculine' within the individual man, at the same time it instructs men that the way to achieve this is by conforming to a universal notion of 'masculinity' which, in fact, neglects or disparages the process of individual self-fashioning through individual experience.

In place of that nostalgic vision of a once-and-future primitive utopia with lots of male-centred ritual now lost to history but partly recoverable from the myths, stories and practices of other cultures, we may draw a more realistic picture: a patriarchal structure in which power circulates unevenly among men who must compete with one another for access to power and privilege, seeking the approval and affirmation of other men in this competitive process. Seen thus, 'masculinity' signifies a constant condition of tension, anxiety and rivalry for males in the culture, because the withdrawal or refusal of masculinity by one's peers often calls forth humiliating penalties, which may arrive swiftly and stay forever. It is, in effect, one's denunciation as a man, marking one insufficiently masculine, and hence, by a rather simple logic, as insufficiently male. Feminised in the eyes of his fellow men, the unfortunate man not only may be the more easily deprived of power, he may also become the butt of scorn, ridicule and sometimes even of violence at the hands of other men. *Pace* Bly, this sort of event—which is commoner than one might suppose, and often makes an early appearance in the form of schoolyard bullying—is engineered by *men*, not by women or the forces of a vague notion of history. Because of the competitiveness encoded in patriarchal discourse and the latter's resultant capacity to reward or penalise, in our culture men punish other men for being men; but they also punish them for not being man enough.

# 3

# *Strictly ballsroom*

We noted in the preceding chapter that it is the penis which identifies men as males across historical and cultural boundaries; but how does such a minor physical difference between the sexes produce such a major sociocultural distinction between men and women, and enable some men to dominate others? After all, as Richard Dyer observes, 'Male genitals are fragile, squashy, delicate things; even when erect, the penis is spongy, seldom straight, and rounded at the tip, while the testicles are imperfect spheres, always vulnerable, never still'.[1] He goes on to remark that 'penises are only little things (even big ones) without much staying power, pretty if you can learn to see them like that, but not magical or mysterious or powerful in themselves, that is, not objectively full of real power' (Dyer, 1985, p. 31). Clearly, then, the diminutive penis must undergo some sort of cultural transformation to become a symbol of power.

The real anatomical penis may be distinguished from the symbolic *phallus* (from the Greek, via the Latin, for 'penis'). The phallus signifies the penis *erect*, a symbol of power rather than the anatomical object itself, which is flaccid most of the time. Our culture is, of course, not the only one to have fetishised the phallus: a number of cultures have done so, including not only the Graeco-Roman one from which our own culture descends, but also, for instance, Hindu culture, in which the *lingam* or divine phallus is regarded as a holy object. The universal anatomical sign of maleness is thus also, for many societies, a cultural or mythic sign of male power, of sexual union by the male with the female, and also of the domination of the female by the male. It is often also the sign of the domination of a powerful male over other less powerful ones.

The phallus thus has become a potent symbol in the ways in which the culture constructs masculinity. The discourse of masculinity is therefore also the discourse of phallic power. Another way of saying this is that masculinity is *phallocentric*, or centred on the phallus as the symbolic sign of power. (It is important to understand, in this connection, that the term 'phallocentric' does not mean—as sometimes it appears to do in popular parlance—that men think about their penises constantly or act simply according to the dictates of the penis, even though at times this may seem to be the case.) For men in the culture, therefore, the social universe is phallocentric, that is, it turns on and privileges the symbolic and powerful phallus, so that men, as possessors of the penis and hence bearers of the symbolic phallus, are the beneficiaries of that social universe. Thus, it is the power accrued about this symbol that motivates men within the patriarchal order and energises their actions and their behaviour.

The phallus as a symbol, however, is not to be identified with an actual penis, because no actual penis could ever really measure up to the imagined sexual potency and social or magical power of the phallus. We might think of the relationship as, in a sense, intertextual: that is, the material penis refers to the symbolic phallus. (Interestingly, this reverses the usual relation between the symbolic and the material, whereby the former refers to the latter.) The distinction between penis and phallus, then, is akin to that which divides sex from gender, in that the former term of each pair is biological/anatomical, the second social/cultural. The first is simply a fact, the second a complex of meanings. For, as social creatures, human beings operate in a world which is made up of more than merely facts: the human world is also the world of meanings, of communication through language and through other social systems. In such a world, then, the physiological fact of possessing or lacking a penis becomes the starting point for a series of symbolic substitutions and correlations which result in a real social status in which the individual may desire, wield or lack social power to a greater or lesser degree. The penis, then, divides males from females not only biologically but socially

That the relation of the penis to the phallus belongs to a discourse of power can be seen by examining one preoccupation of many men and boys, namely, the size of the individual's penis.

In much popular discussion on the subject as well as in pornographic representation, penile size is viewed as though it were for the benefit of a man's female partner that a penis should be as large as humanly possible without actually creating a freak of nature—a sort of human tripod. However, as many studies, both formal and informal, have indicated, penis size does not seem to be an issue for many women, by whom a very large penis may be viewed as aesthetically grotesque and/or absurd, and experienced as physically uncomfortable or painful during sexual intercourse. Yet penis size remains a focal concern for many men. And just as many homosexual men are obsessed with the matter as heterosexual ones, which explodes the idea popular with many heterosexual men that the large penis is man's gift to *woman*. This concern about penis size suggests, moreover, that the individual man must compare his own organ with those of other men, whether actually or in his imagination only. And any such comparison takes its meaning and significance ultimately from a connection with the phallus as symbolic signifier of power. Additionally, it provides the ground for further anxiety since it introduces the (potentially) homoerotic into a masculine discourse that defines itself as heterosexual.

The erect penis not only indicates erotic arousal, it also directly demands the attribution to it of the phallus. The greater the penis, then, the closer its owner comes apparently to appropriating the symbolic phallus and its power for himself—and the greater the threat, consequently, to other men. However, since no man can ever actually finally appropriate the phallus—though many men may try to do so—it remains a free-floating sign in the culture; and it attracts to itself power from a number of sources, and not only from areas to do with penis size and/or sexual performance. These sources include a man's sheer physical size and strength, social position, professional or industrial leverage, and wealth, to name a few.

Though the phallus is not directly or completely accessible to men in the culture, nevertheless some men have better/greater means of access than others. The phallus is equated with male power, and in this context the reverse potential of the equation also comes into play: if a = b, b also = a. So, if the penis = the phallus = power, then power (of any kind) = the phallus = the penis. And if the degree of appropriation of the phallus depends in part on penis size, and in greater part on the power available to an individual man in the culture, the equation becomes somewhat more complicated, but works nonetheless in the same way:

a large penis = greater appropriation of the phallus = a greater proportion of power (assumed or understood)[2]

The equation can also be manipulated and reversed:

much power = greater appropriation of the phallus = a large penis (assumed or understood)

To put it more clearly, the 'well-hung' stud may attract power because of a direct allusion to the phallus; but the powerful businessman, the idolised rock star and the notorious womaniser, among others, may likewise have attributed to them greater penile size, sexual potency or erotic capacity than they in fact possess. Whatever its origin, the fact that power connects all sources of itself acts as a sort of solvent to render invisible the details of those sources of power. In this way, biology, cultural symbol and social conditions become woven into a complex structure which confers power on men.

In order to assert maleness against femaleness on the one hand, and on the other to assert one's masculinity against that of other men, the relation of the actual penis to the symbolic phallus must be simultaneously asserted ('I have one') and shown to be a close relationship ('Mine is a big one', that is, most resembling the symbolic phallus). Accordingly, therefore, the actual fragility and insignificance of the penis—particularly in its normally flaccid state—must be disguised and abstracted. Hence, in popular thought, especially amongst men, the penis is always imagined erect, powerful, emulating the archetypal phallus. For similar reasons, many men remain painfully conscious of penis size, something that makes sense only when the penis is actually erect, since the size of the flaccid penis can be misleading.

However, since the erect penis threatens disruption because of its direct reference to the phallus and its accrued power, patriarchal ideology decrees that it should not be shown. By this proscription the erect penis becomes *obscene*, not only in the word's familiar legal sense but also its original, theatrical sense, namely, as something violent which was not to be represented and shown on stage but instead referred to indirectly. We should recall, though, that the definition of the erect penis as obscene in the familiar sense, together with its attendant socio-legal ramifications (for instance, the charge of pornography) and consequences, *originates with men.* Thus, though the representation of the penis is often officially prohibited on the grounds that it offends women, in fact the problematic if powerful relationship between symbolic phallus and actual penis (and the anxieties that this produces for men in general) requires that the penis (especially erect) remain absent from many kinds of representation because it worries *men* rather more than it does women. The penis, then, is/should be a clandestine, *understood* thing. Indeed, we may say that the phallic power that derives from the possession of a penis depends, precisely, on the *hiddenness* of the penis itself.

As a consequence, representations of the nude male body in art and photography have traditionally shown its penis as flaccid, and quite often of modest size. In this state, the penis does not offer so direct a challenge by reference to the phallus. However, the body itself may often be converted into a phallus by means of different strategies and techniques. For instance, the body may be represented as engorged and swollen with musculature; the pose of the body may be aggressive and/or dominant; the angle of vision may favour the male body against other objects in the frame, and/or in relation to the viewer; and so on. Thus the fragility and insignificance of the real penis may remain camouflaged, even though actually represented; the direct challenge of the penis to the phallus is deflected, and we are offered a representation of the male *body* as powerful, dominant, menacing or heroic. Nevertheless, concealed in and even informing such an image—small, flaccid penis and all—is the symbolic phallus, erect, powerful, dominant.

The affiliation of the penis with social power through the symbolic phallus is one reason that men often become erotically focused on the penis, though it is well known that there are many erogenous zones on the male as well as the female body. If the penis is the individual man's access to the power of the symbolic phallus, then it must of necessity become more than a simple genital instrument. It becomes the man's connection with power, which he must demonstrate in various ways—by conquering and dominating woman, by seeking his own sexual pleasure, and so on. In the last couple of decades, both the various women's movements and a number of sex manuals have attempted to direct men away from this simple economy of penis–sex–phallic power. Nevertheless, cultural discourses still press the individual male to make this connection. As a result, men may be made confused and angry, or confused and incapacitated by such overt directives—perhaps not to the point of impotence, but certainly to the point of making every act of sex a focus for anxiety that the individual man may not be performing up to some sort of standard or not responding to the needs of his partner, while at the same time experiencing guilt, shame and/or embarrassment for responding instead to those ideological imperatives that tell him that his penis comes first and everything else must be subordinated to it.

Next, and this is a corollary of the first point, to be a man must necessarily entail not merely biological, anatomical maleness through possession of a penis, but also recognition *by other men* of one's status as a potential bearer of the phallus, and hence as a rival. This is encoded into ideas about an individual being a 'real' or 'man's' man, as well as into the sort of behaviours associated with *machismo*, which includes seeking to dominate other men as well as women (though Arthur Flannigan-Saint-Aubin interestingly calls for a different notion of the masculine which he defines as testicular rather than phallic, and which he sees as less aggressive and more cooperative[3]). Such ideas and behaviour identify the individual as a declared rival of other men for power, and situate him in the hierarchy of patriarchy. This is a rather different situation from the idealistic, mutually cooperative *ur*-patriarchy imagined by Bly.

A yearning for an *ur*-patriarchal order of sorts is to be found also in *Strictly ballroom*, a widely acclaimed Australian film which won the Prix de la Jeunesse for Best Film at the Cannes Film Festival and was runner-up for the Caméra d'Or prize. It was nominated subsequently for 13 Australian Film Institute awards. In many ways, *Strictly ballroom* belongs to a new generation of Australian film. Instead of the hazy feel, almost pastel colourations and naturalistic lighting typical of the sorts of historical film that put Australian movies on the map in the 1970s—examples include *Picnic at Hanging Rock* and *The getting of wisdom*—we have clear focus for the most part, and bright, even garish colours and lighting; and in the place of vistas of the Australian landscape, whether domesticated by farming or apparently untouched, we are presented with the confines of a suburb of an unnamed Australian city—presumably contemporary, though the costuming and general *mise-en-scène* remain indefinite on this point. (The older style of Australian film is also the object of commentary by *The adventures of Priscilla, queen of the desert*, discussed in a later chapter.)

*Strictly ballroom* refers ironically and parodically to the dance and musical films of the 1940s and 1950s, when the genre was dominated by the MGM studios. The plot line of *Strictly ballroom*, about a star dancer who, abandoned by his partner, chooses an unknown with little dance experience as his new partner and goes on to win acclaim, refers us to at the same time as it borrows from older examples of the genre, such as *Easter parade*. Thus, *Strictly ballroom* on the one hand *distinguishes itself from* an existing Australian tradition and style of film, and on the other *identifies itself with* another non-Australian film genre.

Texts and the cultural representations they encode rely on the presence of, and the viewer's or reader's ability to make connections among, a variety of other texts. That is, we never view a movie or read a narrative in a void, unrelated to any other text. Rather, we make associations between the text before us and the various other texts and kinds of texts we have experienced. Such relationships are *intertextual*, and help to knit together into an apparently logical whole the representations and the texts of a culture.

Intertextual connections may be produced deliberately, through a conscious borrowing or quotation from one text, or allusion to one text by another. Thus, if we recognise a quotation from a particular movie—for instance, Maria von Trapp/Julie Andrews turning and singing at the summit of the hill in *The sound of music*—while we are watching a cartoon (and cartoon series like 'The Simpsons' often make such allusions), we have made an intertextual connection that has been placed there for us to identify.

However, intertextuality is produced by more than simple quotation or allusion. For example, it also allows us to identify different genres and the expectations—of characterisation, of narrative closure, to name a few—which genre prompts. This is how we know to recognise film techniques such as are used in *film noir* when we see them in cartoons or in episodes of television situation comedies; and to distinguish among different kinds of narrative—for instance, romance, fantasy and crime fictions—*even when we commence a text with which we are not yet familiar.*

Intertextual connection not only assists us to identify genres, styles or quotations and allusions, it also increases the 'thickness' of a particular text, which then seems enriched with meaning, or locates itself in a particular textual tradition with which we are familiar. (We might think, for example, of the number of times we have read a text or seen a film, and have picked up implications, inflections or references that our acquaintances have failed to recognise: such instances signal that we have made intertextual connections which our friends have been unable to make.) Intertextual identification serves another purpose also: it embeds the text under consideration in a particular set of textual and ideological discourses. Our recognition of an intertext thus implicates us, as readers, in that discursive configuration.

Intertextual relationships may also be unconscious, produced by the idiosyncratic connections made by an artist within her or his store of literary, film or other experiences; or such associations may be conditioned by the texts and preoccupations of the culture as a whole. Thus, in *Strictly ballroom*, the attempt (ultimately successful) by Scott Hastings (Paul Mercurio) to dance his own steps in defiance of the rules of the Dance Federation and its president, Barry Fife (Bill Hunter), has its own counterparts in other films and may be summarised as the struggle of a young man to assert himself within a pre-existing, usually male-dominated and hence patriarchal structure; this is a narrative we are familiar with from Westerns, 'teen' films, stories of young rebels and the like.

At the same time, intertextual relationships may be set up by the idiosyncratic reading practices and reading history of the consumer of a particular text. This may occur, of course, because she or he is reminded of another text by the one to hand—thus, my reading of *Strictly ballroom* in terms of the *ur*-patriarchy presented in Bly's *Iron John* is produced by my own intertextual connection of the one with the other, rather than by a deliberate association between the two made by the film's screenwriters and director. However, intertextuality is also a mechanism by which each of us *builds up the repertoire* that allows us to identify and distinguish between various genres as well as specific texts. It is through such intertextual association that the viewer of, say, *Star wars* is able to recognise the now famous opening announcement on the screen, 'A long time ago in a galaxy far, far away . . .' as a variation of the code which begins a fairytale ('Once upon a time in a land far, far away'). This assumption is justified by the unfolding of the story of Luke Skywalker (Mark Hamill), Princess Leia (Carrie Fisher)—a princess is *de rigueur* in many a fairytale—and Han Solo (Harrison Ford), who fulfils the function of the hero's helper often required in such stories. The *Star wars* trilogy not only narrates how peace eventually comes to the galactic Empire, it also enumerates the tasks that the story's hero must undertake successfully in order to *be* a hero and, not coincidentally, to find his place in the hierarchical order established by the narrative (the line of succession to the imperial throne is evidently male only: it is Luke, not Leia, who becomes the next ruler). Therefore, Luke's courage, his ability to act decisively in an emergency, his attainment of the status of Jedi knight and finally as the ruler of the Empire are key elements both of the narrative genre and the ideological narrative about how a young man locates himself in the social order. The initial recognition of the narrative as, in part, generically that of the fairytale also suggests that generic identifications are always provisional and must continually be tested as one makes one's way through the text. Intertextual references and connections are central to such identifications.

The opening statement of *Star wars* also signals a second genre, namely, science fiction and its panoply of galaxies, starships, interstellar travel and the rest. This usefully demonstrates not only that *texts may be multi-generic* and so may have more than one project to bring to a conclusion, but also that readers and viewers develop complex, sophisticated notions of genre and genre-attribution, in which the process of making intertextual connections again plays an important part.

Intertextuality may also function to elaborate meaning in a given text. As we noted in our discussion of the Underdaks commercials in Chapter 1, the line 'One day you're gonna get caught' alludes to the slogan for the same product in the commercials of an earlier decade. This is an intertextual understanding; however the line makes sense in its context without this knowledge. Likewise, the closing line of each of the three versions of the commercial carries a weight of meaning when considered intertextually in relation to the others that it does not possess alone.

As we have seen, then, there is an intertextual connection between *Strictly ballroom* and such films as *Easter parade*—which we might dub the theme of dancer-makes-good-despite-abandonment-by-partner. Other connections are the theme of true-love-attained-through-show-biz-connection, as exemplified by Fred Astaire–Ginger Rogers and Judy Garland–Mickey Rooney movies and their ilk; or the familiar story of the ugly-duckling-turned-beautiful-swan, unfolding in *Strictly ballroom* in the transformation of Fran (Tara Morice) from the dismal, unattractive, clumsy creature of the film's beginning to the vibrant, beautiful, passionate dancer at its end. Some of the film's appeal derives from the setting of such familiar story lines in an Australian context, so that there is a comic clash between the urbanity, sophistication and exoticism (because American) of, say, a Fred Astaire film and the somewhat rougher, more provincial and (to Australian audiences) familiar dialogue of *Strictly ballroom*. It is, however, through the knowledge of such intertexts that we are able to predict the eventual union of Scott and Fran in this film.

This predictability, while it may often make for a boring cliché, is also capable of causing the audience to experience a certain satisfaction and thus helps to create the 'feel-good' quality of many a movie. Indeed, the published screenplay of *Strictly ballroom* includes three reviews, all of which indicate to a greater or lesser degree the 'feel-good' appeal of the film.[4] However, 'feel-good' quality is frequently also produced by a text's closure on an ideologically approved narrative ending, so that we are left with the sense that the way things are is all right, and that everything eventually turns out for the best, in life as in the movies.

The ideological power of film and its ability to engage in dominant cultural discourses are, therefore, not to be underestimated. Take, as one instance in *Strictly ballroom*, the way that heterosexual coupling is figured as the social good of each individual: while this is of course so powerful an ideological directive in our culture that such coupling becomes 'normal' and 'natural', it is here tied also to the notions of social and professional success, and to the notion that it is good for each of us to pursue our particular dreams, ambitions or goals, presented in *Strictly ballroom* as Scott's desire to create and publicly perform his own dance steps. The closing sequence of the film invites us to contemplate the realisation of all of these: Scott successfully defies the will of the Dance Federation President Barry Fife (Bill Hunter) and has won over the loyalty of another young hopeful, Wayne Burns (Pip Mushin) and his partner Vanessa Cronin (Leonie Page), as well as of Les Kendall (Peter Whitford), Scott's dance instructor and, up to this point, Fife's creature.

Further, Scott has found love with Fran, and he has been welcomed and encouraged (admittedly after some initial hostility and suspicion) by her father Rico (Antonio Vargas) and grandmother Ya Ya (Armonia Beneditto), who together have taught him to dance the *paso doble* that proves to be both so insurrectionary and so successful in this dance competition. As an added bonus, Scott's father, Doug (Barry Otto), regains some measure of pride and self-respect, enabling him not only to encourage Scott to defy Fife (as he himself did so unsuccessfully before Scott's birth) but also to restore the 'proper' balance in his marriage to Shirley (Pat Thomson), to whom he has surrendered his authority as head of the household. Thus, the heterosexual couple are figured not only as the origin of the family as social centre and model, but also as an integral part of social, personal and professional development and satisfaction. We might note, moreover, that at this point in the film we witness the closing phase of a young male's effort to position himself advantageously within the dominant order, which—unsurprisingly—is patriarchal, heterosexual by definition.

This closing sequence is important also in that it brings together visually two social classes that the film has hitherto kept separate. Scott's gravitation from the dance studio to the house at the back of the Toledo milkbar where Fran, her father and grandmother live, is not only a transition from ballroom dancing to a genre which we might classify broadly as Spanish flamenco: it marks also a move from one social group to another. The ballroom-dancing group is largely middle-class—or so it imagines itself to be: this is signalled, for instance, by the Hastings' living room, shown to us at the beginning of the movie. With a décor strongly reminiscent of the 1950s, the room strives hard for a bourgeois notion of elegance and comfort which it fails to attain—for instance, the sofa's cushions are just a little *too* casually plumped and placed; the display cabinet behind the sofa is so full of ballroom dancing trophies that it speaks of a desire to impress, to make a mark on the world. Likewise, the largely kitsch[5] dance outfits of both the men and the women and their unappealing pastel, acid or candy colours, together with the obviously dyed, teased and sprayed-into-place hairstyles of the women, reach unsuccessfully for some notion of a middle- to upper-class elegance (which the film in fact parodies through the costuming and hairstyling)—yet Les Kendall's dance studio appears to be located in a run-down, dingy part of town. Indeed, ballroom dancing as a genre is presented in this film as a fantasy of escape into a world of upper-class glamour, but which instead topples over into a kitsch universe in which women are constructed as hyper-feminine and men as hypo-masculine. It is as though this world is inhabited by living Barbie dolls, who signify all that is considered appropriate to femininity, but whose partner Ken dolls represent everything *in*appropriate to masculinity.

Fashion is much simpler, if more sombre, in the house behind the milkbar, seemingly not a very prosperous business in an undistinguished part of town: the back of the house (and therefore also of the milkbar) abuts on the railway tracks. At one level, of course, this is a sign both of the family's socioeconomic impoverishment and their marginalisation as working-class people and possibly also as foreigners to Australia. However, Scott's trajectory to this poorer but less pretentious part of town is foreshadowed by his being costumed early in the narrative largely in black and white, whether in tie-and-tails or in his singlet and trousers: this colour scheme marks his difference from the rest of the ballroom-dancing fraternity and his affinity with the family at the Toledo, from whom, of course, he will learn a new style of dance. (Scott's appearance in singlets, incidentally, may be said to signal his masculinity—the singlet has become part of the traditional representation of the working-class 'ocker' Australian man; but at the same time the singleted, hairless or lightly haired, muscular torso has become an icon of the male body desirable to *gay* men. Scott's is thus an interestingly ambiguous image.) Shirley Hastings' concern about Scott's involvement with Fran, therefore, appears to derive in part from the latter's difference from Scott in terms of nationality and class, as well as from Shirley's anxiety that Scott find the appropriate partner for the Pan Pacific Grand Prix competition—that is, someone appropriately compliant with the rules of the Dance Federation as laid down by Barry Fife.

However, we may discern in this transition of Scott's, from studio to milkbar, a movement also from one patriarchal structure to another. The world of the dance studio and of ballroom-dancing championships is a limited world. Shirley works in Les's studio, while her husband Doug appears to be a general dogsbody and factotum for Les. There is no indication that Scott does anything to earn a living, aside from pinning his hopes on winning the Pan Pacifics. Nor does Fife appear to have a day job. The only one in this milieu who does, interestingly, is a minor character, Scott's friend Wayne, of whom we catch a brief glimpse in a hard hat and overalls working on a road. (Wayne's structural function in the narrative is akin to Han Solo's in *Star wars*: to help the hero.) In other words, this is a faux bourgeoisie: it conceals its means of production in order to engage constantly in an activity which others might regard as unproductive and belonging to a leisured class. This is all illusion, however, since the world of ballroom dancing is shown to be quite limited—and limiting.

In this film ballroom dancing, both as an activity and as an institution (with a Dance Federation, which has a president, rules, a judging body and so on) may be understood as metaphors for patriarchal authority and the hierarchical order that this implies. The presiding genius of this world is the absurd Barry Fife who, by virtue of his position—evidently long-held—as Dance Federation president, may be thought of also as its dominant patriarchal figure: aside from Scott, both the men and women of the ballroom-dancing world represented in the film acknowledge and defer to his authority. However, just as the participants in this world belong to and constitute a faux bourgeoisie, so the hierarchy may be understood as a pseudo-patriarchal structure.

For in the genuine article, riven though it is by competition and thus a perpetual cause of anxiety for men, there is always the tacit recognition that change is possible *within* the hierarchy: competitions for power are won and lost, and new individuals take precedence within the structure—otherwise what incentive would there be for men to compete with one another? In the film, however, Fife's efforts to control who dances as well as what steps are acceptable—even, as we discover toward the end of the film, to determine who will win the Pan Pacific Grand Prix championships—signal that this is not a true patriarchal system; or perhaps rather that it is patriarchal domination taken to its logical extreme, in an attempt to freeze the system and render static its intrinsically mobile (and hence potentially threatening) nature.

The other males are ranged in an obsequious subordination to Fife as patriarch: Les Kendall defers to him, as does the young hopeful Wayne Burns, while Doug Hastings is a nonentity—indeed, we learn that he has been effectually, though symbolically, castrated even before Scott's birth by Fife's machinations to prevent anyone dancing steps that he had not authorised. Doug Hastings functions in effect like a eunuch at Fife's court, the latter's sultan-like tastes indicated by his lecherous touchings and pinchings of the female contestants and by his (presumably) illicit affair with a woman judge. Indeed, one might say that Fife's practice is to castrate and disempower any man who might resist him, and thus he is enabled to control that man—Ken Railings (John Hannan), the increasingly alcoholic and out-of-control champion dancer, is a case in point.

Scott, however, refuses to knuckle under, and so much of the film is devoted to revealing Fife's twistings and turnings in his effort to maintain the upper hand—in particular, his use of Les and of Scott's mother, Shirley, as emissaries to do his bidding and bring Scott to heel. Indeed, knowledge of the Bogo Pogo dance step, which poor Wayne keeps asking people—Scott and Fife, for instance—about, acts as a sort of sign of empowerment in this film; and when Fife demonstrates the step with Wayne's dance partner, the unsubtle simulation of sexual intercourse that this entails, at least in Fife's rendition, suggests further that this dance step also signifies potent male sexuality. This has its own significance when we consider that the only other character whom we see dance this step is Scott.

If individual creativity represents a threat to this patriarchal structure and therefore must be suppressed, so, too, must signs of any real sexual activity and potency be curbed and repressed. Though the costuming of the women which exposes much bare flesh and the nature of Latin American dances like the samba suggest sexuality, the latter is subverted through parody and stylisation. (Liz Holt, Scott's vagrant partner, played by Gia Carides, is childish and strident, while the stylisation of certain steps, together with their relatively limited sequencing, removes the suggestiveness of the dance.) Scott presents a further threat to Fife here: in choosing Fran as his partner, he defies the unwritten law that his dance partner is to be decided for him by the dominant order, which includes not only Fife but the servile Les and the submissive Shirley. And when Scott's relationship with Fran becomes an emotional (and therefore potentially sexual) one, the threat to the almost-absolute authority of Fife as patriarch is given new force.

For the young man in social reality, the business of finding a place in the patriarchal order is paramount. Not only is it the most rewarding game in town in terms of the acquisition of power, but the acknowledgment by other men—including those invested with power—of the individual male's right to a position in the order enables him to develop and mature *as a man.* Otherwise, young males are kept perpetually under-age and juvenile (and potentially feminised, therefore). In *Strictly ballroom* this is represented in Fife's control of Ken Railings and Ken's resulting alcoholism as a way of dealing with being kept subordinate; and in Doug Hastings' childlike obedience of Fife, Shirley and Les. Indeed, most of the males in the ballroom-dancing group behave toward Fife like schoolboys toward the playground bully—submissive, eager to please, compliant, complicit. Scott refuses, and in this we may discern his determination to grow up, to become a man, in all senses of the phrase. But Fife's order of things is only a simulacrum of true patriarchy, signalled by the unnatural colours favoured by the dancers, the highly stylised and limited dance routines available to the contestants, and such obvious fakery as Fife's wig, as well as his evident hypocrisy and self-interest.

This, then, is one of the elements foregrounded in the final episode in the film. Confronting it is a different, more powerful style of patriarchal ideology and order, which is introduced into the narrative precisely through Scott's involvement with Fran. Against the provincialism and artificial tradition of Barry Fife and his troop of sycophantic, competitive twirlers and spinners are matched the history of Europe and specifically of Spain, the long and glorious tradition of Spanish dance and its origins in folk and cultural practices, and a discipline which is both rigorous and passionate, whether applied to Fran's comings and goings or to Scott's attempts to learn the *paso doble* as the Spanish dance it. Embedded in this is an ongoing project to masculinise the central character, Scott Hastings—after all, ballroom dancing is not today regarded as a particularly masculine occupation, and this is underscored by the generally 'unmasculine' colours of the men's dance outfits. At the same time, there is a masculinisation—or perhaps a re-masculinisation—of Scott's incarnator, Paul Mercurio: familiar to Australian audiences as a ballet dancer, Mercurio of course runs the risk of stigmatisation as homosexual, since—as we 'know'—all male ballet dancers are gay. (For a useful account of the positioning and sexualisation of the male dancer, see R. Burt, *The male dancer: bodies, spectacle, sexualities.*)

The masculinisation of Scott is accomplished in part by representing Scott as lacking a father figure. Though Doug is Scott's actual father, he is, for much of the narrative, merely a cipher, without presence or authority, and generally bossed around by his wife or ignored by his son. Fife's paternalism is manifestly a strategy to gain the confidence of others, particularly younger men like Scott; there is no true fatherliness there. Les Kendall, though helpful and amiable toward Scott, is too much under Fife's sway to be able to function as a surrogate father to the young man.

Scott therefore looks elsewhere, outside the ballroom-dancing studio and fraternity, and through Fran finds Rico. Where Fife appears to be single and childless, Rico has been married and has a child, namely Fran; and though there is an older woman, Fran's grandmother, her authority in the family is different from and subordinate to that of Fran's father. In taking Scott under his wing and teaching him the *paso doble*, Rico extends a father's hospitality and imparts a family tradition, as it were.

In contrast to the mere formalism and mincing gliding technique taught Scott by his ballroom-dancing teachers, Ya Ya tells him rather first to feel the rhythm in his body and to allow that to direct his movements. In this way, feelings and emotions are introduced into Scott's dance repertoire. This binds him more closely to Fran, who earlier had difficulty with the more bloodless forms of ballroom dancing; and it especially creates a bond between Scott and Rico, who takes over from Ya Ya Scott's induction into Spanish dance, and into the family. That Scott makes the acquaintance of feeling and passion in dance through a woman is paralleled by his initiation into love by that woman's granddaughter: both instances suggest that emotion in a sense emanates from and thus belongs to the realm of the feminine. Scott is able to mobilise these experiences as part of his rebellion against the suffocating constraints of the pseudo-patriarchy headed by Fife.

Though Scott's attempts to dance a *paso doble* are ridiculed by Rico and Ya Ya, their eventual acquiescence to Scott's pleas to teach him how to perform it properly signals, at the symbolic level, their willingness to admit him to the structure of authority that obtains in this domain of the narrative. Aware of the growing attachment of the two young people to one another, Rico and Ya Ya in effect accept Scott as a possible contender for patriarchal power—a feature noticeably absent in the Fife scheme of things.

In the scene in which Scott makes the crucial transition to the new, 'real' patriarchal structure, Fran's family and their friends—and, eventually, Scott also—celebrate by singing and dancing on the back veranda. The camera positions us, the viewers, to see a train rush past the house towards us. At first apparently part of the party, the engine, with its rounded nose and its long array of carriages, suggests an enormous phallus. We may read this scene, then, as indicating that phallicism and patriarchy, in the true sense, inhabit the clearly working-class environment of the Spaniards, not the would-be middle-class hot-house atmosphere of the ballroom.

Spanish dance implies Spanish culture, which in turn invokes Latin *machismo.* The ways the male body is used in Spanish dance tend to accentuate the man's physical power and maleness: the body is held more rigidly than in ballroom dancing, in which it is more pliant. Thus, the *paso doble* which Scott learns lends a new phallicism—absent in ballroom dancing—to his physical presence. This is particularly so in the closing sequence, when Scott and Fran defy Fife and the Federation and dance the *paso doble* as it should be performed: Scott wears a highly decorated and spangled, but traditional, toreador's jacket lent to him by Rico.

This item of clothing exaggerates the shape of the male wearer, widening the shoulders and narrowing the hips and providing a sort of gilded carapace that suggests a heavily muscled body; and it refers us to the tradition of the bullfight, in Spanish culture deemed a true test of a man's strength, agility and power.

The jacket also functions almost literally as the mantle of the patriarch about the young heir-apparent's shoulders. In case we should miss the point, the scene is photographed so that the jacket's decoration produces an aureole of light, suggesting a Grail sought, fought for and won. Though Scott's conflict with Fife has been about his right to dance his 'own steps', in the end it is *Rico's* steps that Scott performs, clad in *Rico's* jacket. And in doing so, he dethrones the fake patriarch and exposes the hollowness of his empire; but—and this is important—at the same time he accepts and submits to the authority of another patriarchal figure.

The two patriarchs, the true and the false, and their values are brought sharply into confrontation in the closing sequence when Fife silences the sound system and orders Scott and Fran off the floor. It is Scott's father, Doug, defecting to the real patriarchy and thus able at last to find a scrap of his own, long-unused masculinity and virility, who effects the shift of allegiance of practically the whole assembled throng, by clapping—not the *coplas* of Spanish flamenco, to be sure, but strongly rhythmical enough to enable Scott and Fran to continue their *paso doble*, and their defiance of Fife.

The intimate and mutually sustaining connections among maleness, the penis, phallocentrism, patriarchy and masculinity produce the phenomenon of male homosociality. '"Homosocial,"' explains Eve Kosofsky Sedgwick, 'is a word occasionally used in history and the social sciences, where it describes social bonds between persons of the same sex; it is a neologism, obviously formed by analogy with "homosexual", and just as obviously meant to be distinguished from "homosexual". In fact, it is applied to such activities as "male bonding", which may, in our society, be characterized by intense homophobia, fear and hatred of homosexuality.'[5] Patriarchal masculinity, then, may be described as homosocial, if we understand by this not merely the practice of male bonding within the patriarchal structure but also—and importantly—a system of surveillance whose purpose is to ensure that men behave in certain ways, if they wish to be accorded the status of 'masculine'.

At the same time, homosocial processes function to protect the dominant model of masculinity—which is above all heterosexual—from confrontation or encroachment by possibly subversive elements. Sedgwick's remarks indicate what the chief of these are: she explicitly names homosexuality, but in her invocation of male bonding she also implicitly indicates that the other element is the female/feminine. Thus homosociality is both an imperative and a set of strategies that instruct and enable men to group together with one another, so that male solidarity emerges through the reciprocal effects of male bonding and the watchful observation by other men.

Such a situation is in effect a political one, and leads to a state of constant anxiety for men, because one of the effects of such a homosocial imperative is that men come to depend for their definition as masculine upon their being recognised as such by other men within a patriarchal dispensation of power; by the same token, that status may also be withheld by other men. All men, therefore, are required by the discourse of patriarchy to demonstrate their manliness to other men. This, in turn, involves the inferiorisation of at least some of these men, frequently accomplished through such behaviours as aggression. Inevitably, therefore, an uneasy cultural and ideological environment results: men are required simultaneously to identify with other males *and* to compete against them (in order to pass muster under their surveillance).

Sedgwick proposes that homosocial relations among men are founded on desire, which she defines as 'not . . . a particular affective state or emotion, but . . . the affective or social force, the glue, even when its manifestation is hostility or hatred or something less emotively charged, that shapes an important relationship' (Sedgwick, 1985, p. 2).

> To draw the 'homosocial' back into the orbit of 'desire', of the potentially erotic, then, is to hypothesize the potential unbrokenness of a continuum between homosocial and homosexual—a continuum whose visibility, for men, in our society, is radically disrupted. (Sedgwick, 1985, pp. 1–2)

Homosocial desire, in Sedgwick's terms, may be seen to function in *Strictly ballroom* in Scott's urgent need for his own identity, expressed through his innovative dance steps, to be recognised and accepted by Fife, and through him by the Dance Federation; in Scott's antagonism toward Fife; and in his developing affinity with Rico. All of these relationships and developments may be described as homosocial, and as reflecting or evoking desire, as Sedgwick defines it.

The principal female characters—Shirley, Fran, Ya Ya, Liz—are not merely subordinated to these homosocial, desiring relationships among the male principals; they are represented as actively involved in fostering and perpetuating them. Indeed, as Sedgwick suggests throughout her exploration of male homosocial desire, women and their bodies often function, in representation, as the sites upon which male homosocial relations may be established and maintained, the presence of the feminine deflecting any suspicion of the homoerotic or, worse, the homosexual. Thus, Shirley seeks to smooth the way between her son and the Dance Federation president and hence to preserve the patriarchal order in which she encourages Scott to find a place, while Fran provides the contact between Scott and her father, as well as functioning as one important cause for the rift between Scott, his mother and Barry Fife; through the metaphor of dance, Ya Ya inducts Scott into the ways of the patriarchal order signified by Rico; and Liz, like Shirley, is anxious to conform to the requirements of the power structure which defines her as a desirable dance partner, and hence to maintain the status quo.

The various homosocially desirous and conflicting relationships and the rivalrous groups they construct are expressed symbolically in the film through the hair of the male principals. (This may seem an odd association to make, but it is not surprising if we recall that hairiness is, in our culture, associated with maleness.) Thus, Les Kendall's coiffure is a ridiculous, minuscule and somewhat effeminate blond pompadour arrangement, a hairstyle echoed by the fuller blond bouffant of the dandyish Ken Railings, Scott's rival: both Les and Ken have submitted to the authority of Fife and indeed are guilty of collaboration with him in his schemes to prevent Doug Hastings and then his son Scott from contesting his authority. The falsity of Fife's own position and authority is reflected in his rather obvious wig—also blond—which becomes dislodged from his head in the rebellion toward the end of the film. Thus all three men are signalled as implicated in the pseudo-patriarchy by virtue of their hair colour and/or styling.

Both Scott and Rico, by contrast, have full heads of dark hair, though Rico's is tinged with silver, as befits a patriarchal figure: this 'coincidence' serves to connect them visually in the audience's mind (as, incidentally, does the fact that Rico, unlike Les and Fife, has a trim body, similar to Scott's). Without wishing to transform the film's narrative into an account of the Battle of the Hair People, we might infer that Scott's luxuriant head of hair is intended as a contrast with those of the ballroom-dancing establishment (the false patriarchy), while it simultaneously foreshadows and is an expression of that belonging to an alien, but strong Other (the real patriarchy).

By contrast, Doug Hastings' head is evidently balding, a fact not disguised by his careful combing of the remaining locks of hair. This interestingly locates him outside the two male homosocial groups defined by hair colour and style, though it aligns him implicitly with Fife, who likewise is bald beneath his wig. This notion is reinforced by the fact that in the dream-like—indeed, cartoon-like—sequence accompanying Fife's account to Scott of his father's failure and resultant breakdown, Doug is shown as possessing a full head of luxuriant, glossy black hair: this, of course, connects him symbolically with Scott and Rico; but the fact that it is quite obviously a wig also allies him with Fife, as does the fact that it is once again a pompadour styling of a man's hair. This, in turn, suggests that the young Doug mistook the pseudo-patriarchy for the real one, and so submitted, in some form, to the authority of the pseudo-patriarch.

Scott's rebellion and subsequent success, then, may be understood not only as a vindication of his impulse to be creative on his own account as a dancer, nor solely as the tale of a young man who competes against other men for a place in the patriarchal hierarchy and proves himself worthy, though it is both of these. It is also the story of a son who more successfully repeats his father's struggle for such a place (and, in the process, erases his father's failure), and thus may be metaphorised as every (young) man's fight for recognition from other men and the rewards that flow from this. In this, the film locates itself intertextually in relation to a range of other similar stories, beginning with the sort of fairytale or folk tale in which the young hero, in gaining the hand of the princess, realises that he is in fact a prince (it is the male version of the Cinderella story), and including films of male adolescent rebellion, one example of which is the James Dean classic *Rebel without a cause*.

*Strictly ballroom*, then, offers us another faultline story, and one which, like Bly's, is conservative. In the linear evolution of the film's narrative is concealed a range of issues within the patriarchal social order, which in actuality men must confront, and if they are to be regarded as 'real' men must surmount. The film makes this challenge seem unproblematic and success inevitable. Scott's triumph masks the fact that he, like all men, must *continue* to compete and will always find rivals. Also made invisible by the narrative is the notion that power gained by one man is almost always also power lost by another; moreover, those that really gain in this politics of the patriarchal order are not always the ones who appear successful—Scott's victory over Fife takes place only at the cost of his aligning himself with Rico, which necessarily augments the latter's base of power as a possible patriarchal figure.

The narrative is so structured as to invite the audience, first, to *want* Scott to make this transition from Fife's false patriarchy to Rico's real and more male one, and, second, to cheer when he does it. Slipping the shackles of Barry Fife's control, Scott appears to launch himself into liberty and independence; what the film causes us to overlook and indeed to accept wholeheartedly is that he has in fact entered into a much more powerful, because less obvious and overt, patriarchal system in which he is the newest comer, and hence the least empowered. The manipulation of the cinema's audience so that it applauds this transition also causes it to accept the idea of a strongly masculine, and therefore powerful, patriarchal tradition; and this is signalled in the film itself by the overflowing of the competition audience on to the dance floor so that all now enjoy the symbolic benefits of patriarchy, each in his or her own way through dance. The audience also feels good at the end of the film not merely because its hero has—apparently—won out against all odds, but also because we have tacitly accepted and approved the ideological directives (about patriarchy, about masculinity, about the place of women, among others) held out to us by the narrative structure and its closure.

Like *Iron John*, *Strictly ballroom* postulates an *ur*-patriarchy in which men both young and old may feel at home. However, whereas Bly seeks this structure in archaic and exotic societies, *Strictly ballroom* proposes that such an *ur*-patriarchy always-already and therefore still exists within the culture: the severe but fair and cooperative order which Rico represents lies outside the world of the pseudo-patriarchy which, by inference, we almost always inhabit. This other order is shown to be in effect within the reach of any man dissatisfied with the (illusory) scheme of things. Scott's success is the dreamed-of fulfilment of all men, the film suggests, and is available to all men; though, as we have noted, in the end his triumph is really Rico's. We recognise the conflict and applaud its successful completion, which carries with it the vindication of the individual male's existence—Scott Hastings as Everyman—and the promise of emotional reward, sexual fulfilment and social security—the transformed Fran as Everyman's prize. In being encouraged to applaud and hence tacitly approve the outcome of this narrative, we are also being ideologically positioned to acclaim the very notion of a patriarchal order. In this way we become—however unintentionally or tacitly—complicit in its continued existence in one or another form.

# 4

# *Degen(d)erates*

In terms of its preferred reading, *Strictly ballroom* recounts to us the ideologically correct narrative of a young male who finds a place for himself within patriarchy by identifying in himself and asserting a masculinity acceptable to the (true) patriarchal order. In thus becoming a man, Scott Hastings implicitly finds appropriate the hierarchical nature of that order. What of the individual male who either fails to live up to the prescriptions and proscriptions of the patriarchal structure or, alternatively, exceeds these?

Such figures suggest alternative ways of being a man, and in so doing call into question the ideology underlying and informing patriarchy. It is necessary, therefore, that preferred readings of any representations of the 'inadequate' or 'excessive' male in the culture's texts show him as excluded and/or punished in some manner, by way of object-lesson to the reader or viewer.

Two texts, William Shakespeare's *Antony and Cleopatra* and Bram Stoker's *Dracula*, belonging to different genres and written several centuries apart, show interestingly that one discursive strategy is to expose the problematic male figure as somehow degendered and hence also degenerate. While it is true that Shakespeare's tragedy belongs to a culture with a different episteme from our own, and therefore articulates somewhat different ideologies and discourses, it is also the case that by the time of its composition (around 1607), English culture had been much perturbed by perceived disjunctions between biological sex and gendered behaviour. Linda Woodbridge, for example, remarks that 'Male effeminacy is a recurrent theme in the formal satires of the 1590s: the satires of Marston, Hall, and Guilpin are full of commentary on foppishness; and other such specialized perversions of true manliness as female impersonation, male prostitution, and buggery in academe receive mention as well';[1] while Lisa Jardine notes that in 1583 '[Philip] Stubbes had been incensed enough at the extravagances of men's doublets; he became even shriller in his denunciation when he drew attention to the fact that women were wearing identical doublets, thus obliterating the customary distinction between male and female costume'.[2] Even the body of Queen Elizabeth I herself had been subject to cross-gender identification (a notion to which we will return later in this chapter).[3]

Toward the end of Shakespeare's play, the Queen of Egypt, immured in her tomb and threatened by Octavius' Roman forces, reconstructs—ostensibly for Dolabella's benefit—the image of the now-dead Antony. It is a famous set piece, in which a colossal Antony is depicted, an Antony who is identified virtually with the universe itself:

> His face was as the heavens, and therein stuck
> A sun and moon, which kept their course, and lighted
> The little O, the earth . . .
> His legs bestrid the ocean, his rear'd arm
> Crested the world: his voice was propertied
> As all the tuned spheres, and that to friends:
> But when he meant to quail, and shake the orb,
> He was as rattling thunder. For his bounty,
> There was no winter in 't: an autumn 'twas
> That grew the more by reaping: his delights
> Were dolphin-like, they show'd his back above
> The element they lived in: in his livery
> Walk'd crowns and crownets; realms and islands were
> As plates dropp'd from his pocket. (V.ii.79–92)[4]

As rhetorically persuasive as this reminiscence may be, it produces an Antony such as we have not in fact witnessed in the earlier part of the play. The cosmic magnanimity (in all senses of the word) which Cleopatra now attributes to him is a transformation of what we have seen to be Antony's more sensual enjoyment of excess, and also of his generosity toward friends like Enobarbus.

That same generosity, from another perspective, however, may be understood as the behaviour of a wastrel. Octavius says curtly to Lepidus, who is willing to give Antony the benefit of the doubt regarding reports about his behaviour reaching Rome:

> You are too indulgent. Let's grant it is not
> Amiss to tumble on the bed of Ptolemy,
> To give a kingdom for a mirth, to sit
> And keep the turn of tippling with a slave . . . (I.iv.16–19)

Since, given the *Realpolitik* of the play, it is Octavius Caesar who finally wins the struggle for power, we should not take his characterisation of Antony as sensual profligate for the merely uncongenial comment of a cold politician. The play, of course, positions the audience so as to favour Antony over Octavius. Nonetheless, the latter's opinions remain important to the dynamics—and especially to the gender dynamics—of the play.

Nor, in Cleopatra's valedictory speech, is the image of Antony as a benevolent colossus straddling the world entirely borne out by our recollection of the cumulative overconfidence, carelessness and political misjudgments which, during the course of the play, lead to his downfall. Indeed, Cleopatra's description of Antony functions less as an accurate memorial of her lover and companion than as a retrospective reinscription of Antony; a reinscription, moreover, that is intended to convince us, the theatre audience, rather than Dolabella, who in any case remains unconvinced. When Cleopatra asks him, 'Think you there was, or might be such a man / As this I dreamt of?', Dolabella bluntly responds, 'Gentle madam, no' (V.ii.93–4). Cleopatra's description is intended to cause us to leave the theatre remembering Antony in her own glowing terms, rather than as we actually saw him on the stage. It is a designer-label Antony that she creates.

Moreover, in thus re-drawing Antony, Cleopatra also adjusts and reconstructs the discourse of masculinity which has targeted Antony as its victim. This discourse centres, inevitably, around the issue of patriarchy, and the position of individual men within the patriarchal hierarchy. As we saw in *Strictly ballroom*, power is wielded differentially not only between men and women but also among men within patriarchy. Indeed, the film enables us to discern two axes of competition and rivalry amongst men under patriarchy. The first may be described as a horizontal axis, and includes the individual male's contemporaries, his social circle, and those work colleagues at the same level as himself—his intimates and equals, therefore. The second axis may be defined as vertical, and includes those males who are his seniors or juniors in age, social status or rank. He struggles, often unconsciously, with these others, whether in an attempt to find a niche as a newcomer in a structure governed by others concerned to defend and protect their established positions, or in an effort to prevent himself from being dislodged by ambitious rising stars. We may therefore conclude that, though patriarchy is a structure which protects male power and authority, it does not protect all *individual men* equally and in the same way. Rather, it protects *certain patterns of power*, promotes those types of behaviour conducive to their preservation, and thence empowers and privileges those individual men whose behaviour conforms to the required pattern.

One arena in which males test themselves against each other is the sexual one, in terms of who is the first to reach adolescent sexuality (that is, to be able to sport pubic hair, erections and ejaculations before any others in his group); who has the biggest penis; who is the first to 'do it' with a girl/woman; and so on, even into adulthood. Penis size remains an obsessional focus for many males, as does one's 'rating' in terms of frequency and kinds of sexual contact: the bigger one's penis and/or the more frequently one has sexual intercourse with women, the more masculine one apparently is. Involved in these sexual preoccupations is also a range of sexual fears—for instance, fears of impotence or of homosexuality—which might deprive the male of his masculinity.

The instance of the discourse of sexuality is particularly interesting in relation to *Antony and Cleopatra*. This discourse may, on the one hand, prompt men toward an active display of male sexuality under certain circumstances. This can be seen in the way in which both adolescent boys and adult men may brag about their sexual experiences or conquests: the point of the game here is to prove through the public profession of one's sexuality that one is 'more a man' than others with less experience (or with greater modesty). Under other circumstances, however, the discourse may require men to restrain their libidinal impulses: this is part of the directive to men in our culture to dominate and control their bodies through the will and reason. It is, moreover, part of the discourse that defines man as mind and intellect, woman as body and passion. (This discourse was encoded early in our culture in the story of the Fall, and in the various commentaries written about this mythic origin of human life.) Thus, men who are overtly chaste or celibate may gain an ascendancy—even if only moral—over others who are less in control of their bodies and appetites: this is, after all, what, in the cycle of stories about King Arthur and his Knights of the Round Table, underlies and explains the story of Sir Galahad, the only knight to achieve the quest of the Holy Grail.

This aspect is indicated by the relationship of Antony and Cleopatra in Shakespeare's play: at one level, the open display of his virile sexuality commends Antony to us as, let us say, a 'real' man. At another level, however, Octavius' self-control and his repugnance toward such sexuality establishes him as a 'true' man, that is, one capable of attaining, wielding and retaining power, whereas Antony, through the very sexuality which identifies him as male, can be seen as submitting to the body, both his own and Cleopatra's. Enobarbus' observations are a useful index of this; for instance, when Mæcenas remarks, after the negotiation for the union of Antony with Octavia, 'Now Antony must leave her [Cleopatra] utterly,' Enobarbus replies, 'Never; he will not . . .' (II.ii.233–4). Similarly, he later tells Menas that Antony 'will to his Egyptian dish again . . . Antony will use his affection where it is. He married but his occasion here' (II.vi.122–9).

It is by now a commonplace in the criticism of *Antony and Cleopatra* that Rome is presented as masculine, Egypt as feminine. What seems to be less frequently noticed is that the play also presents a range of possible masculinities whose radical is the hegemonic, triumphant potency of Rome, symbolised in the calculating and ruthless politician Octavius. Male sexuality here is muted; rather, Rome's masculinity is patriarchal, constructed in terms of military power, conquest and the subordination of all that is not Roman or not conducive to Roman ambitions.

Since the play's definition of masculinity is a homosocial one, Rome represents a familiar patriarchal model of masculinity: Octavius is the patriarchal figure who, intent on subduing all others and all structures to his will, confirms his power by operating through the men around him—he is surrounded by male generals, aides, messengers. The only woman we are permitted to encounter in the Roman sphere of the play is Octavia; and she is constructed as a mere instrument of her brother's will in the project of bringing Antony to heel.

Patriarchal masculinity derives much of its power through the exercise of a particular logic. By imposing upon the flux of events a system of oppositions—for instance, male/female, masculine/feminine, heterosexual/homosexual—which not only produces meaning through difference, but equally gives those differences certain social, moral or ethical values, patriarchal masculinity in effect takes control of both the ways in which meaning may be made in a culture, and the ways in which such meaning is valorised. The positive valorisations are, naturally, those which foreground, support, confirm and protect the structures of masculinity itself (often encoded in the first term of each oppositional pair). The negative valorisations are, therefore, those which oppose, subvert, contradict or otherwise refuse to support those structures.

This is an important feature of the Roman definition of masculinity in *Antony and Cleopatra.* It allows Octavius to define what is 'Other' both to Rome and to himself, and thus as feminine or effeminate He thus reduces its value and renders it both dangerous and vulnerable at the same time. The Roman world understands binaries like victory/defeat, male/female, Rome/Egypt, loyalty/betrayal, Caesar/Cleopatra; typically, the second of each binary is marked as 'Other', and therefore as both antagonistic and inferior to the initiating term of the binary. There are few mediating terms in such a meaning system. Moreover, the shift of emphasis or allegiance from one term of a binary to the other entails a similar shift—in a similar direction—in all related binaries. Thus, when Antony is redefined as non-Roman, he automatically also becomes Egyptian, traitorous, effeminate and doomed to defeat. He becomes, in effect, degendered as a masculine subject.

A significant element in this process of degendering Antony is the Octavius–Mardian axis, which provides the dramatic poles of patriarchal, masculine power and of emasculated, feminised powerlessness. Mardian is a eunuch whose very body has been deprived of the biological signs of maleness, an absence to which Cleopatra scornfully refers: 'I take no pleasure / In aught an eunuch has' (I.v.9–10). Castration is thus made equivalent to the loss of all male power, whether sexual or political, manifest not only in the physical castration undergone by Mardian but also in the fact that the eunuch is servant to a woman whose own sexuality is made a key feature of her characterisation. Moreover, according to the ethics of patriarchy, in serving a woman and thus subordinating himself to her authority, a man degrades himself and thus, under patriarchal norms, risks exclusion as a potential wielder of power. Mardian is therefore represented as having abdicated absolutely from any claim to patriarchal power and to masculinity. He thus serves as an index of Antony's capitulation to the wiles of Cleopatra, a capitulation which is made manifest when Antony follows her from the battle at Actium (III.x–xi).

An important feature of this axis, however, is that both of its poles are defined as asexual, Octavius because he pursues power rather than sexuality, and Mardian because he has been deprived of any active male sexuality (and hence of any power). Seen in this way, the structure of masculinity in the political world of *Antony and Cleopatra* appears designed to exclude that male whose overt sexuality is an integral feature of his personality and dynamic—namely, Antony. Ironically, his very sexuality, which aligns him with body rather than mind, marks him as effeminate (and, it might be added, as beast-like) from Rome's point of view.

Age is another ambivalent way in which men may be ranked within the structures of patriarchal power, for, on the one hand, the older man may claim power by virtue of greater experience and a longer period over which he has attained and secured that power; on the other hand, the older man's position is always endangered by the ambitions of younger men who also seek a place in the hierarchies of power. Thus, in *Antony and Cleopatra*, Octavius is early described as 'the scarce-bearded Caesar' (I.i.21), establishing him through his youth as both a potential subordinate to Antony and as a potential rival. Similarly, Octavius later refers to the failing Antony as 'the old ruffian' (IV.i.4), thus defining his opponent as the ageing patriarch who must be dethroned.

Between the diffuse masculine power of Octavius and the emasculated—'unseminar'd', Cleopatra calls it (I.v.11)—subordination of Mardian lies a range of other possible masculinities. The case of Enobarbus offers an instructive exemplar of the way in which the ideology of masculinity functions in this play. An Egyptianised Roman, Enobarbus is an analogue with Antony, who is seen by Rome as having become feminised by Egypt. His account of Antony's meeting with Cleopatra (II.ii.191–226), as well as his following description of Cleopatra's nature, identifies him as a partisan of things and persons Egyptian, and because Egypt is identified in the play with the sensuous and the erotic, Enobarbus thus becomes a proponent also of things and persons sexual. Such a partisanship must be identified by Rome as a defection not only in terms of politics, but also in terms of the particular ideology of masculinity which exalts self-control and the submission of bodily pleasure to the will. It is significant, therefore, that Enobarbus is presented in Act II scene ii (from line 103) and elsewhere as overstepping the bounds of protocol and/or diplomacy, for this too can be taken as a sign of his Egyptianisation, that is, his loss of Roman self-control.

Enobarbus' return to the Roman camp after it becomes clear that Antony's star is waning (III.xiii.197–201) may be interpreted also as a return from the effeminacies of Egypt to the play's Roman radical of masculinity. Another way of conceiving this return is as a movement back from sensuality and male sexuality to the sterner virtues of patriarchal power and politics, as well as self-restraint. However, Rome, like patriarchy itself, is unforgiving of those who betray its ideology, whether of politics or of gender. It is doubly suspicious of those who, like Enobarbus, betray twice by defecting first from Rome and then from Egypt. Accordingly, therefore, Caesar orders that Antony's former associates be placed in the vanguard of the Roman attack, 'That Antony may seem to spend his fury / Upon himself' (IV.vi.10–11); and Enobarbus mournfully notes that Caesar mistrusts those who have deserted to the Roman army from the Egyptian camp (IV.vi.12–18).

The phrasing of Caesar's command has a triple signification. Its chief meaning, of course, is that Antony should be seen to lay waste his own former associates. A second meaning is that Antony should appear to be maiming himself—a foreshadowing of Antony's mismanaged suicide (IV.xiv). A third sense of Caesar's command—one which develops the second sense in a particular direction—is that Antony should be seen to be castrating himself. This latter sense transforms Caesar's command from a political stratagem in time of war to a moral condemnation of Antony's maleness and sexuality, foregrounded and compromised by his association with Cleopatra and his sojourn in Egypt by her side. It also aligns Antony potentially with Mardian as the male deprived of both maleness and masculinity. Moreover, Eric Partridge gives as a further sense of 'spend': 'To expend sexually; to discharge seminally'.[5] This adds a further dimension to Octavius' command, suggesting that Antony publicly display his lack of manliness (and, implicitly, his unmanning) through a symbolic act of masturbation.

Thus, Enobarbus represents a mid-point between the absolutely masculine model of Rome, as symbolised by Octavius, and the apparent effeminacy and depravity of Egypt, as signified by the eunuch Mardian. Each of these provides an analogue with the treatment of Antony in the play. The play maps Antony's trajectory as, following his departure from the controlled masculinity represented by Rome and supervised by Octavius, he undergoes a process of feminisation by Egypt, until he, in effect, loses his gender identity as masculine, at least as defined by the Roman radical of masculinity. The opening lines of the play establish this particular aspect of Antony's position in the discourse of gender (from the Roman perspective) as Philo and Demetrius comment on the degeneracy and effeminisation of their general through his association with Cleopatra:

> Take but good note, and you shall see in him
> The triple pillar of the world transform'd
> Into a strumpet's fool: behold and see. (I.i.11–13)

The moral disengagement of the two Romans from their general is quite marked, as is the demotion of Cleopatra to the status merely of a strumpet. This opening speech of the play therefore already signifies Antony's decline from the Roman ideal of masculinity, defined in terms of male power ascendant both over women and over non-Roman men. Like Mardian, he has become a servitor of Cleopatra, who represents both woman and female sexuality. Hence the remark of Philo that Antony has become Cleopatra's instrument, 'the bellows and the fan / To cool a gipsy's lust' (I.i.9–10).

Antony's retreat from the play's dominant model of masculinity is marked at several points and, moreover, is inscribed progressively on Antony's body itself. Philo's opening remarks about Antony refer to Antony's behaviour with Cleopatra. However, Cleopatra herself later reminisces about cross-dressing with Antony:

> I laugh'd him out of patience; and that night
> I laugh'd him into patience, and next morn,
> Ere the ninth hour, I drunk him to his bed;
> Then put my tires and mantles on him, whilst
> I wore his sword Philippan . . . (II.v.19–23)

This account is important for several reasons. Though chronologically it tells of an event in the period that precedes the point marked by the opening of the play, the information comes to us after Philo's remarks about Antony's degeneracy. Cleopatra's speech thus functions both as a reminder of Philo's comments, and as an intensification of their import. Rhetorically, then, Cleopatra's account, though alluding to events earlier in the story, registers with the audience as strengthening testimony to the fact of Antony's feminisation. In Philo's speech, Antony is charged with public behaviour inappropriate to a Roman male; in Cleopatra's reminiscence of a private event, Antony's very self-control—in the play, a mark both of Romanness and of masculine behaviour—is gone, and he loses even the outward gestural signs of his masculinity.

Cleopatra's reminiscence shows us that something is more seriously amiss with Antony than merely his unseemly, un-Roman behaviour. Cleopatra's account of teasing Antony, then getting him drunk and putting him into her own clothing is also an account of the weakening purchase of the Roman ideology of masculinity on Antony's very body. That is, the codes of dress which identify and distinguish male and female are violated, so that Antony's body is inscribed with the signs of femininity, an inflection of the actual physical emasculation of Mardian.

Antony's masculinity is interrogated further by his fugitive pursuit of Cleopatra's ship during the battle of Actium. Of this action, Enobarbus exclaims, comparing Antony to 'a doting mallard',

> I never saw an action of such shame;
> Experience, manhood, honour, ne'er before
> Did violate so itself. (III.x.20–4)

What is reprimanded here, as well as his abandonment of the tasks of masculinity, which include steadfastness, valour and aggressive behaviour, is Antony's unmanly capitulation to his female partner. Antony himself confesses as much:

> Egypt, thou knew'st too well,
> My heart was to thy rudder tied by the strings,
> And thou shouldst tow me after. O'er my spirit
> Thy full supremacy thou knew'st, and that
> Thy beck might from the bidding of the gods
> Command me. (III.xi.56–61)

Antony's faltering masculinity is alluded to by a soldier also in Act IV scene iii, in the reference to his abandonment by 'the god Hercules, whom Antony lov'd' (IV.iii.15–16): the club with which Hercules was typically represented in the iconography of the period is unmistakably phallic in its symbolism. The symbolic loss of the phallus is alluded to once more, by Antony himself: 'O, thy vile lady! / She has robb'd me of my sword (IV.xiv.22–3). Here he addresses Mardian, whom we have seen to be already established as a model of masculinity emasculated. At this point, we may assume that Antony has reached the antithesis of the Roman radical of masculinity: without his sword, and deprived of Hercules' phallic club, he is analogous to the 'unseminar'd' Mardian, with whom he now symbolically shares the ideologically shaming and unmanly trait of impotence.

These lines are also a reminder of the cross-dressing episode discussed above, when Cleopatra took and wore Antony's 'sword Philippan'. We might also adduce here Cleopatra's remark: 'I would

I had thy inches, thou shouldst know / There were a heart in Egypt' (I.iii.40–1). Woodbridge suggests that these lines have a sexual *sous entendre*, referring to the penis and to penis size (Woodbridge, pp. 155–6). If so, the lines suggest a further, intended robbing of Antony's masculinity by the Queen of Egypt, whose own gender status can be seen as hyperfeminine, and hence dangerous to men.

The play relentlessly pursues the logic of this process of Antony's emasculation and degendering. As if to set the seal on Antony's diminished masculinity, his suicide is twice botched: first, he asks Eros to kill him (IV.xiv.62–8ff.), thereby transforming himself into a passive object as well as betraying the Roman ideal of a manly death through actively committing suicide. Second, when he is shamed by Eros's example, Antony mismanages his suicide and fails to kill himself outright (IV.xiv.101ff.), thus allowing us to see that which patriarchal culture prohibits us from even thinking: the penetration of the male body, permissible only when—as in Eros's case—death follows immediately.

At this point in the play, Antony has reached the nadir of his fall from the masculine ideal: he has lost his battle with Caesar, he is too strongly attached to Cleopatra, and he has wrought his own death in a fashion which, from the Roman perspective, effectively lacks honour, dignity and manliness. His impotence in terms both of politics and gender is visibly represented on the stage by his body, deprived of its armour and wounded—that is, with a literal gap in its substance.

Cleopatra's description of Antony as a Titan among humans may thus be read as a counter to this degendering of the hero. The gigantic figure she constructs is a figure closely allied to universal nature: 'his voice was propertied / As all the tuned spheres . . . to friends'; but to enemies, 'He was as rattling thunder'; his bounty had 'no winter in't; an autumn 'twas . . .', and his delights were dolphin-like.

More important, however, is Cleopatra's description of Antony's geopolitical splendour and generosity: 'in his livery / Walk'd crowns and crownets: realms and islands were / As plates dropp'd from his pocket.' This image of unthinking, copious generosity is analogous to the iconography of nature found commonly in works of all kinds of the Renaissance. Cleopatra's description transposes the images of fecund, copious, *female* nature into the key of a possible *male* politics, such as is not represented in the play's world by the Roman radical, whether of masculinity or of politics.

In doing so, Cleopatra sets the seal on the feminising of Antony, and transforms it into a positive rather than a negative feature of the once 'triple pillar of the world'. Moreover, she too is identified in the play with fecund, inventive nature. The Roman Agrippa observes of her, 'She made great Caesar lay his sword to bed; / He plough'd her, and she cropp'd' (II.ii.227–8). Enobarbus's famously quoted description of Cleopatra likewise converts the human Queen of Egypt into a goddess of nature:

> Age cannot wither her, nor custom stale
> Her infinite variety: other women cloy
> The appetites they feed, but she makes hungry,
> Where most she satisfies. For vilest things
> Become themselves [become attractive] in her, that the holy priests
> Bless her, when she is riggish [sexually aroused]. (II.ii.235–40)

Cleopatra's rejection of Dolabella's denial that such an Antony as she describes existed is consistent with the discourse identifying Cleopatra with nature:

> You lie up to the hearing of the gods.
> But if there be, or ever were one such,
> It's past the size of dreaming: nature wants stuff
> To vie strange forms with fancy, yet to imagine
> An Antony were nature's piece, 'gainst fancy [contradicting imagination],
> Condemning shadows quite [making works of art inferior].
> (V.ii.95–100)

Cleopatra has imagined a colossal Antony, but now asserts that such an Antony must be natural, for the idea is beyond the bounds of mere fancy. In this way the equation Cleopatra = nature is maintained, as she both creates Antony in her image, and then ascribes that construct to nature. Because she is identified elsewhere in the play with the Nile River and with its reptilian life (e.g. 'my serpent of old Nile' [I.v.25]), the image of Cleopatra nursing the asp at her breast (V.ii.308–9) appears somehow inevitable and logical: she seems at the same time to be both the Queen of Egypt taking her own life and Mother Nature nurturing her creation. This is another instance of the Cleopatra = nature equation in action.

In allocating to Antony facets of herself—her own femininity, her own fecundity—Cleopatra enormously expands the play's discourse of masculinity at this point of the action. Breaking free of the narrow, highly supervised Roman model of masculinity,

Cleopatra's valedictory description of Antony reconstructs and re-genders him according to a new model of masculinity, one in which feminine sensuality and generosity are not excluded and marginalised, but rather integrated into a more spacious concept. It is this, in part, which produces for the audience the sense, first, that Antony has indeed expanded beyond the bounds of the world established in the play, so that he no longer has a place in that world; and, second, that he is a right and fitting mate for Cleopatra, whose own stature becomes likewise colossal.

Antony's sexuality and gender are constructed as progressively more and more ambiguous, and his re-gendering in Cleopatra's speech confirms that ambiguity. His re-gendering may be understood as reflecting and articulating the confusion and anxiety of the late fifteenth and early sixteenth century in England occasioned, for the most part, by the anomaly of a potent Queen Elizabeth—that is, a woman who wielded power usually ascribed to a male ruler.[6] Indeed, the political doctrine of the king's two bodies came to be adjusted in order precisely to accommodate this anomaly. According to this doctrine, the political body remained always implicitly male and patriarchal in nature, whereas the natural body could be, in fact, female.

The effect of this on the culture, as we have seen, was extensive and profound, raising questions about the relation of sex to gender. Such questioning resulted, toward the end of the sixteenth and at the beginning of the seventeenth centuries, in the waves of female-to-male cross-dressing, such as that commented upon by Philip Stubbes and others, and culminating in 1620 in the *Hic mulier-haec vir* debate carried out in a series of pamphlets. (The title of this debate means 'This woman, this man'; but the demonstrative 'this' in each case is in the gender opposite to the noun referred to.) The disruption to the sex–gender system, we may presume, was intensified as the homoerotic proclivities of Elizabeth's successor, James I, came to be more widely known.

(The date of composition of *Antony and Cleopatra* may have been too early for an awareness about James' homosexuality to have filtered through to the public at large: he succeeded to the English throne in 1603. In any case, we should be careful not to identify homosexuality with femininity or effeminacy as presented in *Antony and Cleopatra*: such a correlation may not have been as common in the Renaissance as it is in our culture. Moreover, if the sex–gender system was in a state of crisis, it is precisely such identifications that may have been put in question. In any case, Antony is not accused of homosexuality, but rather of submitting to the will of a woman, which in terms of Shakespeare's culture signified a feminisation of the masculine.)

*Antony and Cleopatra* can thus be read as an attempt to encompass the problems of gender raised by Elizabeth's retention of patriarchal power. In constructing for Antony a roomier definition of masculinity, Shakespeare struggles to arrive at a definition of gender that might accommodate difference without marginalising it as 'Other'. Nonetheless, it is significant that Antony's failure as a (Ro)man is stigmatised as his feminisation, rather than constructed as a masculinity alternative to the traditional patriarchal model; and that his reinstatement, at the end of the play, as a Titan among men is fashioned by a woman, rather than by another man, intimating a further feminisation of the Roman hero.

Bram Stoker's novel *Dracula*,[7] first published in 1897, belongs to an era closer to our own, and to a culture which, according to the central hypothesis of the first volume of Michel Foucault's *The history of sexuality*, was, like ours, saturated by sexual discourse. Foucault's contention is that, despite a popular assumption that the Victorians avoided mention of sex, 'What is peculiar to modern societies, in fact, is not that they consigned sex to a shadow existence, but that they dedicated themselves to speaking of it *ad infinitum*, while exploiting it as *the* secret'.[8] Medicalised, psychologised and pathologised, sex (whether as sexuality or sexual health and practice) came to replace the tradition of sins against religious faith and the canonical rules of daily behaviour as the cause of anxiety, remorse, guilt and dysfunctional social existence, so that the confessor-priest gave way to the confessor-doctor and the confessor-psychiatrist. Thus, suggests Foucault, contrary to being silenced, a discourse of sex flourished in the culture, though inflected and channelled in particular ways.

Accordingly, we might expect Stoker's novel to reflect that discursive anxiety about sex and sexuality. Christopher Craft finds various ambiguities of gender and sexuality in Stoker's novel. He points out, for instance, how, in the scene in which Jonathan Harker first encounters the three vampire women in Dracula's castle, Harker is rendered passive and feminised in his seduction by the vampire woman with the fair hair, while the vampire's mouth becomes an instrument of masculine penetration of the other's body (Stoker, 1979, pp. 51–3). Indeed, Craft traces the way that the vampire's mouth comes to be symbolic of *both* the male genitalia in the ability of the teeth to penetrate flesh *and* the female, especially in menstruation, in the description of red sensuous mouths running with blood.[9]

A masculinisation of the figure of the female vampire is accomplished in the transformation of Lucy Westenra: her aggressive sexuality would have suggested to a Victorian audience less a sexuality proper to a woman (if, that is, readers believed women to be sexual—many didn't) than an inappropriately rampant and hence male one, contributing to her monstrosity. In writing in his diary about his nocturnal visit to her grave in the company of Van Helsing, Quincey Morris and Lord Arthur Holmwood, Dr Seward notes that the now-vampiric woman possesses 'Lucy's eyes in form and colour; but Lucy's eyes unclean and full of hell-fire, instead of the pure, gentle orbs we knew . . . As we looked, her eyes blazed with unholy light, and the face became wreathed with a voluptuous smile' (Stoker, 1979, p. 253).

At the same time, the male vampire is subjected to a series of inflections. In the same scene in which Harker meets the female vampires, Dracula warns them off the hapless solicitor: 'This man belongs to me!' he says. In answer to the fair vampire's response—'You yourself never loved; you never love!'—Dracula curiously replies, 'after looking at my [Harker's] face attentively', that he can indeed love: 'you yourselves can tell it from the past'. Craft suggests that, along with the ambiguous gendering of the vampire's mouth, there is an ambiguity of sexuality, especially in the figuring of the male vampire.

He proposes that the homoerotic begins with the Count's response to Harker's cutting himself while shaving (Stoker, 1979, p. 37), and notes that the homoerotic is diffused throughout the novel, and made to masquerade as the heterosexual, or at least as the heteroerotic (Craft, p. 236). Other instances of the homoerotic functioning covertly in the novel include the multiple blood transfusions from four men into Lucy's veins (the first of these transfusions, involving Lucy's fiancé Arthur, is described in Stoker, 1979, p. 150). The narrative describes this activity explicitly in terms of marriage to Lucy, and Craft comments, 'Men touching women touch each other' (Craft, p. 237). In other words, a certain eroticism is instilled into the concern of the four men over Lucy's health and fate that compounds the gothic perversity of the narrative.

In Craft's analysis, then, that perversity resides in the volatile and unstable nature of sexual identity and its relation to the erotic. These move too swiftly and surprisingly—like the vampire himself—for us to feel entirely comfortable with the narrative. That chameleon subjectivity and sexuality need to be controlled: the Count must be killed. However, as Ken Gelder observes in his book *Reading the vampire*, though Dracula is destroyed at the end of Stoker's novel, he never really dies: instead, he reappears in literature, film and criticism again and again.[10] To invoke the title of one Hammer film, *Dracula has risen from the grave*—repeatedly.

In this, Dracula shares a characteristic with perverse sexuality, especially homosexuality; namely, that no matter how it may be legislated against, repressed, policed, taken through the law court or the doctor's or psychiatrist's office, it seems always to return. This, in part, is what Richard Dyer argues, looking to situate the figure of the vampire within a particular historical context.[11] He notes a connection between the homosexual, as typically figured in late nineteenth- and early twentieth-century culture, and the figure of the vampire (Dyer, 1988, pp. 57–60). Both are marginal and deemed dangerous; both are nocturnal; both are thought to recruit others to their own kind of life. Both live in the shadows or the margins, but are thought to be able to 'pass' in society, and yet each *should* be recognisable through certain signs or characteristics—thus, the vampire novel often focuses pleasurably on how one 'discovers' that so and so is a vampire, just as a certain pleasure is to be derived in 'discovering' that so and so is a homosexual. Both, moreover, confront patriarchal masculinity with the problem of the passive male, since in the vampire tale—as we have seen in the case of *Dracula*—the male body may be represented as passive and vulnerable to the onslaught of the vampire. Moreover, the passivity of the receptive male is part of an ambiguity about homosexual erotics, for the gay man's sexual repertoire often includes both active (penetrating) and passive (penetrated) roles, something that traditional, dominant masculinity finds difficult to encompass. Such an erotics leaves unclear and therefore makes threatening the active/passive role distinction so central to—indeed, so definitive of—heterosexuality.

Dyer discusses the pleasures to be derived from the usually covert but sometimes overt coupling of the figure of the homosexual with that of the vampire:

> One [pleasure] is to identify with the vampire in some sort, despite the narrative position, and to enjoy the ignorance of the main character(s) . . . The structure whereby we the reader know more than the protagonist (heightened in first person narration) is delicious,

> and turns what is perilous in a closeted lesbian/gay life (knowing something dreadful about us they don't) into something flattering, for it makes one superior. Another enjoyable way of positioning oneself in this text–reader relation is in thrilling to the extraordinary power credited to the vampire, transcendant [sic] powers of seduction, s/he can have anyone s/he wants, it seems. Most lesbians and gay men experience exactly the opposite, certainly outside the gay scene, certainly up until very recently. Even though the vampire is invariably killed off at the end (except in recent examples), how splendid to know what a threat our secret is to them! (Dyer, 1988, p. 59).

Thus the vampire becomes a figure with whom the lesbian and the gay man, but also the bisexual, the transsexual, even the transvestite, might identify, because the vampire in various fashions represents both marginalisation and a revenge upon 'normal' society for that marginalisation. Though the individual vampire may be destroyed at the end of the narrative, we 'know' vampirism will survive; and that knowledge generates a certain satisfaction, as well as the fear of 'normal' society.

Insightful though their readings of *Dracula* are, Craft and Dyer pay less attention to a further discursive strategy whereby the Count is aligned with the feminine. The narrative establishes a series of binary oppositions—strong/weak, light/dark, good/evil, holy/unholy, and so on—in which the first term may be identified with those men (Harker, Seward, Holmwood, Morris and Van Helsing) who coalesce as the Crew of Light, their mission to destroy Dracula, the emblem of Darkness. The female characters are either relegated to the periphery, as is the case with Mina Harker, who virtually becomes Jonathan's secretary, or make the transition (symbolised as a descent) from Light to Dark, as is the case with Lucy Westenra when she is herself transformed into a vampire. It is worth noting, too, that Mina hovers in the marginal moral space between good and evil after she is made Dracula's channel of information by being forced to drink his blood (Stoker, 1979, p. 336) and is subsequently unable to tolerate against her forehead the wafer of the (communion) Host when Van Helsing seeks to protect his band against the influence of Dracula and his powers (Stoker, 1979, p. 353).

This movement of the female characters toward Dracula and all he signifies suggests, on the one hand, a heterosexually seductive element in the embodiment of evil, a seduction made explicit early in the episode of Harker's encounter with the vampire women in Castle Dracula. On the other hand, this movement might also propose that the Count's is a feminine realm, toward which women 'naturally' gravitate unless educated against it and supported and protected by those inhabiting the province of the masculine. Moreover, the nature of the binary oppositions indicated above, when aligned with one another, exert a strong pressure to identify darkness, unholiness and so on with the feminine, since the initiating term of each definition is associated with the masculine.

This alignment with the feminine is foreshadowed in Harker's journey to Castle Dracula, which takes him from England, defined by the narrative as a masculine site—a site of boundaries, predictability and certainty, of science, reason, the control of women by their menfolk, and the self-control exercised by the men themselves—to a geographical location in which uncertainty and superstition dominate: 'I read that every known superstition in the world is gathered into the horseshoe of the Carpathians, as if it were the centre of some sort of imaginative whirlpool . . .' says the first entry in Harker's diary (Stoker, 1979, p. 10). A little later he comments on the Slovaks: 'They are very picturesque, but do not look prepossessing. On the stage they would be set down at once as some Oriental band of brigands. They are, however, I am told, very harmless and rather wanting in natural self-assertion' (Stoker, 1979, p. 11). The last comment might suffice as a description also of the 'proper' woman, at least as the novel conceives her to be. It is, moreover, a woman, the old innkeeper's wife in Bistritz, who warns Harker of the possible consequences of his journey to the Borgo Pass on the eve of St George's day, and furnishes him with the crucifix—inappropriate, as Harker himself comments, for an Anglican (Stoker, 1979, pp. 13–15)—which protects him against the vampire Count in a later episode (Stoker, 1979, pp. 37–8). This suggests that feminine knowledge is more efficacious in this region than masculine.

Harker's early description of Dracula, while on the whole it tends to stress his masculinity, power and cruelty, nonetheless contains touches of the feminine—his 'rather white and fine' hands, for instance, whose 'nails were long and fine, and cut to a sharp point' (Stoker, 1979, p. 28) are suggestive not only of the vampire's claws but also of a woman's hands or at least those of an effeminate man who does no manual work. We might note that such manual characteristics also signify aristocratic status, which in a middle-class, capitalist society such as Victorian England would have invited some suspicion, not only about the ambitions of the upper class over its inferiors, but also of the gender identity of individual members of that class. The effete nobleman has a long history in English literature. Likewise, the moment when Harker comes upon the Count acting as servant signifies a confusion both of gender and class function, since both the male servant (Stoker, 1979, pp. 39–40) and woman were customarily defined as inferior, and often performed the same sorts of domestic chores.

More telling of the ambiguous nature of the Count and of the discourses which shape him, is the episode in the tower in which Harker encounters the vampire women. Though the Count, when he intervenes to save Harker's life, is described in terms of demonic, masculine power, there is a grotesque gender inversion when Dracula hands over to his female companions the infant he has stolen. At one level, it is a parody of fatherhood: Dracula gives these women a child to satisfy their hunger, here ironically definable as maternal. However, the child is theirs not to feed, but to feed upon; and at this level Dracula seems to operate as a nurturing mother figure. (The same figuration of vampire as devouring mother-figure is repeated later, when the Crew of Light confront the vampiric Lucy who has brought a child to feed on [Stoker, 1979, pp. 252–3].)

Indeed, a similar ambiguity pervades the vampire's method of recruiting others to his side in his dream of conquering the world. In one sense, this may be described as a dream of patriarchy: the engendering of descendants without the need of women or their wombs—this, incidentally, has often been a charge levelled at the development, chiefly by male medical personnel, of the *in vitro*, or test-tube, baby. In another sense, Dracula's method of increasing his kind may be seen as a kind of maternal process, whereby he *produces* the novice vampire. In this light, the vampire's fabled teeth and red mouth suggest the *vagina dentata*, the vagina with teeth. In the folklore of masculinity and in psychoanalytic theory, the *vagina dentata* is imagined as a fantasy of aggressive, devouring female sexuality, threatening the male with castration by endangering the sign of his maleness and power over the female, namely, the penis.

The episode in which the Count forces Mina to drink from a wound he opens in his breast provides another grotesque parody of motherhood (Stoker, 1979, pp. 342–3). In this respect it is thematically related to the feeding frenzy of the vampire women when Dracula gives them the infant, and to Lucy's victimisation of the children in her guise as the 'bloofer lady' (Stoker, 1979, p.

213). In this episode, the Count metamorphoses symbolically into a mother giving her child suck—indeed, the text explicitly converts the vampire's blood into milk: 'The attitude of the two had a terrible resemblance to a child forcing a kitten's nose into a saucer of milk to compel it to drink' (Stoker, 1979, p. 336). The shifts between the figures of adult and child, and of human and animal, however, and especially the Count's symbolic inversion of sex from male to female, together with the coercion involved, make the scene singularly repugnant.

At the same time, the image of an opening in the body which yields blood produces, in this narrative, a constellation of sexual meanings. At one level, there are overtones of female-to-male fellatio, especially given the volatile status of blood as symbol in the novel: it might be blood, or it might be semen.[12] At another level, it is an image of female-to-female cunnilingus, the wound functioning as the signifier of the vagina; and the presence of blood simultaneously suggests menstruation.

At a still further level, the image of the vampire with a vaginal wound transforms the phallic, penile Count once more into that fear-inspiring thing, the *vagina dentata*. Here, however, we have a sexually still more ambiguous version of it, in which the teeth (or fangs) and vaginal opening are separate from one another, but connected through the identity of the vampire himself. Thus, the possibility of a potent femaleness is coopted by the phallic Count and used against a woman.

All this is not to suggest that the Count is to be considered as in fact female, or feminised or even effeminate, but rather that he *illegitimately* occupies, from time to time, a certain gendered space. He thus both *signifies* that space and *parodies* it. At the same time, however, his ability to enter and leave that space is a sign of his elusiveness, of the difficulty of fixing him in a stable identity. In this way it accords with his various physical disguises, whether human, as the coachman who picks Harker up at the Borgo Pass, or animal, as bat, dog, wolf and so on; and with the fluctuations of his apparent age, depending on whether he has fed or not (for instance, 'There lay the Count, but looking as if his youth had been half-renewed . . .' [Stoker, 1979, p. 67]).

Much of the narrative is given over to establishing the power and guile of the vampire Count. Van Helsing informs us, for instance, that:

> This vampire which is amongst us is of himself so strong in person as twenty men; he is of cunning more than mortal, for his cunning

> be the growth of ages; he have still the aids of necromancy, which is, as his etymology imply, the divination by the dead, and all the dead that he can come nigh to are for him at command; he is brute, and more than brute; he is devil in callous, and the heart of him is not; he can, within limitations, appear at will when and where, and in any of the forms that are to him; he can, within his range, direct the elements: the storm, the fog, the thunder; he can command all the meaner things: the rat, and the owl, and the bat—the moth, and the fox, and the wolf; he can grow and become small; and he can at times vanish and come unknown.

Van Helsing then cogently and appropriately inquires, 'How then are we to begin our strife to destroy him?' (Stoker, 1979, pp. 283–4). This, too, must be the question uppermost in the reader's mind, for Stoker appears to have created an invincible villain who is not to be contained by the stratagems of mere living mortals.

The good professor's solution is an interesting one, namely, to outwit Dracula by sheer force of intelligence:

> As I learned from the researches of my friend Arminius of Buda-Pesth, he [Dracula] was in life a most wonderful man. Soldier, statesman, and alchemist—which latter was the highest development of the science-knowledge of his time. He had a mighty brain, a learning beyond compare, and a heart that knew no fear and no remorse . . . in him the brain powers survived the physical death; though it would seem that memory was not all complete. In some faculties of mind he has been, and is, only a child; but he is growing, and some things that were childish at the first are now of man's stature . . . that big child-brain of his is working. Well for us, it is, as yet, a child-brain; for had he dared, at the first, to attempt certain things he would long ago have been beyond our power. (Stoker, 1979, pp. 360–1)

This sudden introduction of the notion that the vampire's intellect is still in the developmental stages must surely strike some readers as a rather obvious device to find a way out of the narrative impasse Stoker has created for himself, if the Crew of Light are ultimately to succeed. The nature of this information, however, is both telling and characteristic. It articulates a nineteenth-century preoccupation with brain size and intelligence that found expression, first, in the discourse of race. According to the latter, the subjugation, colonisation and inferiorisation of non-European races were justified in part on the basis of the lesser intelligence and the smaller brains of those Other(ed) peoples. Similarly, the discourse of eugenics (a science devoted to the breeding of a better race and nation), which originated in the nineteenth century and found its full expression in this century in the Nazi ideal of a master race, partly distinguished its preferences in terms of brain size and intellectual capacity.[13] Both of these discourses suggest a particular inferiority on the part of Dracula and his origins, an inferiority already implied by Harker in his somewhat scornful commentary about the Carpathians and their inhabitants, and implied in his remark that 'It seems to me that the further East you go the more unpunctual are the trains. What ought they to be in China?' (Stoker, 1979, p. 11).

The claim about smaller brains and lesser intelligence was also employed in Victorian England to explain the 'natural' inferiority of women, and the need, therefore, to submit them to the control of men, who possessed, according to this hypothesis, larger brains and greater intelligence. It was thus also a justification of women's subjugation to men under patriarchy. Van Helsing's account of Dracula's 'child-brain', therefore, may also be understood as signalling the danger that a *feminine* mind might be moving toward a fuller capacity and hence an entry into the masculine, thus consolidating the menace which the vampire offers to the masculine Crew of Light and the social values and structures which it upholds.

However, despite these strokes of the feminine in Dracula's characterisation, Stoker is careful to avoid any direct vampiric contact between Dracula and the male characters. Either it is deflected, as in the shaving episode, when Harker cuts his face and Dracula lunges at him, only to be arrested by the crucifix around Harker's neck; or it is displaced, as when Harker is attacked by the vampire women who, as Craft contends in his article, represent merely a diffusion of the Count's own hunger. One obvious reason for such strategies on the part of the author is to evade any explicit homoeroticism or suggestion of homosexual desire on the part of the Count or of the other male characters. Yet such desire seems to suffuse the narrative, finding indirect expression, including the partial feminisation of the vampire antagonist, and perhaps especially so, since the homosexual is, in patriarchal culture, frequently understood as the (ef)feminisation of the male, and hence the abdication of the individual man from the masculine.

*Antony and Cleopatra* and *Dracula* each signify the failure of their central male characters to observe the patriarchal strictures defining the masculine. This is perhaps especially interesting in the case of Stoker's novel, since Dracula's power, cunning and sheer 'presence' in a differently conceived narrative would not be significantly dissimilar from those of the hypermasculine movie heroes created by the likes of Sylvester Stallone, Arnold Schwarzenegger or Jean-Claude van Damme. Clearly, therefore, something else is happening ideologically in the narratives told in Shakespeare's play and Stoker's tale. In the case of Antony, it is a question of being insufficiently masculine: of surrendering to emotion and passion, jeopardising his public status in the world in order to satisfy his private desires, and ultimately of capitulating, as a man, to a woman. In the case of Dracula, we see a male figure who may be described as excessively masculine: he is almost invulnerable, he clearly keeps well in check what 'softer' emotions he may have (for instance, his indirect assertion of love to the vampire women in the tower), he controls the females at his disposal, and he exults in his own power.

Yet, in terms of the novel's articulation of its ideology, Dracula is feminised as profoundly as Antony. This suggests that the feminine is not merely that 'Otherness' or remote zone to which the failed male may be relegated, but rather represents a fault within the structure of the masculine itself, and hence a source of anxiety for the patriarchal system. What if the feminine were not merely 'out there', but also 'in here', within the body, the psychology and the temperament of the male himself?

Masculine ideology thus establishes boundaries which both demarcate the masculine from the feminine, and enable it to be internalised by the individual male as 'in here'. The feminine then is expelled to a realm conceived as outside the male body and hence beyond the 'true' or 'proper' masculine (whether of behaviour or psychology). It can thus be located conveniently in a bodily morphology different from the male, and invoked as both the threat to and the destination of the disobedient male within patriarchy. This, then, becomes the 'out there'.

The male who, like Antony or Dracula, in some way violates the boundaries and contravenes the codes by which the masculine is maintained as separate from the feminine cannot be permitted to propose some other possible masculine. His exile and punishment, as we see in both *Antony and Cleopatra* and in *Dracula*, despite differences of culture, historical context and genre, not only help to mark and affirm the boundaries of the acceptable in the structure of the patriarchal masculine but also serve as a warning to the reader.

# 5

# *Porn: where men meat*

Like *Antony and Cleopatra* and *Dracula*, the pornographic text tends to create enclaves of 'them' and 'us', to establish sets of signs by which ideological subjects may be recognised and may recognise themselves, while at the same time identifying and marking 'Others' who are not subjects. If, as Murray S. Davis drily notes, 'Pornography seems to be the only social phenomenon that critics find simultaneously dangerous, disgusting, and dull',[1] the range of contradictory readings alerts us to the possibility that the pornographic text may, in fact, constitute a site of *excessive*, or at any rate *plural*, meaning. This, in turn, suggests that the pornographic text may be another form of faultline narrative intended to allay fears that threaten the ideologically dominant with instability and dissolution.

This seems to be confirmed by the desire of critics of pornography to establish clear, unitary readings of such texts which divide up the texts and their readers according to particular issues of morality, philosophy, politics or ideology. The effect has been to oversimplify the possible readings and pleasures that may proliferate on the site of the pornographic text. Porn accordingly has been attacked as detrimental to the sanctity of the family unit, conducing to moral laxity and depravity, contravening the laws of God, corroding the social fabric; destroying the institution of marriage, dirtying sex and making love equivalent to lust; and so on. Those who consume it have been correspondingly stigmatised as antisocial, immoral, anti-religious, decadent, morally bankrupt, renegade breakers of laws both divine and human.

We should distinguish here between the anti-pornography campaign as such, and official censorship. It is the censor's duty to determine whether a text, or parts of a text, are acceptable to a society within the limits imposed by a sense of cultural norms and a knowledge of legal definitions and proscriptions. The censor thus deals with specific textual objects. (It is unfortunately beyond the scope of the present book to explore such issues as obscenity and its legal definitions, or the debate about the difference between hard- and soft-core porn, though these do inevitably have a bearing on representations of gender in the culture.[2]) The anti-pornography campaigner, by contrast, is more likely to wish to ban pornography *as a genre.* Such an encompassing, general censure, rather than the censorship of a specific text or passage of a text, is both problematic intellectually and critically, and dangerous politically, since in practice it often does not distinguish between pornography as a *textual genre* and as a *narrative mode.* The offensive porn film or novel is thus made identical with an offensive television commercial, though the latter's *generic* function is not simply to represent human sexual activity, as is the former's.

The broad-brush approach has often been favoured by anti-pornography campaigners, whether they begin with a couple of specific instances and then generalise from these, or deal broadly from the beginning with the 'pornographic'. Feminist critics of pornography in particular have tended to regard it as not only degrading to women but actually fostering a culture of male violence toward women—Andrea Dworkin's influential *Pornography: men possessing women*, first published in 1979, may be taken as a radical statement of this position (and it has been widely criticised, by feminists among others).[3]

Porn-inspired violence the feminist anti-pornography camp fears might include physical abuse, rape and death. Thus the argument takes the pornographic text out of the realm of an apparently innocent male pleasure in smut and relocates it in an arena in which women continue to fight for rights over their bodies, their lives and their social existence. For feminist anti-pornography theorists and critics, porn is part and parcel of the patriarchal, masculist discourse by which women are subjected to men. In pornographic texts, whether verbal or visual, women become the objects of the male gaze, and are thus reified (that is, turned into things) and subordinated to male desire. The female body is fetishised and in the process is dismembered conceptually and ideologically. Woman ceases to be an integrated identity with a subjectivity, becoming instead merely a collection of body parts with erotic potential. The rendering of the woman as passive object to the desiring gaze of man prepares the ground for more extreme, more violent practice, such as rape. Put more simply, if woman's body can be subjected passively to the male gaze, her body can also be actively and physically subjected to male desire.

Because so much of this critique has been conducted—and conducted powerfully—by feminist writers, its focus has frequently been the effect of pornography on the bodies and lives of women. Certain other issues have, as a consequence, either been sidelined or overlooked. The first of these is whether men use or enjoy pornography *solely* for its evocation of power over the female body, or whether this genre of text serves other functions, apart from the obvious one of erotic titillation, within the construction of the masculine.

Second, though it is unquestionably true that historically women have been marginalised and victimised by men, the anti-pornography position often takes it for granted that *all* men like and want to view or read porn, and that *all* men respond similarly to it; that is, because pornography is a representational system that positions men as consumers and women's bodies as that which is consumed, men who read or view porn implicitly approve of violence against women and hence are, potentially at least, rapists. A case may be made, of course, for the idea that many men *do* like and want to view or read pornography; but any move from this to the hypothesis which constructs men universally as rapists in intent if not in deed seems much more problematic. It does not take into account an individual man's general life experience, his experience of relationships with women, his sense of ethics and morals, or his psychology. Moreover, it takes for granted that *only* men are interested in pornographic texts.

Nor does the anti-pornography argument always examine at a particularly sophisticated level the structure and dynamics of the pornographic text *as text*. Some of its proponents, as Andrea Dworkin's book demonstrates, appear to assume an unproblematic relationship between the pornographic text and behaviour in reality, as though each reflected and affected the other directly, in a way unmediated by any sense of the *textuality* of porn. Of course pornography, like any other kind of text, participates in and reproduces certain ideological assumptions and the behaviours grounded in these. However, we should be cautious about any simple and unitary theory that sees the text as exercising an immediate and direct effect on the reader's social behaviour. (This echoes, of course, the arguments often made about the impact on young people of representations of violence on television.) We might note, however, that this approach to texts has venerable antecedents: Plato, after all, wished to expel the poet from his ideal republic because he identified the poet as encouraging the populace to immoral, ungodly behaviour through textual representation.

The anti-pornography argument, moreover, sometimes articulates a position which insists upon a transhistorical and transcultural relation between pornography and violence. Dworkin, for example, considers figures as diverse culturally and historically as Georges Bataille, D. H. Lawrence, the Marquis de Sade and Norman Mailer as essentially the same male identity. Equally troubling in her work is the assumption that pornography is a primary, if not the sole, cause of violence by men against women without considering, first, that pornography itself may be a *symptom* of a violence in the culture rather than its cause; or, second, the possibility that men may themselves be caught up in a dynamic of violence which is independent of pornography, and of which violence against women is only one manifestation. Lynne Segal points out, for instance, that the phenomenon of rape appears to be related to the specifics of the cultural construction of gender and of gender roles, so that in some cultures rape is virtually unknown.[4] Segal also suggests that rape and the more direct general violence against women may, in fact, be both class-related and historically conditioned, so that generalisations about all men at all times become questionable (Segal, pp. 238–41).

Indeed, Segal's analysis of Dworkin's work is penetrating, and points out, among other things, that Dworkin fails to identify pornography as fantasy, or to acknowledge that readers/viewers may recognise it as fantasy, a variant of my point above that the pornographic text should be considered as a *text* (Segal, p. 222). Moreover, observes Segal, Dworkin neglects the possibility that violence is a dynamic amongst women as well as men (see, for instance, her section entitled 'Is violence masculine?', pp. 261–71). She also takes to task Dworkin's condemnation of sexual activity itself as another instance of male violence against women, protesting that many women actually do enjoy sex, and that, for many sex workers, prostitution may be an occupation preferable to others—pornography, for instance (Segal, pp. 226–8).

Perhaps the most disturbing aspect of Dworkin's analysis of porn and its effect on male behaviour is her implication of a misogynist violence inherent in maleness itself. Not only does such a position simply dismiss the possibility that such violence is constituted historically and socially as a characteristic of masculinity, but logically it also implies that male violence is inevitable and ineradicable. Hence, the possibility is by-passed that by changing the construction of masculinity, men's attitudes toward women may also be changed. Instead, Dworkin's position tacitly accepts violence against women as a general and constant feature of masculine behaviour. It also assumes that certain definitions of the feminine and the masculine are exclusively inherent in female and male bodies respectively; that women are naturally gentle, nurturing creatures while men are—equally naturally—violent, competitive ones. Again, the possibility of the historico-cultural construction of femininity and masculinity is ignored, or at any rate backgrounded.

There is also the issue of not only *how* but also *whether* homosexual pornography fits into the feminist critique. It may be a fundamental error to assume that the erotics of gay porn are identical with those of standard, commercial straight porn, and that therefore the politics of each is the same. If, as Davis remarks about pornography in general, 'The most proscribed literary forms—like the most persecuted social deviants—must reveal unsettling truths about society that it does not want to hear' (Davis, p. xx), then the general condemnation of gay porn, even sometimes by those who regularly consume straight porn, suggests that something more is at stake than simply the graphic representation of a disapproved or actually prohibited sexual behaviour—that perhaps gay porn unsettles certain certainties both within straight porn and within dominant models of masculinity.

The focus largely on heterosexual pornography would seem to imply that male homosexual pornography functions on identical lines—yet gay men do not go out into the streets to rape passing males (though no doubt this is an alarmist fiction that some homophobes may find convenient). This is not, of course, to assert that homosexual rape *never* occurs: indeed it does. However, as much sociological and anecdotal evidence indicates—say, from prisons—such rape is generally occasioned by professedly *heterosexual* men, for whom the first step is the refusal to attribute masculine status (and hence also masculine power and privilege) to their victims. That is, the victim must first be feminised in some way to enable the victimisation to take place.

A more interesting argument is that which proposes that since men already enjoy power and privilege within masculinity, male homosexuals cannot easily disempower one another in the way in which a man can victimise a woman through violence and pornography. This, however, is not a persuasive argument: male homosexuals are as capable as their heterosexual fellows of seeing one another as sexually feminised; and even the most cursory glance at gay video pornography will reveal the operation of differential power relations similar to those obtaining between heterosexual men and women. Rape by one homosexual of another remains a possibility, perhaps especially in situations involving domestic violence. However, given still generally hostile attitudes toward gays and the public recourse to legal and other (often illegal and violent) forms of containment of the homosexual presence in society, the rape by a homosexual male of a heterosexual one seems unlikely: the probable consequence to the former, if exposed, would probably act as a significant deterrent.

Another possible assumption about gay porn is that it is different in its structure and dynamics from the straight kind, in which case we are entitled to ask how and why this might be, though this information is usually not forthcoming in the debate about porn. Or, alternatively, the assumption is that homosexual pornography is negligible and need not be considered seriously, in which case the critique of pornography is both heterosexist and ignorant of the large body of gay pornography that circulates in the culture. Indeed, as Susan Gubar observes, '. . . recent efforts to emphasize the female figure in pornographic representations have virtually erased a long and significant tradition of (male) homosexual pornography'.[5]

We might note, too, that the critique of pornography has, until comparatively recently, paid scant attention to lesbian pornography, and especially to sado-masochistic tendencies sometimes to be found in such texts. We may conjecture that this reluctance has been due to the tacit assumption in the anti-pornography stance of the essentialism we have already noted, which sees women as naturally gentle, unprovocative, even asexual creatures. The forceful (if simplistic) argument, therefore, that pornography is an objectification of women by men and hence a violence committed on them by men becomes difficult to sustain in a consideration of lesbian pornography, and still harder in the face of the latter's sado-masochistic strain.

The feminist critique of the anti-pornography arguments has taken various forms. While often these critics may find porn debasing or repugnant themselves, they have taken to task the logical, philosophical and ethical bases of the feminist condemnation of pornography and find these lacking or flawed, or have observed that because 'pornography' as a concept in much of the antagonistic criticism often remains ill defined or only narrowly defined, a good deal of the writing against pornography has been weakened. Still another school of criticism, often characterised as 'anti-censorship' feminism, is concerned that the anti-pornography stance makes feminism the inappropriate bedfellow of many a right-wing group whose agenda otherwise has little sympathy for other feminist concerns—for instance, women's rights, including employment outside the home or access to contraception and abortion.[6]

The anti-censorship faction also questions whether it is pornography as a genre that should be condemned, or rather the way human sexuality is currently portrayed in erotic and pornographic texts. For such representation—and this is a powerful element in the anti-pornography argument—positions woman, and especially the female body, as simply the object of the male gaze and of male desire. Indeed, the argument is frequently made that the very etymology of 'pornography', that is, 'the representation [verbal or visual] of a whore', already places woman in a weakened and morally doubtful situation: as simultaneously the object of desire and a commercial identity trafficking in the satisfaction of that desire, she loses credibility in a number of ways. She makes public and commercial an act and its prologue which culturally have been defined as private and as linked with emotion ('true love'); she makes herself available to anyone able to satisfy her pecuniary needs, often redefined as her own commercial or social interests or ambitions; and the mercenary nature of the transaction may transform into an act of willing participation what is actually a coercion, whether through financial need or physical threat (the latter was an argument made, for instance, by Linda Marchiano, a.k.a. Linda Lovelace, the star of the feature-length hard-core porn movie *Deep throat*, in a document cited in 1983 by Andrea Dworkin and Catherine MacKinnon in support of the proposed amendments to the civil rights law concerning pornography in Minneapolis [L. Williams, p. 112]).

It should be noted that pornography, as many feminist theorists point out, also imposes upon women a set of signs which, in turn, constitute the criteria of feminine attractiveness or sexiness. Dworkin and others are thus perfectly correct in claiming that the pornographic text both refers to and mediates the culture's ideology to the consumer/reader of such a text. However, ideology is not trapped in a text like a fly in amber, but rather is pervasively constructed as much *through* the text as *by* the text; and, moreover, is not as univocal and totalising as some, like Dworkin, may lead one to believe: as we have seen, resistance to dominant ideology is built into the idea of dominance itself.

Nonetheless, it is true that subjectivity is effectively limited to the male figure within the pornographic text on the one hand, and on the other to the presumably male reader or viewer of the text. However, as some of the proponents of the anti-censorship feminist position argue, pornography may be reconceptualised as a celebration of eroticism and sexuality that can be both liberating and instructive. Segal suggests that 'Perhaps . . . we need more women pornographers to confront misogyny with new images, less divorced from social context and featuring different types of emotional relationships' (Segal, p. 30). What is sought is an alteration of the structure and dynamics of porn so that it is able to include a viewing position for women, as well as an acknowledgment that women also experience sexual desire that may be articulated and represented in a variety of ways. This argument often cites the increasing presence over the last decade or so of a pornography by and for women.

Generally, however, though the feminist positions on pornography focus on how men's attitudes and responses to porn affect their attitude toward and treatment of the women in their lives, indications that men are by far the largest consumers of pornography[7] support the idea that pornography is significant also in the cultural construction of masculinity. Arguments to the effect that cultural conventions, as well as economic constraints, have debarred women from access to pornography, or that pornography for women has largely been (at least until relatively recently) nonexistent, in fact, offer additional support to the notion that masculinity and pornography are somehow imbricated in one another. Femininity, by contrast, may be constructed for women without reference to pornography (for instance, through imperatives to be companion to men, bear children, make homes, as well as through various narrative genres, such as romance fiction).

Of course, in the wider view patriarchal culture no doubt defines and controls female sexuality; and what amounts to the denial of pornography to 'decent' women is simply one aspect of such definition and control. 'Indecent' women who remain unshocked by pornography or indeed seek it out for their own pleasure, represent the threat to patriarchy and to masculinity of the phallic—and fully sexualised—woman. On the other hand, they may be defined as susceptible to masculine censure because apparently sexually available to all men; such censure may take the form not only of moral condemnation but also of mistreatment of different sorts. (Further, some evidence that it is largely younger men who require access to pornographic materials [Hawkins & Zimring, pp. 56–7] may point not only to a higher sexual drive in such men, but also to their greater need to confirm their masculinity in and through pornography.)

Left largely unexplored in the attack on pornography, then, is how a man, reading a pornographic novel or watching a pornographic film, responds—and perhaps may even be encouraged toward the degradation, actual or ideological, of women, not excepting violence against them—*even when he recognises that the text before him is fictional and fanciful* in its depiction of human sexuality and desire. We need, then, to explore pornography not only from the perspective of women who fear the effects upon themselves of the the sorts of porn texts consumed by men, but also from the point of view of men who look at or read it, in order to understand what its interest for them might be, how they might respond to the several cues coded in such a text. We are concerned, in other words, with how a pornographic text might interpellate the male reader or viewer as a subject and hence may represent him. This implies, of course, that pornography functions ideologically, but it includes more than an assertion about male supremacy over women and their sexuality. That is, what counts as pornographic depends on current cultural values, which in turn means that the pornographic is determined historically also.

Since much of the debate about pornography centres on questions of pleasure, both licit and illicit, afforded by such texts, it is appropriate that we explore the nature and function of some of these pleasures. We have considered in our discussion that one such pleasure is that of the exercise of patriarchal power over the female body, and hence also over the feminine and over women in society (though whether this pleasure necessarily and inevitably leads to actual rape is another question). A different issue, and one that has been raised particularly in feminist psychoanalytic writing on pornography, is that which argues *scopophilia* (the love of looking) or visual pleasure as a masculine pleasure, as opposed to *haptic* pleasure, or the pleasure of touch, which it characterises as feminine. With its origins in the work of feminist theorists of film (for instance, that of Laura Mulvey), this argument proposes that the male pleasure in pornography is produced by *seeing* sex happen, of witnessing, as an observer rather than a participant, the pleasure of the sexual partners.

That pleasure, however, references a certain politics and ideology, for to be the subject of the gaze is, in a sense, to control its object, and to possess it visually. Scopophilia as a male pleasure thus constructs masculine subjectivity as dominant. This idea, as we have seen, underlies the anti-censorship argument that producers of pornography need to rearrange the traditional dynamic of the genre so that women are able to occupy the position of gazing subject, instead of remaining the gazed-at object. It is not that, in enjoying porn, women violate some biologically determined essence of femaleness by departing from the category of haptic pleasure, but rather that, like men, they are enabled also to incorporate the possibility of visual pleasure as part of the erotic. Women thus become capable of control and possession through the gaze. This, of course, signifies a serious challenge to the structures by which men are able to dominate. The difference here—and it is an important one—is that women presumably would not lose the capacity for haptic pleasure, whereas men, for the most part, have still to acquire it.

Though haptic pleasure is in fact common to both sexes, it is argued that men are often so focused on the penis as the sole, and not merely the primary, source of sexual pleasure that they do not recognise the potential for pleasure through touch that the male body as a whole offers. In this way, haptic pleasure quickly becomes assimilated to the idea of passive pleasure (being touched rather than touching), whereas the male pleasure of looking can be likened to (and in the work of some theorists is actually made equivalent to) the sexual invasion of the female body by the penetrating penis.

One difficulty with this line of thinking is that it runs the risk of essentialising such things as visual and haptic pleasure, so that scopophilia may come to mean maleness and vice versa, just as haptic pleasure and femaleness may become interchangeable. Moreover, it may allow a certain slippage between the notion of *visual* pleasure and *sexual* pleasure, as experienced by the male consumer of porn. This confusion may become manifest in a number of ways. In the first place, there is the inclination to understand the pornographic text as collapsing together desire, pleasure and sexual fulfilment, so that somehow the text both *substitutes for* 'real' sex and *offers* it at the same time.

The notion of substitution is, of course, present in the common view that those men who purchase porn are pathetic, lonely creatures unable to find a sexual partner: you don't need porn if you have a real, live, naked person waiting in bed for you. Sexual intercourse, then, is conceived as real, unmediated—the full presence of desire, the erotic, and physical contact, culminating in sexual satisfaction. However, this fullness of erotic presence may also be understood as illusory, because *our very notion of the full presence of the erotic and the sexual comes to us from our cultural representations of sex*, whether these are via formal instruction (the 'sex talk' given by parents to teenage children, as well as sexual initiation by seniors or peers), sex manuals, soft- or hard-core porn, or the erotic content of various sorts of text (the Hollywood movie, for instance, has for a considerable time dictated notions of love and sex in particular ways). Such cultural representations generally comply, or course, with dominant ideology, and therefore will tend to foreground heterosexuality as *the* sexual discourse. Heterosexual desire and its physical fulfilment are thus instead proffered, not only as 'natural', but also as *the* most satisfying forms of sexuality, satisfying because of their assumed plenitude of presence of desire and gratification. What lies outside such dominant representations of sexuality, therefore, becomes classified as fetishistic, sick, morally depraved and corrupting.

It is further supposed that we 'naturally' know how to engage in sex, that it is instinctual. While, of course, from the perspective of biology and the survival of the species it is no doubt true that sexuality is instinctual, its *meanings* in the culture—meanings linking desirability with power, and desiring with subjectivity—are not. Depictions of a 'natural' sexuality, as in the 1980 American remake of the 1949 British movie *The blue lagoon*, are thus fantasies of the plenitude of sexual presence.

It can be demonstrated that pornography is no mere artificial substitute for 'real' sexual activity. For instance, many men consume porn because it may offer pleasures other than or additional to those of actual sexual intercourse—for instance, scopophilic pleasures, which are not always available in actual sexual engagement. Moreover, more and more couples now consume porn, whether as an aid to improve and extend their sexual skills, or simply as a method of arousing one another and heightening pleasure.

Interestingly, men may consume pornographic texts, especially visual ones, as members of a group rather than as single individuals pursuing solitary pleasures. Such groups may be made up, for instance, of all-male crews working at remote sites who watch porn videos together; schoolboys, especially in single-sex schools, poring over 'girlie' magazines like *Playboy* or *Penthouse*; or mechanics in a workshop with a calendar like the famous Pirelli calendars featuring naked or nearly naked women in inviting poses. Such instances suggest that the pornographic text may, in addition to offering erotic arousal, mediate moments of male–male bonding and other forms of male homosociality.

Frequently, however, a connection is customarily made between the pornographic text as object and masturbation as an activity. That is, the consumption of the porn text is seen as merely preparatory to or as inciting the act of masturbation. Indeed, a semiotic connection is often made between the two: to consume porn is to signify masturbation, while to masturbate is to imply the consumption of porn, if only imagined, recalled, or constructed from actual sexual events in the masturbator's life. Both porn and masturbation are therefore often defined culturally as substitutes for the 'real thing'.

Hence masturbation becomes a pleasure guiltily sought and enjoyed, but not often bragged about by men, as their sexual conquests are. However, Jacques Derrida's theory of the supplement offers a different way of seeing the relationship between the 'real thing' and masturbation. A supplement is usually thought of as that which can be added to another entity without in fact disturbing its original structure and function—a bit extra, as it were. In his essay "'. . . That dangerous supplement . . .'", however, Derrida observes that what is perceived as a supplement to another activity or idea is, in fact, more often than not part and parcel of that activity or idea. His reasoning is that that which can be added to cannot be complete; and that which can be added must already belong to that to which it is added.[8]

Discussing a passage in Rousseau's *Confessions of a solitary walker*, in which Rousseau berates himself for succumbing to erotic thoughts and finding release through masturbation (one is tempted, therefore, to re-christen Rousseau's book 'Confessions of a solitary wanker'), Derrida argues that if the 'language' of the erotic and the sexual is able to substitute a symbol for the real presence of a person (that is, a fantasy for the real person), then that person was never 'really' present, but was always enmeshed in a mobile system of signs and symbols which continually substituted for one another (Derrida, p. 154). This position raises questions, of course, about whether, when we have sex with someone, we are physically and intimately engaged *with that person*, or whether we are rather inserted into a system of signs and significations which the other person with us represents or points to. This is seen most clearly, perhaps, in the man or boy who brags about having had sex in order to demonstrate that he is a sexual being, but for whom the identity and subjectivity of the sexual partner are secondary.

Derrida's argument, however, also beats down the boundaries between 'real' sex and its substitutive forms that culture normally erects. If sex occurs, not so much between *people* as between *subjects constructed in, through and by various sign systems in the culture*, and if the signified is, let's say, 'erotic pleasure', does it make much difference if the act is real or imagined, or if at least one of the participants is fantasised? After all, masturbation usually satisfies sexually—at least temporarily—the man who engages in it. It cannot therefore in fact be *simply* an adjunct to or substitution for sexual intercourse.

At the same time, however, an argument may be made for the *fantasy* nature of the pornographic text. The fantasy component is manifest in a number of obvious ways. For instance, in the pornographic text women are represented not only as both beautiful and desirable, but also as lusting reciprocally after the men who desire them, something that doesn't always follow in real life. Female sexual desire is of course generally shown as subordinated to male sexual desire, but in porn it is also often shown as active: the woman enjoys sex with the man, is voracious for it, and never seems to have any trouble reaching orgasm, not only once but often several times. In this sort of text, women apparently are always sexually available and accessible. Likewise, porn customarily represents men as generously endowed by nature in the genital department. Moreover, they are always capable of performing sexually, whenever and however the circumstances might dictate, for they are indefatigable, apparently never experiencing brewer's droop, impotence or premature ejaculation; and they are always capable of producing what looks like litres of semen, apparently often able to send a jet a remarkable distance across the partner's body and/or the set.

Obviously, these features derive from and feed back into a particular masculine myth about women—for instance, that women *should* be available and accessible—and about men—that men *should* be capable of performing at the drop of a pair of knickers. However, everyone knows that this isn't the case. Women are often, for various reasons, not always able to comply even if they wish to; and men can often lose both their lust and their erections if the circumstances aren't just right. Indeed, part of the fascination about male porn stars is the viewer's knowledge that these men have had to perform sexually with cameras and lights trained on them, and with a director and some sort of crew watching and moving about them, sometimes also issuing instructions to them about what they should be doing, or doing next. Thus, the male porn star—at least in his manifestation on the screen—represents a mythic ideal to which men are encouraged to aspire, but which most are aware they are unlikely to attain.

In this sense, then, pornography is already framed as a sort of fantasy about how things might be or ought to be in sexual terms. Other features include the enhancement of the erotic—in video porn, by repeat shots of the copulating invidivuals in their ecstasy, so that the viewer can recapture such moments as he or she never can in reality (the print porn text of course allows its consumer to reread or review its contents at will). On video there are slow-motion shots of penises ejaculating, not only allowing the male viewer to observe the process and to see how other men ejaculate—an important detail to which we will return shortly—but also aiding, particularly in older video porn, in the construction of a world in which semen is not viewed as nasty and slimy or, these days, possibly infected with HIV, but rather as an ambrosial fluid which can be consumed through the mouth as well as the body, and which can be treated like some sort of beauty cream, and rubbed all over the partner's body. This is not the response to their ejaculated semen that many men experience in real life, especially in a sexual culture bedevilled by questions of HIV infection and safe-sex procedures.

However, there are other aspects of fantasy in porn important to our consideration of the ways in which the masculine is represented textually. One of these aspects is the tendency of the pornographic text to conflate the actual physical penis with the culturally significant symbol of the phallus—this explains in part why the positively presented male protagonists of porn texts often sport large genitals. Sex, sexuality and power, intricately involved in other cultural discourses but often in somewhat indirect fashion, are, in the pornographic text, so closely linked as to become equivalent to one another in a sort of palindrome: the sexually active stud has a large penis and thus wields power/the wielder of power must have a large penis, and hence is necessarily a sexually active stud. Since, as we have seen, power is an integral part of the construction of masculinity within patriarchal ideology, sexual activity and prowess, together with a generous genital endowment, are important signs in the semiotic of patriarchal masculinity, and most obviously so in the pornographic text.

Another important element in the construction of pornographic texts—and this is true also of specialist pornography directed toward those with interests in sado-masochism, cross-dressing, and so on—is that the producer of the text cannot predict with absolute accuracy the kinds of people who make up the audience or readership. Thus, in order to work and to produce pleasure, the text must include a broad spectrum of erotic possibilities and fantasies in order to appeal to the greatest number of the readership or the audience. Hence the frequent changes of partner (dark/light complexion, dominant/submissive, active/passive, even on occasion male/female, and so on); of sexual activity (fellatio/cunnilingus, vaginal/anal penetration); of locale (city/country, indoor/outdoor) and of *type* of setting (from spa bath to desert sheikh's tent to executive office). These are all intended to engage certain fantasies in the audience, but not necessarily of every member simultaneously. Viewers or readers thus can dip in and out of the text, registering interest when one of their particular or idiosyncratic fantasies is activated, either in the narrative frame (clandestine meeting or exhibitionist public performance), or in the combination of types of actor, setting, décor, sexual activity, and so on. Even porn texts intended for a narrow audience—for instance, those interested in bondage and discipline—must throw out some lures of this sort of fantasy to the various members of the audience or readership.

Such lures satisfy two demands. The first, obviously, is visual pleasure and its concomitant, curiosity—about what 'it' looks like, how other men ejaculate, what women look like when they experience pleasure, and so on. The other demand is that the text leave gaps in the narrative so that consumers may enter and 'inhabit' it, by inserting themselves into the narrative at the various points where their own individual erotic interests and fantasies are triggered and aroused. This process is different from that described by Linda Williams in her discussion of stag films, in which she proposes that both the techniques and the narrative structures of this genre make the male participants in the film the surrogates for the film's (male) audience. In this way, she suggests, the male viewer *identifies with* the male actor in the film (L. Williams, p. 80). Thus, though making a rather different point, Williams' argument approaches that of Dworkin, for example, for whom the identification of the male consumer of porn with the male protagonist within the pornographic text is the identification of subject with surrogate. At the same time it is an ideological representation which becomes an imperative issued to the consumer via that identification.

However, it is likely that in any practical use of the pornographic fantasy—whether in engaging sexually with another person or persons or in masturbating—the elements of the narrative are actually reworked in the imagination, so that only certain scenes or events are replayed, and details are rearranged imaginatively to suit and satisfy the needs of the sexual participant or masturbator. That is, the protagonist in the pornographic text may be thought of less as a surrogate in a given narrative sequence of actions than as a placeholder for the consumer in a system of meanings whose signs may be rearranged by the consumer in different configurations. The relation of the consumer of porn to the protagonist in the pornographic text is thus made both less direct and less fixed.

If so, porn may be understood to provide a sexual fantasy principally *in order to stimulate other such fantasies* in the reader's or viewer's mind. Commercial pornography, though itself often quite formulaic and predictable, can thus open the way to an infinite play of erotic signifiers whose signifieds are unforeseeable by porn's producers, and require particular imaginations and desires to be filled with meaning. In this sense, porn proffers to the consumer what we might think of as a fugal fantasy of desire. In a musical fugue, a particular motif or figure is introduced which is then played off contrapuntally against another musical theme or themes, the two motifs pursuing or, literally, 'flying' from one another. The fugue's conclusion is the resolution of the two competing motifs.

The fugal nature of pornography can be seen in the introduction of the theme of the erotic and the satisfaction of sexual desire, which undergoes its variations in the various representations of sexual activity on the screen or on the page. The counterpointing theme is introduced by the viewer or reader, and depends on his (or her) fantasies, needs and desires. The resolution is the consumer's appropriation of the original motif and its blending into his or her particular fantasies and needs.

Pornography and masturbation thus are not merely supplementary to 'real' sexual activity but, in terms of Derrida's argument, integral parts of male sexuality which, having been disconnected and uncoupled from each other, are then placed in a hierarchy which sees penetrative, vaginal intercourse as primary and everything else as secondary or less: 'between auto-eroticism and hetero-eroticism, there is not a frontier but an economic distribution' (Derrida, p. 155). Derrida describes specifically the underlying system of meanings in Rousseau's work, in which 'hetero-eroticism' refers to erotic activity with a woman, as opposed to the self ('auto-eroticism'). However, the prefix 'hetero' actually means 'other', so we may extend Derrida's observation to include erotic activity with any other (male or female, singular or plural), as opposed to the self. The reference to 'economic distribution' between auto- and hetero-eroticism implies, then, that in the fantasies which help to constitute the act of auto-eroticism—that is, self-masturbation—there is already present an imagined or imaginary other.

At the same time, however, despite its fantasy elements, porn apparently offers 'real' sex for voyeuristic and vicarious enjoyment. Linda Williams notes that porn attempts, at one level, to render as a sort of documentary *vérité* the experience of desire and of sexual activity: 'hard core is the one film genre that always tries to . . . see the visible "truth" of sexual pleasure itself' (L. Williams, pp. 49–50). Williams suggests that, given the male orientation of much pornographic material, part of this curiosity is focused on issues of the difference between the sexes and sexual difference in pleasure, as well as the difference of sexual acts (L. Williams, p. 31). Ironically, however, 'while it is possible, in a certain limited and reductive way, to "represent" the physical pleasure of the male by showing erection and ejaculation, this maximum visibility proves elusive in the parallel confession of female sexual pleasure' (L. Williams, p. 49).

Citing Foucault, Williams proposes that a further pleasure afforded by pornography is that of knowledge: the pornographic narrative delivers 'the pleasure of knowing pleasure' (L. Williams,

p. 3). She traces in the structure and the history of cinematic porn a desire for what she terms the involuntary confession of pleasure, a confession which is easier to represent in the male than the female, for 'Anatomically, female orgasm takes place . . . in an "invisible place" that cannot be easily seen' (L. Williams, p. 49). For Williams, therefore, porn seeks to obtain that female confession of pleasure: the 'meat' shot (the shot of the penis entering the vagina) is merely the initiatory move in this process. However, there is no female equivalent of the 'money' shot (the ejaculating penis) which announces the male's confession of pleasure; and so the pornographic narrative searches for signs and sign systems which might be made equivalent.

As persuasive as Williams' argument is, it tends to background or downplay the male consumer's interest also in the *male* confession of pleasure. To understand how and why this may be, we need to recall that patriarchy, as a structure experienced by men in the culture, is hierarchical, so that as a result men are positioned in relations of power differential and struggle. Part of this struggle consists in the confirmation of the individual's sexuality, and in particular of his *hetero*sexuality, since male homosexuality enjoys few rewards under patriarchal norms and incurs many retributions. That heterosexual confirmation must be diffracted somehow back through the patriarchal structure, then recognised and authorised by other men.

This explains the boasting of locker-room talk, the requirement that a man's female companion, whether friend, wife or lover, be attractive to other men, the 'scorecard' of sexual conquests, as well as other evidence of virility, for instance, getting women pregnant, and so on. It is this, too, which underlies the Jules Feiffer cartoon cited by Harry Brod:

> We see two men talking over drinks, with one announcing to the other that he's 'quit going out'. Perplexed and disturbed, the other asks why. The first proceeds to tell a tale of 'the loveliest, purest experience I ever hope to have—a fantasy come true—me with the most beautiful, delightful girl in the world—and she *loves* me! She loves *me*!' The story includes superb food, conversation, lovemaking, etc. The punch line has the lucky fellow telling his companion, 'And all that time do you know what I was thinking? . . . Wait till I tell the fellas.'[9]

In other words, the confirmation of a man's sexuality through a woman is imbricated in his need to be validated as masculine *by other men.*

Within this economy of the masculine, pornography may serve a number of functions. As an opportunity for men to engage in a communal activity, porn offers the opportunity for male homosocial bonding, and hence an affirmation of the individual's acceptability by other males, simultaneously marking his entry into the patriarchal hierarchy or confirming his already-existing position within it. Even if the consumption of porn were a solitary activity, the individual male's engagement with it constitutes him as a member of an imaginary male community with similar tastes and pleasures.

In this way, some of the value of pornography to men may lie in what could be termed its educative function. This function of pornography operates on at least two levels. The first of these is purely informational: as we have seen, part of the pleasure for men as consumers of pornography is the satisfaction of curiosity about the act/s of sex; about the way in which men and women differ physiologically; and so on. Many adolescent boys therefore turn to pornography precisely as a form of sex education—akin to the pleasure of knowing pleasure of which Williams speaks—independent of any illicit thrill or masturbatory pleasure they may derive from such texts.

However, at the second level of educative function, pornography is particularly pertinent to the construction of masculinity in the culture. An interesting strategy by which to explore this is through René Girard's notion of the triangle of mediated desire.[10] Girard's study limits itself to the examination of a range of types of novel, focusing chiefly on those of Flaubert, Stendhal and Proust. Its interest for us lies in his perception that in these novels there is a repeated dynamic of mediated desire centring on a desiring subject and on an object of desire (which, incidentally, need not be erotic: Girard points out that social position and status may also constitute objects of desire in the works he analyses). Interrupting the flow of desire from subject to object is the figure of a second subject of desire, a rival who constitutes both a *model of desire for the first subject* and *an obstacle to the fulfilment of the first subject's desire*. In this sense, therefore, the second subject *mediates* the desire of the first subject for the object. Desire, for the first subject, is thus routed toward its object through the second desiring subject (Girard, pp. 7–9 and *passim*).

Eve Kosofsky Sedgwick uses Girard's notion of mediated desire in her study of male homosocial desire in literary texts, but significantly shifts its emphasis.[11] For Girard, when we have a triangle of desire whose object is a woman and whose mode is erotic, we see that both male subjects of desire are locked in a relationship in which one models desire to the other and obstructs the other's desire through his rivalry with him. By contrast, Sedgwick proposes that the two desiring subjects *are bonded in homosocial desire by means of and through the stated object of desire.* Woman becomes a site on which men may meet and confront one another, and thereby bond with one another (see for example her analysis of Shakespeare's sonnets, pp. 28–48). This appreciably alters the tenor of Girard's original hypothesis, and transforms the female object of desire into a vehicle by which homosocial desire may be mediated and—importantly—by which any potential homosexual desire may be masked or deflected.

If we apply Girard's idea and Sedgwick's manipulation of it to the study of pornography, some rather interesting and important new contours for our understanding of it emerge. In the first place, Girard's notion of mediated desire suggests that pornography may function not only as an erotic fantasy for men, but also as a means of identifying and then confirming their own masculinity *vis-à-vis* that of other men.

In such a reading of pornography, the viewer or reader is situated as the desiring self, and the fetishised female body is, of course, the object of that desire. The potential rival subject of desire in the pornographic text may be defined as the viewing/reading position privileged by the text and generally constructed as male. That position may be occupied by a central character who participates in the erotic activity; and/or by a voyeur figure, a function often re-presented as the text's narrator or the eye of the camera. This position thus both models for the reader/viewer what male sexual desire is and how it is to be fulfilled, and at the same time, by virtue of the nature of the text's textuality, is also the obstacle that prevents the male reader from achieving that satisfaction—except, of course, in his own fantasy.

This relation of the male reader/viewer to the virtual male protagonist (whether actual or notional) within the text is a significant one. To begin with, it enables men—particularly young men—in the culture to identify what male sexuality and male desire may be, and to model themselves upon it. In effect, then, the figure of the woman in such a text becomes a device by which the male viewer can align himself with the sexual dynamic of masculinity, and can confirm himself a man among other men.

Put another way, a teenage boy might look at pornography

in order to find out how he should feel and act when confronted erotically with a woman; for him, pornography provides information that goes beyond merely technical and mechanical data—it helps him construct himself within the dynamic of masculinity and within the discourse of male desire. For the adult male, by contrast, pornography provides a way of confirming his own sexuality and desire by comparison with other men, something that he cannot easily and comfortably do even if he leads an active sex life. There must inevitably arise a desire amongst men to know what sex looks like—after all, when men are actually involved in sexual intercourse, they are not in a position to examine it out of detached curiosity. This also has a component of the dynamic of visual pleasure in it: to give oneself over entirely to the sensations of sex is—potentially at least—to make oneself passive, and hence feminine, according to the canons of hegemonic masculinity; whereas to place oneself in a position where one can *look at* sex, as well as derive pleasure from sexual activity, is actively to retain a measure of control, and hence one's masculinity.

There is, further, a desire to know what other men involved in sexual activity look like, and to make comparisons: as one writer engagingly puts it, 'Of course, I know what my own erection looks like, but so much stress is placed on the nature of erections that it's difficult not to wonder what the erections of other men look like (and how mine looks in comparison)'.[12] That is, the graphically educative function of pornography assists the individual man to place himself conceptually and ideologically within the discourses of masculinity and male sexuality.

Sedgwick's use of Girard's thesis of mediated desire produces interesting results when applied to pornography. Homosocial desire, in its pornographic aspect, distances the female not only as subject but also as presence: she is simply the conduit by which the reader can affirm his maleness by comparison with the male position or male figure in the pornographic text. As David M. Halperin remarks, 'To study the various strategies by which men simultaneously construct and coopt female "difference" . . . is not at all to study men's attitudes towards (real) women; rather, it is to study the male imaginary, the specular poetics of male identity and self-definition'.[13] In this way, women are excluded not only by being transformed simply into objects of desire—a principal theme of much feminist criticism, as we have seen—but also by becoming merely a means to an end: not just sexual stimulation, but indeed the affirmation of those very structures which already exclude and oppress women.

It is this reduction of the female subject, as well as the female body, to the status of a cipher in the calculus of masculinity and of male desire that facilitates the degradation of women in pornography and that hypothetically permits the possible connection between pornography and rape: if pornography is an erotic fantasy whose function it is to affirm male homosocial desire, the pornographically represented and constructed female body becomes simply a device to enable the achievement of this end. Woman then may, in a sense, be ignored as a significant factor; and such diminution of her importance may well figure in the relation of pornography to rape, though it is worth signalling that the evidence of such a relation remains a little unclear, according to some of the theoretical literature on the subject.[14]

What of homosexual pornography, often conveniently forgotten or mislaid in the critique mounted by feminist anti-pornographers? The case of gay pornography raises certain critical issues relating both to the nature of heterosexual pornography and to the construction of masculinity in the culture. The application of the Girardian triangle of desire to homosexual desire and homosexual pornography reveals that distinctions between the rival subjects of desire and the object of desire become more blurred and more difficult to make—both the subjects and the object of desire are of the same sex and with the same gender construction, foregrounding the dynamic of male homosocial desire. It also signals the danger to men of the explicit exposure of such desire, since homosociality may be confused, conceptually as well as lexically, with homosexuality.

Ideologically, woman is constructed as penetrable, hence passive and inferior to man, who is penetrator, and thus active and superior. However, homosexuality in our culture interrogates and subverts that construction of man, for if man can be penetrated, where is his superiority? This vexing question lies at the heart of popular representations of the homosexual, in which the nature of the homosexual's actual lifestyle, his emotional and social problems, and his sexual practices amongst other things, are elided into a single point, namely, that this is a man who allows himself to be penetrated by other men. Thus, the homosexual becomes an object of fascination, fear and disgust because by his very existence—regardless of what his preferred sexual practices are—

he challenges the hegemonic model of masculinity in the culture, a model which insists on the impermeability of the male body.[15]

And thus we return to the attempt to apply Girard to the matter of gay pornography. In the heterosexual model, the roles of subject and object remain fixed and determined chiefly by the questions of who penetrates and who is penetrated. This fixing of subject and object enables the voyeur function to operate within the pornographic text, and to both model and mediate the desire of the reading subject. However, in gay pornography, subject and object of desire become interchangeable, a state of affairs which also renders the voyeur function unstable. While there is still the virtual rival subject of desire constructed in and by the text, the distinctions of subject and object of desire are no longer hard and fast. The subject of desire may be penetrator or penetrated; its object, conversely, penetrated or penetrator, thereby confusing, interrogating and subverting the sexual roles familiar to men through the lessons of hegemonic masculinity. Whereas, in the heterosexual model of the pornographic text, the rival desiring subject mediates desire to the reader and obstructs the latter's desire by virtue of the text's textuality, in gay pornography the fact of obstruction appears to be converted into a multiple modelling of desire, which questions that of the heterosexual model. The presence and the dynamics of male homosocial desire are exposed and eroticised as they cannot be in heterosexual pornography or, indeed, in actuality.

In sum, then, the male consumer of gay porn finds himself confronting a text whose codes allow him to suture himself into the representation either as subject of desire or as its object, however the fancy takes him; and, moreover, to switch these identities as further fancy might dictate. This fluidity may not be available to the consumer of heterosexual pornography, which is, as we have seen, more carefully fixed in order to protect the hegemonic model of masculinity, which refuses homosexuality as an approved practice or identity, and which limits and controls the nature and extent of male homosocial desire.

True homosociality, as Sedgwick observes, implies a spectrum of acceptable male–male relationships: 'To draw the "homosocial" back into the orbit of "desire", of the potentially erotic . . . is to hypothesize the potential unbrokenness of a continuum between homosocial and homosexual—a continuum whose visibility, for men, in our society, is radically disrupted' (Sedgwick, 1985, pp. 1–2). If feminist criticism of pornography tends to neglect the circulation in the culture of homosexual pornography, this is because the debate is principally concerned with the effect of pornography on women. This focus, in turn, obscures the function of pornography as a device enabling male homosocial desire. However, the general *moral* criticism of gay pornography may be traced in part to its undisguised mobilisation of male homosocial desire, and its exposure of such desire as potentially (homo)erotic, a desire which is masked in heterosexual pornography by the presence of the woman-as-desired-object, whose body, as Sedgwick points out about the speaker and the young man in Shakespeare's sonnet sequence, functions as the ground on which homosocial and even homoerotic relations between men may be played out (Sedgwick, 1985, p. 38).

This is not, of course, to aver that men are fundamentally homosexual in nature. Rather, it suggests that in a structure of masculinity which is broken and disrupted in terms of the sorts of male–male bonding it permits, as well as the kinds of emotions it licenses amongst men, and one that impels men into conflictive, rivalrous relations with one another, men require strategies, whether textual or extra-textual, by which they may assert and affirm a sense of belonging to a gender and a sexuality that goes beyond the superficialities of drinking together, being involved in sport together, and boasting together of sexual conquests. For better or worse, it would seem that pornography assists men to the sense of solidarity with other men that they need, and which their very masculinity, in the fear that the homosocial may shade into the homosexual, attempts to deny.

The pornographic text, then, becomes a fugue not only of fantasy and erotic desire but also of scopophilia, male homosociality and the desire for knowledge, whether simply of the mechanics of sex or also of pleasure, as Williams suggests. It attracts consumers with the hope of engagement in a fully present sexuality and with the promise of erotic satisfaction; however, as a discourse, the pornographic cannot but ultimately disappoint its consumers, since, as Derrida's work suggests, it is a constantly shifting play of signs and their meanings. Moreover, no commercially produced pornographic fantasy could hope to reflect *precisely* the individual fantasies of each consumer, and so satisfy him (or her). The play of signifiers in such texts thus both enables fantasies of desire and deconstructs them at the same time by signalling the impossibility of their fulfilment in the terms required by the reader. In this respect, then, we may say that the pornographic text promises what Roland Barthes calls *jouissance*, or bliss, but in fact delivers only *plaisir*, or pleasure. ('Bliss' is the English equivalent for *jouissance* in Richard Miller's translation of Barthes's *The pleasure of the text*, though Richard Howard, in his introduction, points out that the French *jouissance* also includes the ideas of orgasm and ejaculation, or 'coming'.)[16]

Barthes concedes that the two are not easily distinguished, but he proposes that bliss, as a textual experience, is an indeterminable site:

> Does writing in pleasure guarantee—guarantee me, the writer—my reader's pleasure? Not at all. I must seek out this reader (must 'cruise' him) *without knowing where he is*. A site of bliss is then created. It is not the reader's 'person' that is necessary to me, it is this site: the possibility of a dialectics of desire, of an *unpredictability* of bliss . . . (Barthes, 1975, p. 4)

At one level, then, the pornographic text is ignorant of 'where' its consumer is, so there is always the promise of bliss in the text's 'recognition' of the individual consumer's desire: 'The text you write must prove to me *that it desires me*' (Barthes, 1975, p. 6).

Bliss, in Barthes's terms, is related to the psychoanalytic notion of desire as a sense of lack in the subject that can be met and satisfied only temporarily, provisionally: it is, in fact, never completely satisfied, though it may take any number of objects in its quest for the sense of completeness in the subject. Thus, Barthes defines the text of pleasure as 'the text that contents, fills, grants euphoria; the text that comes from culture and does not break with it, is linked to a *comfortable* practice of reading'. The text of bliss, by contrast, is riskier, and shorter lived in its satisfaction of desire, 'the text that imposes a state of loss, the text that discomforts (perhaps to the point of a certain boredom), unsettles the reader's historical, cultural, psychological assumptions, the consistency of his tastes, values, memories, brings to a crisis his relation with language' (Barthes, 1975, p. 14). In this sense, then, the pornographic text, as a commercial product of culture that reproduces cultural messages and ideology, can offer only comfortable readings, readings that coincide neatly with cultural expectations of the erotic and the sexual, and with dominant ideologies of gender relations and politics expressed sexually. It is perhaps only in those specialist pornographies—those dealing with and representing paedophilia, sado-masochism, fetishism, transgender identities, and perhaps also those aimed at gays, for gay porn remains both shocking and titillating to all men given the ideological normativisation of male heterosexuality—that the shock and concomitant ecstasy of bliss might be experienced; and this would be precisely *because* of the marginal, challenging nature of such pornographies, their violation of cultural messages, rules and ideologies.

Nonetheless, because pornography as a genre is proscribed, relegated to the region of the indecent and made the transactional coin of an underworld of shady characters on the margins of the decent, law-abiding citizenry, it ironically carries with it the imprint of the lawless, of the unimaginable, and promises bliss, rather than pleasure. But Barthes remarks that ultimately, because it submits to and reproduces dominant ideology, porn is unable to deliver that sought-for experience of *jouissance*:

> The text of pleasure is not necessarily the text that recounts pleasures; the text of bliss is never the text that recounts the kind of bliss afforded literally by an ejaculation. The pleasure of representation is not attached to its object. Pornography is not *sure*. (Barthes, 1975, p. 55)

Barthes states that 'pleasure can be expressed in words, bliss cannot', and, further, that 'Bliss is unspeakable, inter-dicted' (Barthes, 1975, p. 21). The representations of apparent bliss in the bodies and on the faces of the sexual performers of the pornographic text, then, do not necessarily mean that its *consumer* experiences bliss also, though its representation, as Williams proposes, is what he seeks—and, one might add, what he hopes will in some way be reproduced in actuality through the process of reading or viewing the text in question. In this way, the representation of *jouissance* in the text and the text's allusions to it promise the consumer a share in the experience, but in fact produce in the reader only *plaisir*, which is in the end the pleasure of the conventional, the familiar, and the safe.

# 6

# *Do men have a gender? or, I'll show you mine if you show me yours*

Speaking of the erotic work of the Marquis de Sade, Barthes remarks that 'pornographic messages are embodied in sentences so pure they might be used as grammatical models', an observation which prompts him to suggest that two 'edges' are brought into being and into juxtaposition with one another:

> An obedient, conformist, plagiarizing edge (the language is to be copied in its canonical state, as it has been established by schooling, good usage, literature, culture), and *another edge*, mobile, blank (ready to assume any contours), which is never anything but the site of its effect: the place where the death of language is glimpsed . . . These two edges, the compromise they bring about, are necessary. Neither culture nor its destruction is erotic; it is the seam between them, the fault, the flaw, which becomes so.[1]

A little later he asks:

> Is not the most erotic portion of a body *where the garment gapes?* In perversion (which is the realm of textual pleasure) there are no 'erogenous zones' . . . it is intermittence . . . which is erotic: the intermittence of skin flashing between two articles of clothing (trousers and sweater), between two edges (the open-necked shirt, the glove and the sleeve); it is this flash itself which seduces, or rather: the staging of an appearance-as-disappearance. (Barthes, 1975, pp. 9–10)

If *jouissance* resides in the collision witnessed between the legitimate and the illegitimate, between the seen and known and the hitherto unseen and the unknown, then the pornographic text encodes a discursive possibility which simultaneously assists in constructing and maintaining the patriarchal masculine, and in threatening its deconstruction and possible dissolution.

Though much porn, as we have noted, promotes an ideologically approved notion of sexuality—namely, a heterosexuality in which woman is dependent on man for the satisfaction of her own desires—the identification of such texts as fantasies of desire also isolates for us certain dangers within them. For, whether the male protagonist of the porn text is thought of as a sort of surrogate for the actual consumer or rather, as I have suggested, a placeholder within the text's narrative and discursive structure, there is a risk that the consumer will *identify* with that protagonist. Moreover, within the context of eroticism proffered by the genre, this identification will be not only ideological, narrative and discursive but also erotic in nature.

The Girardian triangle of desire allows us to put it more simply: in finding his desire mediated via the second textual subject, there is the possibility that the consumer may come to desire that mediating male subjectivity itself. The complicated relations of desire articulated by the pornographic text among power, success, phallic status, the erotic and the sexual both command attention from men who seek the ideological familiarity of the patriarchal masculine, and invite homosocial desire, together with the concomitant possibility of homoerotic desire. This clearly constitutes a problem for the patriarchal masculine, which refuses such homoerotic identifications, particularly when they become overt.

Ironically, in order to avoid this proscribed identification and desire, the male consumer may instead find himself driven to identify at least provisionally with the *female* protagonist in the text, an identification invited and reinforced by what Linda Williams perceives to be the male desire to see female pleasure involuntarily 'confessed'. Here, too, reside certain dangers, particularly as focused on the feminisation of the male consumer's desire, for this ultimately leads to the same destination as homoerotic desire as understood within patriarchal ideology: the male body and masculine subject rendered passive, (ef)feminised.

These two kinds of identification, while rarely invited overtly in the standard commercial porn text, nonetheless remain as ghostly forbidding—and forbidden—presences, glimpsed intermittently in the fashion that Barthes suggests, and sketched against the more conventional, patriarchal notions of sexuality and erotics. In this way, the vertiginous moment in which *other* possible subjectivities, indeed other masculinities, might be recognised and used as a means of self-identification, holds out to the consumer who recognises them the thrill of *jouissance*, the disruptive moment when a gap opens that threatens the comfortable reading of the pornographic text which Barthes defines as textual *plaisir*.

Male consumers of porn become aware, to some degree and in some fashion, of this danger to their identities as patriarchal, masculine subjectivities. For the strong insistence by the commercial pornographic text on the power of the phallus, on the penis's unmediated identification with the phallus, as well as on the primacy of heterosexual erotics and on the subordination of the female body to male desire, suggest that other possibilities are being backgrounded and silenced. Indeed, we may conclude, given such an emphatic restatement of dominant patriarchal ideology, that *the male pleasure in looking*, especially in regard to the pornographic text, *constitutes a risk to the subject who looks.*

Nonetheless, porn requires the male consumer to identify a particular configuration of signs as signifying 'masculinity', a recognition which at the same time interpellates him as an ideologically obedient male subject, that is, as 'masculine'. However, though such signs may at first appear evident and beyond question, we should note that sign systems may prove dangerous in their signifying capability. As we have already seen in our reading of various texts, constellations of signs can be read as signifying *other* meanings in addition to the preferred one, and thus potentially extend to the reader an *excess of signification*. This is as true of the signs of gender in the culture as of other, perhaps more obvious sign systems. Therefore, suggests Judith Butler, a key element is its repetitiousness, or what she calls its 'citation'.[2] That is, it is apparently not sufficient in a patriarchal (and therefore phallocentric) culture that a body of a particular sex be marked as belonging to one gender or the other. Instead, it seems to be necessary that the relevant and appropriate gender be cited repetitiously through various means (words, acts, behaviours, attitudes, and so on) in order continually to reinforce the idea of that particular gendered subjectivity. In this sense, the signs of gender are *performative*, a term which Butler borrows from the linguistic work of John Searle and J. L. Austin, who propose that certain verbal expressions actually *do* what they *say* (Butler, 1993, p. 10; see also pp. 12–16). Thus, to say 'I promise to do such and such' is in effect to make the promise itself: it is a performative. For Butler, then, it is not so much that, as subjects, we 'have' gender, as that as subjects we 'do' gender, through an array of signs and sign systems. This suggests, in turn, that gender assignments are neither natural nor perpetual, and that the culture enforces their citation continually in order to reinforce patriarchal, phallocentric structures and the way these disperse and assign power. In this fashion, the culture seeks to disguise the fact that gender is constructed and thus potentially fluid.

The cultural construction and operation of masculinity in particular depend not only on the citation of gender but also on what we might (at the risk of sounding a bit like a revival of an old Beach Boys number) call the *ex-citation* and *in-citation* of gender. By *ex-citation* I mean, first, an analogy with Barthes's notion of *ex-nomination*, an operation by which a social group contrives to vanish as a named identity through a naturalising process.[3] The same process may be observed with reference to the construction of gender. For instance, in binary pairings like *man/woman* or *boy/girl*, it is the *second term* in each which appears to encode difference. In this way, *man* and *boy* take on the semblance of an incontrovertible fact of nature, while *woman* and *girl* seem to be the deviance or divergence from that fact. (The same is true, in racist discourse, of the *white/black* pairing: *white* is normalised and universalised, whereas, as we saw earlier in the case of Othello, *black* becomes the deviant and exceptionable term.)

This has, of course, been remarked on by a number of feminist theorists, who have suggested accordingly that the masculine is considered the degree zero, or the silent criterion. Thus, for instance, Monique Wittig argues that it is really only the female who is considered to 'have' or 'be' a sex, since that sex is perceived in a patriarchal culture as a deviance from the male and, moreover, as inferior at that.[4] For such feminist thinkers, then, the male and the masculine are constructed as the norm. *The implication, then, is that men are in a special sense gender-less, precisely because the masculine is thought of as the universal and neutral/neuter term.*

We may pose the relationship between the performative nature of gender and its ex-citation thus: the citation of gender—its performativity—implies that, discursively, gender is in fact a weak attribute and must be reinforced constantly, and hence made visible to people in the culture; the ex-citation of gender, by contrast, seeks at the same time to make that gender performativity invisible, so that it appears *natural*, and hence beyond question.

The concept of gender ex-citation has some convergence with

what Sedgwick calls a contradiction in the culture's minoritising and universalising views.[5] Though her specific focus is the way in which homophobia creates a minority of (i.e. minoritises) the male homosexual population and thus affirms the normativity of (i.e. universalises) the heterosexual majority, her perspective has much in common with Butler's mobilisation of the notion of the *abject*, or that which is unthinkable and therefore has no place in the system, nowhere to inhabit (Butler, 1993, pp. 2–3 and *passim*). Butler proposes that the feminine constitutes such an abjection in a patriarchal, heterosexist culture, as indeed does the homosexual. The category of the abject does not consist merely of that which comes along to find that it does not fit into the ideological scheme of things. Rather, it is that *which has already been anticipated* by ideology and relegated to a position which then allows ideology to invoke a boundary between the acceptable (or, more properly, that which may constitute the subject or which has subjectivity) on the one hand and, on the other, the abject (that which has no real or significant subjectivity). Put otherwise, if the feminine and the homosexual constitute the abject in patriarchy, it is not because patriarchy is in absolute terms neither feminine nor homosexual, *but because it has anticipated these and expelled them.* That expulsion, in fact, helps to constitute patriarchy itself, and to draw the line between what is and is not patriarchal, masculine and possessed of subjectivity.

If the ex-citation of gender produces a politics of gender and especially of masculinity, the relation between the normative, patriarchal masculine and that which it minoritises or abjects is what we might call the gender *in-citation* of the masculine. That is, within the ex-citation of the masculine—its disappearance from view as the ground zero of gender—we find a system of relationships which are not those merely of difference, but rather of *self-definition through difference.* In other words, the in-citation of gender, and especially of the masculine, refers to the structuring relationships that constitute it. *The masculine is thus defined in the first place as a gender category which is allocated to only one sex: the male.* Women cannot be—or, more properly, ought not to be—masculine. Indeed, a woman so defined becomes an anomaly, even monstrous. This, then, is a definition by sex; and historically it has been a way of policing men, via the threat of (ef)feminisation or indeed even the perception of effeminacy.

*In the second place,* in more recent cultural history, *the masculine is defined by sexuality: properly speaking, the masculine is heterosexual.* A homosexual, then, though male by sex is excluded or marginalised by virtue of the fact of his sexual preference for members of his own sex. However, this has not always historically been the case: studies of same-sex relations among men in classical Greece or in European history until the eighteenth century show that it has at times been possible for a man to retain the status of masculinity independently of his sexual preference for other men, provided he could also avoid the charge of effeminacy (and we should note that what constitutes 'effeminacy' changes historically and across cultures).[6] Thus, the masculine is defined negatively in modern Western culture in two ways, once by sex and once by sexuality: the masculine is *not* female, and it is *not* homosexual.

This way of thinking of the masculine challenges its apparently absolute primacy by shifting focus from the notion of the masculine as a given positive term in relation to which the feminine and the homosexual must find their (marginal) places, to a notion of the masculine as a category within *a system of categories.* Seen thus, the masculine now appears as in fact *dependent categorically and systemically on a negative relation to both the feminine and the homosexual.*

In order to preserve its independence as a category and to avoid being identified either with the feminine or the homosexual, the masculine deploys several strategies, and it should be noted that these are not necessarily related serially, but may function—and often do so—simultaneously.

One of these, preventing the slide toward the feminine, is the encouragement of what Eve Kosofsky Sedgwick calls male homosocial desire.[7] This prompts strong emotional or emotion-producing bonds, not only positively—for instance, in what is commonly referred to as male bonding or mateship—but also negatively, often manifested in the rivalry with, suspicion of and hostility toward other men that is—as we have seen—prompted by the differential distribution of power amongst men under patriarchy. The classic Western or the war film provide ample illustration of this principle. Whether the male characters are figured as lawman and outlaw, for example, or as good soldier and bad, as officer and soldier, or as one of 'our side' or one of 'theirs', they are connected by a shared set of experiences and emotions, and demonstrate different facets of the masculine, some approved, some not. (Indeed, we might say that the conflict between such characters is often driven by competing definitions of the masculine: the same is true of the rivalrous situations we noted in *Strictly ballroom*, and in the hostility between Dracula and the Crew of Light in Stoker's novel.) Thus, the individual man is inextricably linked emotionally and psychologically with other men, regardless of the nature of that link or its social consequences. In this way, then, the slide of the masculine as a category toward the feminine is arrested and controlled.

A further strategy to evade and resist the feminine is to be found in misogyny, which may be articulated and inflected in a range of attitudes and behaviours toward women, commencing with the ignoring and disparagement of women, and including such phenomena as wife-beating, rape and murder. It should, however, be noted that *misogyny does not definitively exclude heterosexual desire*; and indeed misogyny may even be heteroerotically charged, as is evidenced by some cases of rape (others, of course, may be chiefly or solely motivated by a politics of power, rather than by desire). The chief function of misogyny, though, is to distance the feminine from the masculine, and this is achieved by the inferiorisation of the feminine, and hence also of women.

Male homosocial desire and misogyny, then, are strategies whose goal is to keep the masculine away from the feminine as categories in the culture's system of gender. A similar pattern may be discerned in the ways the distancing of the category of the homosexual from the masculine is accomplished. In many ways, of the two categories, the feminine and the homosexual, the latter is the more dangerous: the gay man is morphologically identical to his straight counterpart, and, importantly, because of popular assumptions abroad in the culture about the homosexual's erotic practice, such as passivity, penetrability and so on, the homosexual is often read as the gateway to the (ef)feminisation of the male.

The most obvious of the strategies to distance the homosexual as category is the privileging—in all ways, including, often, the law of the state—of heterosexual desire. Indeed, one might go so far as to say that heterosexual desire is fetishised in being made normative for the culture, to the exclusion, marginalisation, or reduction in importance or validity of other forms of sexuality. Yet such desire ought logically to contradict misogyny (though in practice heterosexual desire often fuels it), as illustrated by Western culture's rich treasury of stories about the disastrous sexual enslavement of men to women—disastrous, that is, chiefly to men, according to the focus of the stories. This catalogue of tales begins with Adam's devotion to Eve, and encompasses further accounts such as that of Samson and Delilah, the Homeric stories of Circe and the Sirens, the legends of figures like Antony and Cleopatra, the historical as well as legendary account of Mata Hari and her victims, and many others. (We might also include in the woman-as-siren motif such stars as Mae West, Madonna and Sharon Stone.) Such cautionary tales—which seem to be a persistent genre in Western cultural history—lend weight and authenticity, via inter-textual confirmation, to the notion that woman is in fact a threat to man. Moreover, they signal that men's submission to hetero-sexual desire may be understood as an implicit surrender to the feminine, and the individual male's consequent (ef)feminisation, since these stories frequently link heterosexual desire to woman's control over man.

The foregrounding of heterosexual desire as a strategy to resist the category of the homosexual is reinforced by the deployment of another strategy, namely, homophobia, which, just as misogyny disparages women, belittles gay men and may even subject them to the same sorts of violence—beating, rape and murder—that many women have experienced, feminising those men still further and disavowing the possibility of their enacting masculine sub-jectivities.

Yet homophobia implies the homoerotic—it doesn't otherwise make sense. That is, homophobia is not simply a reaction by 'real' men to the existence of homosexual Others and their sexual activities: it is also a fear of the possibility that homoeroticism may in some way blur the categorical boundaries between the masculine and the homosexual; and, because the homosexual is often classified as on a par with the feminine (whether as 'failed' or feminised masculinity), there is the danger that the distinctions between the masculine and the feminine might also become less defined, threatening the collapse of all categories.

Now, I am not here proposing those fantasies of the gay culture, namely, that men are really all homosexual deep down, or that any man can be 'had' by a gay man—though, as we saw in our discussion of pornography, it is significant that what often motivates homophobia is precisely the same sort of fantasy, read rather as seduction, recruitment, rape or other contamination of the heterosexual man by the homosexual. I am instead suggesting that dominant forms of masculine behaviour are, in our culture, predicated on a dual dynamic: *the fascination of the possibility of same-sex attraction* and, simultaneously, *its prohibition and perse-*

*cution*, which in effect helps to produce the abjection of the homosexual from the masculine proper by anticipating it and then defining the masculine in contradistinction to it. This process renders the latter vulnerable to the imposition of a range of negative attributes, many of which are already associated with the feminine, including, for instance, sexual, moral and physical passivity, physical frailty and 'effeminate' behaviour.

The new macho image of the gay man as it emerged in the 1970s contested this strategy of marginalisation of the homosexual, and thus disrupted the definition of the masculine by interrogating its ideological assumptions and by demonstrating the performative nature of gender subjectivity. Indeed, this phenomenon raises a variety of interesting questions; for instance, the ways in which the male homosexual has been constructed and made visible by the dominant model of the masculine. In *Speculum of the other woman*, Luce Irigaray proposes that patriarchy transforms woman into a specular object which mirrors aspects of the masculine back to man.[8] Thus, woman loses both her subjectivity and her unity as a subject. The conventional image of the male homosexual as effeminate may likewise function as a specular object for mainstream masculinity, in that he reflects a distorted and disjointed image of what the masculine is not or should not be. However, the macho gay as a specular object reflects a recognisable image of the masculine as aggressive, muscular, non-effeminate, and so on, *but remains differentiated in terms of sexual orientation.* It thus presents a much more troubling image to patriarchal masculinity. Indeed, we might say that, whereas the stereotype of the homosexual offers to patriarchal masculinity an acceptable parodic version or contestation of the feminine—namely, what the masculine is not—the macho gay offers a parodic version or contestation of the masculine, that is, what patriarchal ideology defines as admirable and worthy of emulation, and which it therefore enjoins upon men in the culture—and which, in the macho gay, therefore becomes unacceptable because it creates the anomaly of a homosexual masculine.

The fear of the homoerotic as well as its fascination for men can be illustrated by men's obsession with penis size, which of necessity must cause the individual man to think of the penises of other men, though—if he is heterosexual—he is explicitly forbidden to do so. Hence, the stories of men furtively surveying the genital equipment of other males in the public lavatory, the changing room and shower at the gym, and so on—to say nothing of the accounts of pissing competitions, masturbation contests and the like, especially among adolescent males. The homoerotic nature of these activities may be masked by homophobia and by homosocial desire; but its presence may nevertheless be sensed, perhaps particularly in situations where there is an emphasis on homophobia or on male homosocial desire.

Indeed, the presence of homophobia frequently precipitates a concentration of male homosocial desire: a group of men jeering at or otherwise persecuting a homosexual is a group bonded as much by homosocial desire as by homophobic behaviour. In this way, therefore, male homosociality always runs the risk of toppling over into at least covert homoerotic, or perhaps even homosexual, bonding. This, in turn, suggests that the discourse of masculinity in our culture relies on a simultaneous recognition and disavowal, via the homosocial, of the homoerotic and the homosexual.

These various strategies of the masculine (and there are no doubt others) highlight not only a radical disruption, as Sedgwick has it,[9] but also a radical ambiguity at the very heart of masculinity, at least as it is constructed in our culture: heterosexual desire, yet misogyny; homosocial desire, yet homophobia. It also suggests that misogyny and homophobia are the twin motors which drive the patriarchal machine, distancing the disturbing categories of the feminine and the homosexual from the masculine, protecting the masculine and preserving it from dissolution into one or the other of those categories.

If this is so, we may think of masculine power as the *effect* of the struggle enjoined on men by patriarchal discourse to sustain and protect the category of the masculine. Its privileges, therefore, function in part to camouflage the anxieties and tensions created by this need of the masculine to protect itself from that which it has abjected, but which it nonetheless requires in order to sustain and define itself.

Despite the abjection of homosexual subjectivity under patriarchy, a casual perusal of the personal columns in almost any newspaper will yield the information that a prime quality in the partner sought by many gay men is that he be 'straight acting'. Such a description references not only the 'masculinised' or 'feminised' social behaviour of the individual ('butch' versus 'femme'), but may often be taken, especially in the larger heterosexual community, also to signify sexual behaviour, in terms of activity or passivity. Much has been written and said about how such assumptions and the terms which enunciate them reproduce within homosexuality, male or female, the structure and power relationships of heterosexuality. However, analytic and theoretical attention needs also to be paid to the way that the idea (or ideal) of 'straight acting' among male homosexuals reflects a tangled issue of homosexual subjectivity in a heterosexual ambient culture. Additionally, the importance of 'straight acting' to men and women in general requires some exploration. A number of questions consequently arise: what, for instance, is the meaning of 'straight acting', as a mode of social being in the discourse of patriarchal masculinity, and in its associated oppositional discourses of heterosexuality and homosexuality? And what does it mean that male 'straight acting' is—or can be—eroticised in the discourse of male sexuality, and especially of male homosexuality?

Patriarchal discourse not only assumes heterosexuality in individual males: it requires *all* men to be 'straight acting' if they are to function under patriarchy, and imposes punitive consequences on those individuals who fail to comply. Male homosexuality offers a threat to patriarchal discourses of gender and sexuality which female homosexuality evidently does not. For instance, 'mannish' dress and social behaviour among women have, since the middle of this century, become more generally accepted and indeed even fashionable, whereas 'womanish' dress and behaviour among men remain subject to deep suspicion and criticism. Moreover, lesbian activity has for a long time been eroticised by and for heterosexual men, especially in the porn industry, and is understood by (heterosexual) men to be a female sexual orientation reclaimable by men; whereas male homosexuality, whatever its covert erotic value for heterosexual men, officially remains intransigently coded as both un-erotic and reprehensible, since it signals the absolute failure of the norms of masculinity in the homosexual male.

The culture's sex–gender system, as Gayle Rubin defines it,[10] takes for granted a particular connection between *sex* identity (male/female) and *gender* identity (masculine/feminine), and thereby effectively conceals this connection by naturalising it. The system moreover assumes gender properly to be grounded in heterosexual desire. In this way, sexuality—that is, the development of erotic desire for an object of a particular sex—functions as a link between biological sex identity, on the one hand, and (apparent) social gender identity, on the other.

It is thus not only a general gendering of behaviour but also a particular sexuality which has the important function of locating the body in a social context. Sexuality is a bridge, as it were, between the body (sex) on the one hand and society (gender) on the other. This bridge is generally conceived as leading naturally *from* biological sex *to* social gender identity. The important point here is that the conventional linking of sex to gender—that is, of the body to society—through sexuality is performed by defining that link as heterosexual.

Within this discursively produced framework, *the orientation of desire itself becomes a marker of gender.* In our culture, therefore, masculinity and heterosexuality, as both erotic desire and sexual orientation, are intimately intricated with one another, and acquire the status not only of norm but also of normality, that is, both universality and behaviour according to nature. Thus, if the male individual's sexuality develops along expected and encouraged lines so that he desires the other sex, the transition from biological sex to social gender identity appears uni-directional, seamless, unproblematic and, indeed, inevitable.

Though it may be commonly thought of as uni-directional, however, that bridge may also be a two-way thoroughfare, traffic running *between* sexual fact and gender identity, and not merely from the one to the other. Thus, masculine behaviour seems to be appropriate only to male bodies, and when witnessed in an individual male, appears to promise or confirm a heterosexual orientation in that man. Sexuality, as a link between sex and gender, thus permits a slide between the social and the bodily, a slide which often becomes an ideological convenience in a patriarchal culture. So, for instance, though women have long resisted the idea that biology is destiny, the bi-directional pathway created by sexuality between sex and gender in fact encourages people in the culture to think precisely in those terms, so that gender, for all its social construction, is reconceived as located in sex, that is, in the body.

For men, sexuality as bridge provides a convenient recourse to justify the practices of male sexual and erotic activity. The myth (in the sense of 'cultural belief' rather than 'fable') that male sexuality is a tidal phenomenon that brooks no resistance and must find release is sustained and confirmed by the linking of sex to gender through sexuality. Such a definition of male sexuality becomes 'natural', because it is understood as being of the body. This 'natural' urge becomes assimilated as part of masculine gender identity, and can then be invoked to justify such phenomena as rape (whether of women or other men).

The fact of same-sex desire, however, contradicts and disrupts the discourse which unproblematically sees sexuality as the connection between sex and the privileged (heterosexual) gender identity. For the homosexual man, the same sexual bridge arrives nowhere licensed and authorised by the culture. He is thus in the anomalous position of being male-identified through his anatomical morphology, yet having to assume a gender identity which not only fails to encode his sexual orientation but actually refuses it. From this fact proceed the arguments that gay men have few or no role models on which to pattern themselves, and that effeminacy of behaviour may become a likely option for gay men uncomfortable with the anomaly of the subject position created by the clash among sex identity, sexual orientation and gender definition.

Another possibility for gay men is, of course, to emulate their heterosexual brethren. Straight acting, which presumes heterosexuality, becomes the social and public demonstration of gender normality, and is articulated—in Butler's term, cited—through a particular repertoire of verbal and gestural signs which are understood to be tokens of heterosexual masculinity. Such behaviour is both reinforced and enforced by the structure of patriarchal masculinity, which in turn produces a sort of undeclared police-state mentality among men, establishing guidelines of attitude, behaviour and other sorts of practice in order to assure the culture that its males will act in required, approved ways; and to warn those males who are unable to do so, or who refuse those guidelines, that there will be punitive consequences for their noncompliance. In this way, heterosexual masculinity takes on the guise, not merely of normality, but of essence. Men who conform, whether they are homosexual or heterosexual, to the dictates of the discourse of patriarchal masculinity thus seem *essentially* masculine and therefore apparently heterosexual.

The bi-directional nature of the bridge between sex and gender identity consequently invites assumptions about the sexual orientation of an individual based on the latter's gender behaviour. But appropriate gender behaviour, as we have noted, may in fact mask desires and sexualities deemed inappropriate to that sex. The straight acting of the homosexual male, in subverting the premises of the sex–gender system, therefore represents a threat to it, and thence to all men in the culture.

The term 'straight acting' is rich in meanings. In gay parlance, 'straight' is opposed to 'gay'. It signifies not only heterosexuality but also normality, 'straightness' or non-deviance from a norm of some kind. Its meaning, therefore, in the personal columns may be put thus: 'simulating, or behaving like, a "straight" or heterosexual (man)'. However, 'straight' may also mean 'direct, honest', as in the phrase, 'I'll be straight with you'. The term 'straight acting', considered semantically, thus begins to gather complexity, meaning both 'acting as heterosexual' and 'acting honestly'; yet the two are contradictory, for a homosexual acting like a heterosexual is not acting honestly, at least according to the canons of patriarchal discourse. And it raises a further question, namely, whether there is or may be a behaviour both appropriate to and typical of each sexual orientation.

These complexities increase when we include as possibilities in the term the dual sense of 'acting', namely both 'performing' and 'doing, behaving as agent'. This implies that the *doing* of a kind of masculinity is also its *performing* (here understood as a form of representation, not as a perform*ative*)—and, of course, vice versa. The play of potential meanings in the phrase is, therefore, highly suggestive—about the placement of the homosexual (as adjective) on the cultural map of meanings and values, about notions of conformity and honesty, and about the relationship between behaviour and performance. In the stipulation of gay personal ads that the person sought be 'straight acting', then, is concealed a complicated network of discursive meanings.

Performing the heterosexual—acting the straight—then may become a strategy whereby the homosexual can 'pass' undetected, and hence unpunished, in the culture. It requires the individual to use the gestural and verbal sign system—stance, hand movement, voice inflection, clothing, conversation topic, and so on—appropriate to heterosexual masculinity; and it often requires him, too, to keep his sexual orientation undisclosed or backgrounded. That this is the case can be seen in how a gay man who in every respect reproduces the conventional signs of masculinity in his body language, his aggressiveness, competitiveness, bravery and so on may nonetheless be stigmatised because of his sexual orientation, and his social being invalidated as a consequence. Moreover, the same promiscuity which marks the heterosexual 'stud' as an approved figure with a validated mode of being can be denounced in the male homosexual, in whom it becomes a sign of innate perversity (an interesting use of the body-as-nature figuration). Thus, in the early phase of the HIV/AIDS epidemic, homosexual promiscuity was stigmatised as a major cause of the spread of the disease. While this may indeed have been so, the point to understand here is the culture's shifty seizure and subsequent projection of this notion as defining the homosexual against the more 'normal', heterosexual male, now rather righteously redefined as *less* sexually active than his homosexual counterpart.

Homosexual desire and the homosexual as social being together thus disrupt a normative discourse which wants to be seen as natural and therefore universal. We can trace this rupture in the way that the male body is culturally constructed in the processes of defining the masculine, in which that body becomes uniquely the subject of heterosexual desire. Homosexual desire, by contrast, sees it also as its object.

As we saw in our exploration of *Strictly ballroom*, men, empowered by the hierarchical structure defined by patriarchy, learn at an early age that to be a man is to compete successfully against other men. Manliness thus is defined for the individual by the structure of patriarchy as well as by discourses of the body. Cultural practices, say of courtship, sports or business, foreground competition, and reward those who win, not those who merely take part. The experience of individual men also indicates that they daily operate under the assumption that they must show other men that they succeed where others fail, professionally, personally, sexually. Given such conditions (and conditioning), it is hardly surprising that men prove anxious to enact their manliness at every turn.

Nor is it surprising that they attempt to conceal or suppress elements which might betray them to other men as *insufficiently* manly. These include lack of 'drive', whether social, professional or sexual; the refusal of confrontation; and the expression of emotion, sensitivity, passivity—in short, the demonstration of *vulnerability*, as defined by patriarchal discourse. Invulnerability, that is, non-femininity, becomes so highly valued that even the male body comes to be understood as impervious to shock, pain, or emotion. Thus, masculinity is seen also as the demonstration of the individual male's independence and self-containment, his body likewise integral and whole. However, the insistence on these lead one to suspect that they mask a crucial fear of betrayal. A useful metaphor here is the citadel, invoked by Antony Easthope in his *What a man's gotta do*:

> For the masculine ego the body can be used to draw a defensive line between inside and outside. So long as there is very little fat,

> tensed muscle and tight sinew can give a hard, clear outline to the body. Flesh and bone can pass itself off as a kind of armour. A hard body will ensure that there are no leakages across the edges between inner and outer worlds. Nature, it seems, has betrayed the perimeter of the male body. It has opened up there a number of gaps and orifices, though mercifully fewer than for the female body. What holes remain must be firmly shut . . . Tensed, the whole frontier can be kept on red alert.[11]

'Typically' masculine behavioural characteristics—such as aggressiveness, endurance, resilience and so on—thus become both equivalent to the impermeability of the male body and complementary with it. The male body and masculine behaviour become in turn the basis for a masculine subjectivity which wants to see the male self as impregnable, defended but not merely defensive, and integral, whole.

The boundary willed by the male body has two purposes. First, it prevents the incursion of the outside world. Second, it seals in that which is within the male body, preventing illicit desires or menacing emotions from finding expression in and blending with the outside world—for instance, through the consummation of those desires, or finding objects for those emotions. The male body is thus constructed in opposition to the female body, which is perceived as lacking such boundaries. Instead, the female body becomes a gateway at which the interior and the exterior meet and merge, for through this gateway issue forth into the outside world the infant during birth, as well as menstrual blood and other matter; and, in sexual intercourse, the male body gains entry from the outside world.

It is partly on this definition of the male body (and therefore also of the masculine) as closed, complete and whole that the subjectivity bestowed on men by patriarchy rests: if woman is constructed as open and incomplete, she can achieve only a partial subjectivity at best, subjectivity itself being produced by the imagined sense of self as complete and closed. By this logic, then, desire can be experienced actively only by such a closed, complete subject, namely, a man. Woman can desire only passively, that is, she can desire to be desired. Hence, the notion of woman's need for man (and, more precisely in the terms of psychoanalytic theory, his penis or, symbolically, his baby) as a means to achieve temporary completeness and closedness. Here again the metaphor of the citadel of the masculine body is suggestive: its inhabitant, deeming himself safe behind its fortifications, can allow himself the periodic foray outside his walls, because he can always return to their protection.

In ancient days, fortresses looked impregnable, but they often contained a secret passage by which inhabitants, escaping from the overwhelming force of a besieging army, could find their way from the perils of siege and the certainty of defeat, and issue forth in safety some distance from the citadel they had abandoned. Of course, that secret exit could sometimes be discovered by the enemy, who then had a means of ingress into the hitherto apparently impregnable hold, and could wreak destruction on the people sheltering there. Its whereabouts, therefore, had to be kept hidden, and carefully guarded. So it is with masculinity, and with the male body: the discursive patriarchal insistence on the integrity of the male body and the autonomy of the masculine prompts us to suspect that in men there may be a flaw, a gap which must be protected and kept secret from the outside world.

Easthope's description of the male body suggestively indicates that such discursive gaps occur where the bodily surface is pierced by an orifice. The homophobia built into the dominant model of masculinity in our culture suggests further that the orifice most feared and protected by men is the anus, which Guy Hocquenghem identifies as the first bodily site we make our own, and which thus becomes a signifier of privacy, and of subjectivity.[12] (We might recall that an older term for the anus is 'fundament', etymologically related to 'foundation', and hence indicates that on which the rest of the body and the subjectivity of the individual are built.) Though of course the sexual repertoire of gay men is not limited exclusively to anal penetration, this identification is the one commonly made in the culture; and Hocquenghem argues that homosexual desire, so construed, makes the anus, as it were, public. This in turn constitutes a scandal in the culture, since it demonstrates the penetrability of the male body. That body can then no longer be defined as integral, and hence as masculine. The anus becomes in effect the secret of the citadel, to be protected at all costs—hence the warning by heterosexual men to others when entering the site of the homosexual: 'Backs to the wall, boys!'

This view of the specifically male anus as sacrosanct is already articulated in an early modern erotic (or pornographic, depending on one's definition) text, John Cleland's notorious *Fanny Hill, or memoirs of a woman of pleasure* (published in two volumes 1748–49). Fanny, pausing at a public house during a journey, sees two young men enter the premises, and spies on them through a hole in the wainscot.[13] To her moral indignation and horror, the two start to engage in erotic games with each other, and eventually turn to anal sex. The older youth enters the younger:

> And now, passing one hand round his minion's hips, he got hold of his red-topped ivory toy, that stood perfectly stiff, and showed that if he was like his mother behind he was like his father before . . . (Cleland, p. 195)

Whatever we might conclude about Fanny's scopophilia or her occupation here of the moral high ground, we must also recall that she is the fictitious narrator of a male author, and that through her Cleland was probably expressing his culture's official attitude toward the violation of the male body's integrity. We might note, moreover, that the possibility of anal penetration of the *female* body does not seem to be so severely criticised in this text: Fanny, meeting a sailor, allows him to have his way with her:

> . . . he leads me to the table, and with a master-hand lays my head down on the edge of it, and with the other canting up my petticoat and shift, bared my naked posteriors to his blind and furious guide. It forces its way between them, and I feeling pretty sensibly that it was not going by the right door and knocking desperately at the wrong one, I told him of it: 'Pooh,' says he, 'my dear, any port in a storm.' (Cleland, p. 178)

(As an explanatory aside, we should note that the exclamation 'Pooh!' in the eighteenth century signified dismissiveness or disparagement, and was not an indicator that the speaker had caught a whiff of something unpleasant.)

Fanny's remark about the homosexual young man highlights the grotesque incongruity of a body which is male before, but female behind, insisting that his sexual activity robs the male body of its masculinity by defining it as partly feminised, because physically and sexually permeable by the outside world. Moreover, through Fanny's voyeurism and her moral outrage, Cleland affirms and reinforces patriarchy's imperative that masculinity be performed *for others to see*. The surveillance of those others then becomes the means by which the individual's performance of masculinity is acknowledged and confirmed, or refused and either corrected or punished. The youths' appearance initially characterised them as attractive but otherwise unremarkable, and hence masculine. However, through Fanny's voyeuristic observation of the two, that appearance is exposed as a sham, for they are not 'proper' men. Their masculinity is likewise shown to be merely a masquerade—a public performance to disguise a private and shaming reality.

The discourse constructing and controlling the male body is thus not merely incidental to patriarchy. Masculinity, which assumes heterosexuality, is predicated not only on the integrity of the male body, but consequently also, as we have noted, on the contrary existence of the homosexual (as an adjective), since this both underlies and reinforces the definition of the male body as heterosexual, that is, as closed to homosexual desire and impenetrable.

The performance and recognition of masculinity relies, therefore, on a system of signs prescribed by the culture. This system, it is important to note, is something that *all* males in the culture learn from infancy onward, through observation and imitation of older males, and through the effects of noncompliance meted out socially, for instance, by colleagues at school and work, as well as by superiors including parents, teachers and bosses. It is, thus, a performance of masculinity which all males can *do*; the question, however, is how conscious a performance is it? Or, to put it another way, does the doing of masculinity always remain an impersonation, or does/can it become rather an assimilated behaviour, apparently natural to men and therefore inevitable?

That masculinity, as culturally conceived and approved, can be aped to perfection so that the non-masculine (as the culture defines it) can 'pass' with relative ease is clearly a cause for concern in the patriarchal structure. This is why, every so often, we are treated to a media 'exposé' about homosexuals, homosexuality, and/or the gay lifestyle; and why shock waves are felt when a man in a field deemed reserved for 'real' men announces that he is gay, as happened relatively recently in the United States in the cases of David Kopay, a football player, and Joseph Steffan, a cadet whose career was cut short when the disclosure of his homosexuality precipitated his expulsion from the Naval Academy at Annapolis. Such instances reveal, if only momentarily, that *masculinity is not only a construct, it is a performance*; and that men may be described as better or worse interpreters of masculinity-as-act. One implication of this is that the culture must be ever-vigilant to identify the 'impostor' (namely, the man who refuses or falls short of performance), expose him and submit him to the appropriate punishment.

The heterosexual male's behaviour is therefore kept under

scrutiny. Parental injunctions to young boys not to cry, because big boys don't do that, and name calling by other boys ('Faggot!', 'You throw like a girl') are clear warnings about what is considered acceptable male behaviour. This suggests, in turn, that, like homosexuals, heterosexual men must also monitor their behaviour, lest they incur the same penalties as gay men, namely, hostility, marginalisation and perhaps actual persecution. The interesting case here is the effeminate heterosexual man, who signals the non-correspondence between effeminacy and sexual orientation. Nonetheless, men who fall into this class often receive the same treatment meted out to homosexuals, effeminate or not.

Masculinity as implying heterosexuality, then, may be perceived as an act for all men, in the senses both of performance and doing. However, because of the dominance of heterosexuality in the cultural discourse of masculinity, such masculinity and such performing and doing of it come to seem natural to heterosexual men. Of course, every so often the heterosexual man must encounter moments when that doing seems like performing, for example, when boasting to other men of his sexual exploits or concealing sexual failure. For the gay man, by contrast, 'doing' masculinity in the manner approved by the culture often feels like performance, because its basis, heterosexual desire, is always simulated or present only by absence.

In a discursive structure which allocates subjectivity and desiring to the masculine, objectivity and being desired to the feminine, the acknowledgment, whether voluntary or involuntary, of his homosexuality frequently places the gay man in the same category as woman, so that he becomes the object not only of male sexual desire, but also of male violence, as cases of male rape and gay-bashing indicate. When a gay man requires that his partner be straight acting, therefore, he may be simply deploying a strategy of camouflage, so that two homosexual men may be seen in each other's company without causing stir or comment in the ambient vigilantly anti-homosexual culture. However, *the eroticisation of the signs of male heterosexuality* suggests that something else may be going on at the same time.

Because the gay man is perhaps more acutely aware than his straight counterpart that masculinity is a performance rather than an essence, he is able to challenge assumptions about gender and sexuality, and in this he deconstructs the apparent bedrock of the masculine. Moreover, in his own performance of the masculine, he demands that the subjectivity of heterosexual men be accorded him and not rescinded, as it frequently is in cases of social and media exposure, juridical procedure and gay-bashing. There may be, therefore, a political purpose and agenda in the gay man's eroticisation of the signs of heterosexual masculinity which might be understood in three ways: first, as a rejection of a stereotyped effeminacy popularly attributed to all homosexuals; second, as a denial that the gay man is less of a man than others on the grounds merely of his sexual orientation; and, third and consequently, as an insistence on the right to a voice in patriarchal discourse, including the capacity to alter and direct that discourse—in short, the right to masculine subjectivity.

The enactment of homosexual desire is further interesting because it proposes the possibility of desire between two subjects. That subjectivity of course may reinforce the cultural endorsement of the (heterosexual) masculine subject of desire; but it is also capable of creating a space for the subjectivity of the one desired, as heterosexual desire often does not:

> In the construction of the homosexual subject, two parallel and simultaneous movements may be distinguished. The dynamic of heterosexual desire emphasizes the alterity of the (male) active subject and the (female) passive object. However, the dynamic of homosexual desire is that of a modified narcissism: since both subject and object are male they are each potentially desiring *and* desired, each potentially acting and acted upon. This is a palindromic relationship in which subject and object of desire are reversible, interchangeable. They are the same, but different: identical selves, as it were, yet other to one another.[14]

The homoeroticisation of male heterosexuality, therefore, at one level demands a place for the homosexual man in the intersecting discourses of masculinity, subjectivity and social empowerment which privilege the heterosexual male, while at another level questions the very assumptions on which that heterosexual privilege is erected, namely, the authority of heterosexual desire—which implies the subordination and objectification of the Other, woman—and the impenetrability of the male body.

Homosocial relations among men, Sedgwick argues, are discontinuous: disrupted by rivalry, suspicion, competitiveness and fear. She contrasts these with homosocial relations among women, for whom:

> At this historical moment, an intelligible continuum of aims, emotions, and valuations links lesbianism with the other forms of women's

> attention to women: the bond of mother and daughter, for instance, the bond of sister and sister, women's friendship, 'networking', and the active struggles of feminism. (Sedgwick, 1985, p.2)

What seems most disruptive, then, in male homosocial relations is the potentiality, together with the fear, of homosexual desire. Homophobia, then, is the mark of that discontinuity.

Sedgwick is careful to insist that 'it has yet to be demonstrated that, because most patriarchies structurally include homophobia, therefore patriarchy structurally *requires* homophobia' (Sedgwick, 1985, p. 4). It would seem, however, as we have seen, that our own culture *does* require homophobia, as well as misogyny. Another way of putting this set of relationships among gender, sex and the orientation of sexual desire is to say that dominant cultural constructions of masculinity *require* the differences established by anatomical sex (male/female) as well as by desire (heterosexual/homosexual). To do away with any of these terms is radically to alter the definition of the masculine itself. In this fashion, therefore, dominant constructions of masculinity are locked systemically into differences of sex and sexuality. Masculinity thus discursively *produces* homosexuality, and *is in turn produced by its relationship to it.*

Homophobia thus patrols the bridge of sexuality which connects sex identity with masculine gender identity, and though it is therefore commonly thought of as simply the instrument of patriarchal heterosexuality, it may also be conceived as the go-between of patriarchal masculinity and homosexual desire. Or, to change metaphor, homophobia is the membrane connecting patriarchal masculinity with homosexual desire, and it cannot be severed without radically altering the nature of these and their relationship. (We may also, therefore, argue that femininity is the discursive product of the same system, and fulfils similar functions to homosexuality in helping to construct and sustain the masculine. Thus misogyny is likewise intrinsic to the structure and dynamic of patriarchal masculinity.)

The question then arises as to whether—and how—the homosexual feeds back into the masculine. Here it is helpful to distinguish between the *homosexual* and the *homoerotic.* The term 'homosexual' I take to mean an acknowledged and specific sexual desire for members of one's own sex, whether or not that desire is acted upon and satisfied. 'Homoerotic', I suggest, indicates a vaguer, often unacknowledged capacity for erotic arousal through the voyeuristic contemplation of, fantasising about, or engagement in physical but not overtly sexual contact with others of one's own sex. The homosexual implies a certain mode of existing in the world that is at present marginalised and in many ways proscribed; the homoerotic, by contrast, is able to persist within dominant patriarchal culture precisely by remaining unacknowledged, and hence interpretable in various less dangerous ways than the homosexual *per se*, deferring through a system of relays the fact of erotic arousal by another or others of one's own sex. The homosexual and the homoerotic are clearly connected—the homoerotic is a precondition for the homosexual. However, where the homosexual is specific and limited to particular individuals or communities, the homoerotic is widely dispersed through the culture.

Thus Jonathan Rutherford is able to observe:

> Despite the marginalisation of homosexuality, it is ever present in our relationships with one another. Heterosexual men's common response is to render it invisible, to assume that it exists in crude, easily identifiable stereotypes. Yet men's language and behaviour is full of homoerotic content. In the City, a bastion of male power, markets are penetrated, good stocks are sexy, firms that are merging are getting into bed with each other, and their directors are referred to as likely bedfellows . . . Workplace banter, men's horseplay, mocking references to effeminacy and the mimicking of 'queens' are practices that spell out [heterosexual] men's own separateness from them [homosexuals], yet reveal their fascination.[15]

The ubiquitous presence of the homoerotic may be traced also in social structures like mateship, in preoccupations like men's hero-worship of athletes, in actions like footballers patting one another's behinds, and in texts like 'buddy' movies. It is present also, as I have suggested, in the fetishisation and totemisation of the penis, which necessarily inscribes the man so preoccupied in a homoerotic relation with other men, if only by drawing his eyes to their groins.

How, then, is this incursion of the homoerotic into the heterosexual discourse of the masculine managed so as to avoid dissolving the boundaries which that discourse has erected in order to stake out its area of definition? The Russian theorist Mikhail Bakhtin provides one way of answering this question in the notion of *monoglossia*, by means of which an official culture and authority seeks to reduce meaning to a univocal, unproblematic, authorised, single signification.[16] We may say, then, that the discourse of patriarchal—that is, heterosexual—masculinity seeks the status of monoglossic authority by defining the world in terms of itself and its interests. However, as Bakhtin notes, language, and hence discourse in general, because socially and historically produced, are actually *multi*-vocal, permitting various perspectives to find expression.[17] This *heteroglossia* thus allows the polyphonic articulation of ideas and sentiments different from or contradictory to those preferred by the monoglossic discourse of official culture.

We might propose a further term based on Bakhtin's to encapsulate the discourse of masculine desire in our culture, namely *homoglossia*. This is not intended as a simple pun on the term *heteroglossia*—or, at least, not only that. Rather, it encodes several possible meanings within the discourse of the masculine, meanings which are simultaneously invited by the prefix *homo-* and thus coexist in the definition of masculinity. The first of these is that which derives from the Latin *homo*, meaning 'man'. In this sense, then, *homoglossia* refers broadly to the discourse of masculinity as appropriate to males (and, we might note in passing, therefore also appropriated by males): this signification thus includes also the language, behaviours, gestures, attitudes, activities considered proper to men. The other two meanings, however, open up within this apparently unified discourse a contradiction which is analogous to that of monoglossia versus heteroglossia, but here specific to masculinity and to male desire. This contradiction, moreover, points precisely to a fissure within the would-be monoglossic discourse which is likely to be a cause of anxiety to men.

These two meanings are those derived, first, from the Greek *homos*, meaning 'the same', 'identical'; and, second, from the abridgment of *homosexual* (as in 'homophobia'), which in effect, within the terms of this discourse, is equivalent to 'the Other'.[18] The first of these, 'the same', 'identical', suggests both the discursive production of heterosexual masculinity as a sort of template for men in the culture, and also the mechanisms by which that conformity is surveyed and supervised. Thus, for instance, men are all supposed, among other things, to be heterosexual: on this the definition of masculinity relies, and therefore men are kept under surveillance to ensure that this requirement is neither refused nor flouted.

The remaining sense of *homoglossia* as pertaining to the homosexual is isomorphic phonetically with the others, just as gay men are isomorphically similar to straight ones; but it contradicts its twinned meaning by offering homosexual desire as a component of the discourse of masculinity. It thus subverts the intended monoglossic identification of the masculine with the heterosexual. In this way, then, male desire, which seeks to establish itself as unequivocally heterosexual, remains ambiguous and troubled by its own ambiguity.

This troubling ambiguity is present also in *Fanny Hill*. Ostensibly the memoirs of a country girl who, upon arriving in London, is pressed into prostitution, and now, her career as a woman of pleasure ended, offering her story as a moral lesson to other women, the novel's author, as we have seen, is in fact male, and we may assume that his intended readership was likewise male, implied, for instance, by the discrediting of lesbian sex as mere 'foolery from woman to woman' (Cleland, p. 71). Yet there are many extended descriptions of penises flaccid and erect, which one would have thought of little interest to the presumably heterosexual male reader; and the episode of male–male sex cited earlier likewise seems inexplicable in terms of the readership, though a case of sorts of course can be made for its inclusion in terms of the psychology (such as it is) of the female narrator. In fact, there is every indication that *Fanny Hill* and the narrator-heroine of the title, instead of re-presenting the monoglossic discourse of male heterosexual desire, serves rather as another instance of the way in which homosocial desire is articulated that Sedgwick finds in a range of works from the canon of English literature. This enunciation of male–male desire, even when not explicitly sexual but rather homosocial and/or homoerotic, requires the presence of woman, and often also of woman's body, to serve as a pretext and as the sign of heterosexuality under which that desire can function without attracting the attention and resulting censure of patriarchal authority. It is, in other words, another, more subtle instance of 'straight acting', but this time by ostensibly heterosexual men.

The simulacrum of masculinity, as performed by both heterosexual and homosexual men in the culture, may thus be described as a guise which confers subjectivity and the capacity for desire on men. However, because it assumes heterosexuality, it may also be a *dis*guise for homosexual men, in that it at once conceals their proscribed sexual orientation, and exposes or dis-guises the fictions of patriarchal masculinity. In this, masculinity becomes semantically equivalent to the term 'straight acting', dishonestly honest, a performance by men largely for other men.

The subtitle of this chapter, 'I'll show you mine if you show me yours', is intended, then, to encapsulate that need of the masculine for the Other's continual self-revelation so that the masculine may thereby establish its own credentials and identity—in short, its subjectivity. It is another instance of the ritualised repetition or citation—what I have called the in-citation of gender—which Butler sees as indispensable to the performative maintenance of gender distinction in a phallocentric, heterosexist culture. This is one reason why the homosexual male tends to be figured stereotypically in modern culture, for if he were to be accepted as indistinguishable from the heterosexual male (as are many gay men whose gender performativity complies at least with the apparent refusal of the effeminate in behaviour), one of the key anchoring points of the (heterosexual) masculine would disappear, and the system by which the masculine defines itself rendered unstable.

This idea has a number of implications, the first of which is that masculinity, rather than comprising the single, unitary, monolithic block that it is often supposed to be, if only implicitly, is in fact a rather fragile construct that *depends upon* a system of gender and gender meaning instead of actually dictating it. A second important implication is that any change in the definition of the feminine or the homosexual not only necessarily has an impact on the definition of the masculine, but is also likely—as is shown by various historical and cultural studies—to induce a state of crisis in the masculine and its self-definition, and, as a corollary, in the attitudes and behaviours of men-in-the-culture.

The masculine deals with the anxieties raised by such questions in ways intimated by another meaning of each of the terms which I have been employing as a theoretical frame. 'Ex-citation' in the sense of 'arousal' (which is, of course, its normal sense) suggests that the vanishing trick performed by the masculine actually depends on a constant vigilance and expectancy in the discourse of patriarchal masculinity in order to protect the interests both of patriarchy and of men-in-the-culture. It is, if one likes, a wakeful absence-as-presence, and not necessarily a benign one, though it may frequently appear so to men who are concerned that males grow up to be 'proper' men.

At the same time, that wakefulness is sustained and goaded by gender in-citation in the sense of 'incitement' or 'provocation'. This involves, as we have seen, keeping the feminine and the male homosexual as categories at bay, and at the same time inferiorising and rejecting them in order to maintain the exnomination—the ex-citation, as I have been using the term—of the masculine, so that it continues to appear normal and natural, and the unmarked grounding term for the deployment in the culture of a certain politics of gender. The alternative would be to allow the categories to collapse into one another, and the reappearance of the masculine as nominated, cited and visible—and hence vulnerable, open to challenge and to change.

The strategies I have been discussing as protective of the ex-citation of the masculine are enacted each day by men in relation to women and to other men, and especially those known or even only suspected to be gay. However, given the structurally fragile nature of the in-citation of the construction of the masculine, each such enactment must raise and restate questions about sex, gender and sexuality which are profoundly troubling to dominant patriarchal discourses. Textual representations of gender, and of masculinity in particular, are thus very important instruments in eliciting gender citation in order to interpellate the reading subject successfully. In the ideological reproduction of gender definitions and assumptions through the text, people in the culture are reassured about their approved performance of gender and warned off other possibilities of gender performance, whether by direct threat or by the 'invisibilising' of those possibilities. The interpellation of subjects through textual representations of gender thus makes them compliant with and quiescent about the culture's dominant—that is, patriarchal—ideologies.

# 7

# *And then a queer thing happened . . .*

The first-person narrator of Jeanette Winterson's novel *Written on the body* presents an unsettling subjectivity to the reader, for it is impossible to determine whether that narrator is male or female, adopts masculine or feminine gender behaviours, or is heterosexual, homosexual or bisexual.[1] To put it more precisely, the narrator, who is also the central character, seems over the course of the narrative to be or to do all of these things. The reader thus is left in a quandary as to how to understand and evaluate the statements and actions of the narrator, rendering problematic not only narrative itself but also the culture's ideological need to identify sex, gender and sexuality and the relationships among them.

The title of Winterson's book, *Written on the body*, raises some interesting questions also. At one level, it refers us to a central notion of gender theory, namely, that it is *sex* which is written on the body, making the body legible to the culture in particular ways, and of course also then subjecting it—in all senses—to the requirements of the dominant gender ideology. At another level, the title refers to the ways that experience and age may be written on the body, in the form of scars, torsions, wrinkles, stretch marks, a musculature that is taut or slack, distortions of bone and limb, and so on.

These bodily signs are not always read the same way. Wrinkles on a man, for instance, are often read as the *gaining* of the wisdom of worldly experience. The signalling of age is often then made to signify a greater emphasis on subjectivity and, for many, an increased sexual attractiveness. The same wrinkles on a woman, by contrast, tend to signify the *loss* of youth and beauty, and with these, of sexual attractiveness and even of subjectivity, however inferiorised. Winterson's novel refuses the possibility of such identifications, creating still greater difficulties for the reader in making conventional sense of the narrative.

In *Othello*, as Iago whispers poisonously to the Moor about Desdemona's alleged lack of chastity and fidelity, Othello fiercely demands incontrovertible evidence, snarling at his ensign, 'Be sure of it, give me the *ocular* proof' (III.iii.366; emphasis added).[2] Ocularity, the quality of being able to be viewed, plays no insignificant role in both the construction and the representation of masculinity in the culture. As we have seen, it underlies not only the pleasure of looking, but also the way in which the masculine itself is constructed: in order even to become visible and hence legible the masculine requires the simultaneous and oppositional presence of the feminine and the homosexual. But what happens when those presences become indefinite, mutually substitutable or indistinguishable from one another, as in Winterson's novel?

Ocular proof thus can be challenged, subverted. So, too, what we might call experiential proof, which grounds itself in the irreducible material fact of the body. A key element in feminist writing of the 1960s and 1970s was the invoking of the commonality of women's bodily experiences, whether biological (menstruation, orgasm, conception, childbirth, and so on) or social (women's bodily oppression through the allocation to them of menial tasks, for instance). Those materialities of the sexed body are also invoked in the call to women by some French feminists to engage in *écriture féminine*, feminine (or women's) writing which articulates those bodily 'truths': 'I feel,' says Chantal Chawaf, 'that feminine writing is social, vital. I feel the political fecundity of mucus, milk, sperm, secretions which gush out to liberate energies and give them back to the world'.[3] However, what if the body were *not* an irreducible material reality or truth? This is precisely the argument advanced by those who identify themselves as gender dysphoric, that is, unhappy in the bodily sex configuration with which they were born and which requires them, under the ideologically coercive gender system of the culture, to behave in ways they feel uncomfortable.

Such subjectivities, among whom we may also count the transgendered and the transsexual, create anomalies in the culture's sex–gender system, and seriously contest the apparently incontrovertible truth of the body. The argument from experiential proof thus becomes less substantial when an individual presents himself or herself as transgendered. Nor is the argument convincing that, once one has undergone the sex-change operation (often interestingly called 'gender reassignment surgery', which implies that the *sex* of the patient remains stable), one is repositioned in terms of such experiential truth to become a 'conventional' man or woman. Kate Bornstein, once anatomically male, remarks:

> I've no idea what 'a woman' feels like. I never did feel like a girl or a woman; rather, it was my unshakable conviction that I was not a boy or a man. It was the absence of a feeling, rather than its presence, that convinced me to change my gender.[4]

Bornstein argues powerfully for the position of androgyne, that is, a subjectivity that is neither male nor female, masculine nor feminine; and the very difficulty that many might find in accepting such an idea indicates how deeply and firmly rooted in the male/female binary our gender ideology is.

Bornstein's response to a question asked of her by an audience member during her appearance on the 'Geraldo Rivera' talk show is highly provocative, but ideologically and theoretically suggestive at the same time. 'Can you orgasm with that vagina?' asked the audience member. 'Yah, the plumbing works and so does the electricity', replied Bornstein (Bornstein, p. 31). Her answer deconstructs the body as a transhistorical reality, as a natural given and as a universal law, and reconstructs it as a dwelling which can be 'produced' and moved into, just as we might move into a newly built house. In this, she reminds us that even for those of us who are content with our native sex, our bodies are not entirely natural and innocent objects: that is, they are framed for us by culture, given meaning and value by ideology, and thus are 'produced' in ways not unlike that of the artificially altered body. That reconstruction of the body, of course, is sharply at odds with the argument from the experiential proof of gender via the sexing of the body.

The undecidability of sex, gender or sexuality and of their relationship which we have traced in both Winterson and Bornstein is part of what has come to be called 'queer'. Queer theory, a recently emerged constellation of other theories and strategies of textual reading, examines cultural behaviours, patterns and objects with a view to finding what Sinfield calls their faultlines, here located specifically in the relationship among sex, gender and sexuality, but also with attention to other components, such as class and race or ethnicity.

'Queer', as a critical or theoretical concept, is rather elusive. Primarily associated with non-heterosexual, non-traditionally gendered individuals and groups, it appears to have different significations, depending on its context. When found in relation to activist groups, whether associated with HIV/AIDS (for instance, drawing the attention of governments to the plight of people living with AIDS and the need for adequate funding for treatment and resourcing for research) or activities such as 'outing' celebrities and persons in power (to demonstrate that homosexuality is neither so limited nor so easily stereotyped, contained and persecuted as a generally homophobic culture might imagine), the term 'queer' takes on a powerfully aggressive connotation. It is, in this regard, an 'in-your-face' assertiveness of difference, of refusal to be categorised in terms of dominant ideological taxonomies; an angry rejection of the demand for complicity with the ideologically dominant. (It is also, as the French put it, to *épater les bourgeois*: to scandalise and thrill the conventional middle class.)

At the same time, 'queer' is also the recuperation of a term that formerly was used not only as an insult to homosexuals, but also as a means to accuse, condemn, inferiorise and victimise them. 'Queer', then, becomes the homosexual equivalent of 'nigger' to a black person: it signifies marginalisation, oppression and humiliation as part of its history. However, when appropriated by a member of the marginalised, oppressed and humiliated group denoted, the term becomes a political rallying point. This adds to the assertiveness and aggressiveness of the term, and inflects it in a particular way. However, it should be noted that many older homosexual men and women find it difficult to accept 'queer' as a positive term, given their own experience of its earlier history as a means by which to denigrate and repress those whose sexual proclivities do not correspond with those of the larger ambient culture.

'Queer' seems also to have been adopted by many younger male and female homosexuals and bisexuals, to demarcate a generational or age difference *vis-à-vis* those older men and women who might still prefer to call themselves 'gay' or 'lesbian'. The deployment of the term often has the tactical advantage of refusing the gendered and political differences encoded in alternatives like 'gay' and 'lesbian'. While 'gay' emerged in the 1960s as the homosexual-positive term for both men and women who were homosexual, by the mid-1970s it was being used to signify 'homosexual man', many homosexual women preferring to return to the term 'lesbian'. This was an effect of the increasing disappointment felt by lesbians over the direction gay politics seemed to be taking: more and more these women perceived that their political agenda lay closer to that of various feminist groups, since gay men appeared to exhibit the same sort of sexually exploitative and misogynistic tendencies as their straight brethren. Gay liberation meant, it seemed, simply the liberty for homosexual men to have sex more openly and frequently, rather than the pushing back of political horizons and of social practices oppressive to more than such men alone.

'Queer' seems, further, to have been taken up by younger men and women as a more modish descriptor. That is, given the fondness of a postmodern youth-oriented culture for labels that are not only themselves disposable but which often signify disposability in the things labelled, 'queer' in its reincarnation as a homosexual-friendly term seems pre-eminently suitable, since it comes—for this generation—without a particular historical, ideological and other sort of baggage which would make it somewhat less trendy and 'cool'.

How does 'queer' affect the construction of masculinity? Let us begin by considering why 'queer' has been reinvoked as a contra-distinction to 'gay' and/or 'lesbian'. While 'gay' itself was a reinvocation of a term used as early as the 1890s (a 'gay' woman was one who was easily available sexually; a little later, 'gay' applied to homosexual men signified the passive partner in homosexual intercourse), in the 1960s it had a particular political signification: one was 'gay' only if one had 'come out' to one's family, friends and professional or business associates. Later, of course, it became a popular term, much as 'queer' has, to separate *the life and culture* of the homosexual from *the simple medical or clinical fact* of homosexuality. 'Gay' simply sounded better, friendlier and more sociable than 'homosexual'.

Why now introduce—or, more accurately, *re*-introduce—'queer'? One reason is that 'gay' and, for that matter, 'lesbian' are terms that, on the one hand, invite a particular identification, but which, on the other, leave in place the idea that heterosexuality remains not only dominant but norm*al*, as well as norm*ative*. From the 1960s until comparatively recently, the ideas constellated around 'gay' and 'lesbian' as terms have been important as part of a politics of identity: gay and lesbian movements and groups have fought for recognition and for social and political rights, though perhaps not always successfully. For a younger generation of homosexual/bisexual people, and of theorists in particular, while those struggles have been important and remain so, they remain implicated in a politics of dominance versus subordination, and of marginalisation and tolerance rather than acceptance. One logical extreme of such a politics is separatism in various forms, ranging from lesbian separatism as a political and personal strategy to the establishment of gay and lesbian ghettoes in cities which have large populations of gays and lesbians. As a strategy, however, this leaves intact the sense of living at the margin, ultimately of being unacceptable to the main community, and of being at best merely tolerated, even through—maybe especially when there is—legislation against discrimination on the grounds of sexual preference or orientation.

Another logical extreme of this politics is assimilation. In many instances, this happens already—after all, not all gays are nancy poofters, nor are all lesbians diesel dykes: in most instances, homosexual men and women are indistinguishable from heterosexual ones in terms of mannerism, dress, behaviour and way of living. However, this is seen by some as a strategy of camouflage and mimicry; and while it denies the authenticity and acceptability of being gay/lesbian in whichever mode one might choose, it also invites assumptions that the homosexual person is in fact heterosexual, another form of denial, subordination and self-refusal or self-abnegation.

Another complication is that the terms 'gay' and 'lesbian' can be understood as exclusive. Bisexuals, therefore, may feel that they are marginalised both by the heterosexual *and* homosexual sectors of the community. And what of the transvestite (one who cross-dresses), the transgendered (one who feels him- or herself to be in the body of the wrong sex) and the transsexual (one who undergoes surgical procedure in order to occupy a body felt to be closer to that of the 'correct' sex)? The transvestite is often assumed to be homosexual; however, many individuals cross-dress because it affords them certain pleasures, but are heterosexual in their object choices. (The transvestite should not be confused with the drag queen, who often *is* homosexual, and whose exhibitions of cross-dressing may often have rather different ideological drives and goals.) The transvestite thus contests certain assumptions about behaviour, gender and sexuality abroad in the culture, namely, that the cross-dressing individual must be homosexual since otherwise s/he would dress according to the appropriate—namely heterosexually defined—gender identity.

Transgendered and transsexual people offer even more direct challenges, not the least being the confrontation that such people and their feelings of being in the 'wrongly' sexed body set up to gender theories about essential versus constructed gender identity. For example, how does such a person *understand* or *know* him-/herself to be in the 'wrong' body? Is such a sense of outrage essential, or is it rather constructed by the culture's refusal of certain possibilities? Moreover, the technology that has enabled the sex-change operation has also opened the door to new gender and sexual identities, perhaps the most astounding being the male lesbian. This is a biological male who has undergone the operation to become an apparent woman, in order to establish and maintain sexual and emotional relationships with other women. Bornstein again provides interesting insights into this, for although as a woman she has had relationships with men, at the time of writing her book her partner was another woman. And just to add spin to this idea, her partner was about to undergo the operation in the other direction (Bornstein, p. 4). Bornstein's book asks a number of questions about the relationship of sex to gender, of each of these to sexuality, and of all of these to power. What kind of couple would a pair of transsexuals, one male-to-female, the other female-to-male, make? Gay, because one is a biological male, the other a reassigned male? Lesbian, because one is a reassigned woman, the other a biological one? Heterosexual, because each will have been biologically of the other sex, and will have been reassigned to each of the two sexes? These sorts of permutations of identity, of gender and of sexuality cannot be contained in a binary system which recognises only biologically male or female sexes, masculine or feminine behaviours, and straight or gay/lesbian sexualities and erotics, and which, moreover, assigns power hierarchically and differentially in terms of that binary.

What, then, does 'queer' offer? In the first place, 'queer' seeks to defy and thence destabilise such binaries, first, by *demonstrating that they are ideological* and not natural or inevitable; second, by *blurring the boundaries* among male/female, masculine/feminine and heterosexual/homosexual; and, third, by *advocating instead a range or spectrum* of various subject-positions in regard to sex, gender and sexuality. According to these lights, any one of us might occupy any of those positions at any point in our lives, but would not necessarily feel obliged to *maintain* a *single* position. What 'queer' seeks, therefore, is an opening up and a loosening of categories, first, so that the culture can take account of all the sex/gender/sexual possibilities that its members are capable of embodying and enacting; and, second, so that the members of a culture are enabled and freed to experience different positions in relation to sex, gender identity and sexual desire.

Annamarie Jagose traces the genealogy of queer theory back to the gay liberationist theory and politics of the 1960s and early 1970s, noting certain continuities with these, but she also foregrounds strongly queer theory's antecedents in and connections with Marxist (particularly Althusserian), Freudian (and Lacanian), structuralist (especially Saussurean) theories, as well as certain feminist theories and politics, and Foucault's historical analysis of power relations, especially in relation to sexuality.[5] She notes that 'queer' contests the minoritising, ethnicising identity politics which liberationist theory espoused (Jagose, pp. 61–71, 77 ff.), and indicates that 'its denaturalising project is being brought to bear on axes of identification other than sex and gender' (Jagose, p. 99). Queer theory thus continues to evolve and develop, coalescing out of a range of theories, disciplines and approaches, rather as a new star is born out of the cosmic dust which is brought within range of its gravitational pull and the pressures it is increasingly able to exert.

Queer theory both draws on and articulates subjugated knowledges. That is, in Foucaultian terms, if knowledge is power, and both circulate through a range of intersecting and converging discourses in the culture, then those knowledges which are least known are both the most marginalised and yet, at the same time, the most dangerous to dominant discourses and knowledges, for they are capable of articulating 'truths' and disciplines not accounted for, screened, controlled and/or marginalised by the dominant discourses. It would appear, then, that queer theory and the readings it engenders may be considered resistive to the readings preferred by dominant theoretical and ideological grids.

Indeed, despite at least one strand of thought about 'queer', I suggest that it is precisely in this resistance that queerness resides. That is, one may *be* male or female, and gay, lesbian, bisexual, straight or whatever in and through one's sexual inclinations; but one *performs* or *does*—and perhaps more to the point, one *chooses to perform or do*—'queer' through resistant behaviours and resistant readings. In other words, 'queer' is not an invitation to a new politics of *identity*, but rather the announcing of oneself or a text as in some way possessing *agency* in the challenging and subversion of dominant ideological 'truths', if only to test their validity or to offer the culture a different 'take' on those 'truths'. This notion of agency is suggested by the titles of many queer theoretical and critical materials, for instance, the main titles of Alexander Doty's *Making things perfectly queer*, or of the collection *Queering the pitch*.[6]

There are two chief ways one might queer cultural representations. The first of these takes place in the production of a text: existing codes of representation are consciously manipulated so that new significations emerge. We can see how this works in two Australian films which were released at around the same time: *The sum of us* and *The adventures of Priscilla, queen of the desert*. Both films deal with the questions of heterosexuality (assumed as a norm), bisexuality (both Jeff Mitchell, Russell Crowe's character in *The sum of us*, and Tick/Mitzi, Hugo Weaving's character in *Priscilla*, have 'tried' heterosexual sex) and, of course homosexuality (Jeff is gay, and so are Tick/Mitzi and Adam/Felicia, Guy Pearce's character). *Priscilla* also includes a treatment of transsexualism (Terence Stamp's character, Ralph/Bernadette, is a male-to-female postoperative transsexual).

*Priscilla* won significant international acclaim and notoriety, claiming the Prix de Public at Cannes in 1994, an Oscar in 1995 for its costume design, as well as nomination for nine Australian Film Industry awards. Its plot is succinctly, if disdainfully, summarised in a scathing review by Evan Williams: 'Two Sydney drag queens, Mitzi and Felicia, and an elderly transsexual, Bernadette, travel in a dilapidated bus to central Australia and perform in desert pubs and resorts.'[7] We may surmise two chief causes for this film's popularity. First, the representation, in a major feature film, of homosexual subjectivity was bound to attract the attention and support of gay and bisexual audiences. These members of the film-going public are more accustomed to the silencing of their subjectivity and its being rendered invisible in mainstream movies, or to its inferiorisation and parody;[8] as a consequence, therefore, a gay-positive rendering of that subjectivity would elicit an enthusiastic response. However, as important as it is to provide gay-friendly representations of the homosexual, one such instance does not necessarily, *ipso facto*, mean that it is also a *politically* positive one.

This brings us to the second reason for *Priscilla*'s success, namely, that the film may be understood as, ultimately, not only *not* challenging dominant notions about the male homosexual, but in fact domesticating this subjectivity and making it safe—and hilariously entertaining—for heterosexuals. For, after all, what does the average straight audience member discover about homosexuals? Why, what she or he has always 'known', namely, that they are flamboyant creatures who like dressing up, give good advice on fashion and make-up, are witty and bitchy at the same time, and who are, at bottom, rather pathetic creatures. The three central characters are in fact caricatures of 'the' gay man: Tick/Mitzi is a confused, neurotic personality who once got married and sired a son but now prefers to dress up in extravagant female attire and mime ABBA songs; Adam/Felicia is a bitchy queen with more than a tinge of malice in her; and Ralph/Bernadette is a world-weary, been-there-seen-that-done-it-all transsexual. (In fact, Bernadette's character seems to affirm the popular notion that the gay man really wants to be a woman.) These are all guises of the homosexual with which audiences are already familiar, and from which they need not expect any worrisome questioning.

Moreover, the three central characters appear, to all intents and purposes, asexual. Though we hear about past sexual escapades, Tick/Mitzi appears to have no sex life; Adam/Felicia's full-drag gatecrashing of a party in Coober Pedy, though filled with sexual innuendo, does not appear to be a serious attempt at finding a sexual partner, and in any case the episode turns nasty; and Ralph/Bernadette's relationship with Bob is very muted, from the sexual point of view. This is a curious phenomenon, since after all it *is* gay men's sexuality which is the crux of the gender and sexual politics surrounding the issue of male homosexuality. Thus, *Priscilla* appears to fashion homosexual identity not from sexual orientation, but from a rather cartoon-like representation of theatrical gesture, mannered behaviour and clichéd coding. From this critical perspective, then, the heterosexual audience is not confronted by ideas or images that actually challenge their ideologically privileged position as heterosexuals.

There are some other elements in the film that invite questions about its politics. For instance, the encounter with the Aborigines in the desert seems rather gratuitous, motivated less by the plot than by issues of political correctness external to the film. Moreover, it might be interpreted as demeaning: the Aborigines' own campfire gathering is transformed into a rehearsal for a drag number, one of the Aboriginal men indeed being drafted into service in clownish get-up. The fact that his experience of the outback provides Tick/Mitzi with the inspiration for an 'Australian' number later, when the bus arrives in Alice Springs, might also be regarded as problematic, for this routine commences with the 'girls' (billed as the 'Sisters of the Simpson Desert'[9]) dressing up as extravagant versions of native wildlife, and ends with them costumed *à la* Marie Antoinette in an ingenious and parodic representation of the Sydney Opera House. At once, this routine takes in notions of the natural and the cultural, the indigenous and the colonial, the oppressed and the oppressor, but does so unquestioningly and uncritically; or rather, by parodying them all, the film reduces them to the same level. Thus, at points when there is an opportunity to make significant commentary and observation—for instance, drawing a comparison between the gay 'community' (if such a unified group actually exists) and Aboriginal groups in terms of their marginalisation by mainstream culture, their tribalism, their use of face and body paint, as well as their degree of mutual acceptance—the film swerves, preferring instead to give the audience a feel-good experience.

Further, many women were offended by the way women were presented by the film. True femininity, it seems, resides with the drag queen, the transsexual and the lesbian, or at any rate bisexual, woman: for instance, Shirley, the aggressive woman in the bar at Broken Hill who challenges Ralph/Bernadette to a drinking contest, is represented as loud and 'butch'-looking, but there is no indication that she is supposed to be understood as lesbian. Rather, she stands for a particular female 'country' type. Bob's Asian wife, Cynthia, though attractive, is exoticised and orientalised, so that her rebellion against Bob's authority is seen as out of character for an Asian woman; and her party trick, being able to fire ping-pong balls out of her vagina, transforms her into an object of quirky eroticism and general derision. Marion, Tick/Mitzi's erstwhile wife in Alice Springs, seems impossibly patient, understanding and charming by comparison with these other two women; but this is explained when we learn from Benjamin, their son, that his mother once had 'a girlfriend': clearly, Marion benefits from her sexual variety, as opposed to Shirley and Cynthia, who remain caricatures of women.

And yet the film is queer in certain respects, and thus carries a certain political edge to its feel-good quality. For instance, the film appears to conform to the generic conventions of the road movie, a typical, if not indeed archetypical, instance of which is *Easy rider*, a narrative in which men not only prove themselves to be men in the face of various dangers but also simultaneously learn about male bonding: such a text thus teaches men something about male homosociality and its value to patriarchal structure. However, in focusing on the adventures of two gay men and a transsexual, *Priscilla* challenges and subverts the assumption that such movies are only about heterosexual men (who remain anatomically male). Moreover, since road movies are often also buddy movies—that is, about the developing relationship between two men (or, in the case of *Thelma and Louise*, another road/buddy movie, between two women, and hence another text which, when read intertextually, violates the convention that such films are about men)—*Priscilla* also challenges the assumption that men are heterosexual only. This, in turn, introduces an element of homoeroticism into the film which road and buddy movies are usually careful to exclude or minimise. (Gregg Araki's *The living end* is another road-and-buddy movie which is confronting in that its two central characters are both gay and HIV-positive.) In this way, therefore, a particular filmic generic code is queered by being, as it were, 'homosexualised'.

Another example of the queer potential in *Priscilla* is the incident at the opal-mining town of Coober Pedy alluded to above. Bob, who has friends in the town, plans to join them in a drinking party. Adam/Felicia wants to join him, but is vetoed by Tick/Mitzi and Ralph/Bernadette, who give him the choice either of dining with them or of staying in the hotel room to watch TV. Bored, Adam/Felicia finds a small plastic bag filled with white powder, which we understand to be cocaine, since the next time we see Felicia (now in drag) she is sniffling, which suggests that she has inhaled some of the powder. After astonishing the insipid young man acting as attendant in a video store (batting her eyelashes, she asks him, 'Do you have "The Texas Chainsaw Mascara"?' [Elliott, p. 56]), Felicia invites herself into Bob's drinking group, but is identified as male by Frank (Ken Radley) when he sees the hairs on Felicia's knuckles (Elliott, p. 57). Pursued by the enraged Frank and his mates, Felicia is finally cornered. Frank hits him/her, and makes ready to kick the fallen Felicia in the testicles. Bob intervenes—earning Frank's disgust—and is followed by Mitzi and Bernadette. The latter, upon Frank's repeated taunt to 'come on and fuck' him, knees him in the balls and drops him, commenting with satisfaction, 'There. Now you're fucked' (Elliott, p. 59).

While this episode no doubt gives considerable satisfaction to many gay and/or effeminate men who have found themselves in similar situations but with no rescuer in sight, it is also a moment in the narrative which brings about that dizzying moment which Barthes identifies as *jouissance*, and which helps the film to 'queer' certain ideological assumptions and imperatives. For Frank's fury is aroused, not by being flirted with by an attractive person who appears to be female, but rather by the discovery that that person is in fact male. In that instant, the cut-and-dried assumptions of a heterosexual ideology—that one not only should not be attracted to members of one's own sex, but that one *could not possibly be* so attracted—are exposed as ideological constructs.

Bernadette's presence and role in this episode similarly provides a moment of queerness. She is both less and more than she appears: seemingly a woman, she is in fact a man; once anatomically a man, she now lives as a woman. A similar deficiency/excess pattern may be identified in Bernadette's behaviour: though throughout the narrative she tends toward the polite and the 'ladylike', this scene shows that her conventionalised behavior is both underlain and defined by a masculine brutality that has little in common with gentlemanliness. Thus, whatever the poetic justice of her well-delivered blow to Frank's groin and her punishment of him as he intended to punish Felicia, Bernadette brings about a certain ironic figuration in the narrative which we might compare to the rhetorical figure of chiasmus, or a criss-cross pattern of elements and signs in the text. While this might appear not only like the return but also the revenge of the repressed, it further signifies the interdependence of the various categories, and their mutual self-definition in terms of the Other. The male homosexual exists *because of* the male heterosexual, and vice versa. Bernadette's role, moreover, in addition to erasing conventional notions of ladylike behaviour appropriate to female appearance, also blurs the boundaries between male and female.

However, it is important to note that notions of 'queer' are not limited simply to drag performance and transsexualism, though this is often where the understanding by some readers of Judith Butler's notion of gender performativity reaches its limits.[10] Butler proposes that the distinction between sex as biological and gender as social silently reproduces the relation of nature to culture, so that an apparent homology is produced: sex is to gender as nature is to culture.[11] Yet, if we consider the nature/culture binary, we find that the very notion of 'nature' is itself cultural, and that it is produced *from within culture* in order to define a boundary between itself and that which it constructs as 'non-culture'—for reasons of ideology and the consequent distribution of power. After all, what *we* call 'nature' does not run about announcing itself as such.

Indeed, the very notion of nature that we are capable of grasping is produced only by and within language, and therefore only by and within culture. Nature is, then, by a kind of sleight of hand, made to appear to be prior to culture, and as a consequence attracts attributes like 'primacy', 'rawness', 'innocence', 'purity' and the like. Thus, the beauty and curative powers attributed to 'the country' or 'the beach' (that is, 'nature') make sense only in relation to culture; and Simon Schama, in *Landscape and memory*, suggests that even 'unspoiled nature', by definition ancient and untouched, has been meddled with, framed and otherwise constructed by culture.[12] The very notion of a landscape is a cultural one, not a natural one. As that which appears to come *after* nature, therefore, culture is understood to be simultaneously the domestication and refinement of nature, *and* its contamination and destruction.

Butler suggests that the sex-gender pairing may be similarly deconstructed. Accordingly, she points out that though sex appears to be the bedrock on which the behaviours and signs of gender are erected, in fact the *idea* of sex is already predicated on the prior existence of a notion of gender (Butler, 1990, pp. 6–7). Thus, there would be no point in identifying an infant as male or female unless the culture had already set in place a gender system which *required* such identifications for other purposes. In other words, sex may not be a raw, innocent primary 'fact' but is rather itself an *idea produced by gender*, just as the idea of nature is produced by culture.

In *Gender trouble*, Butler seems to suggest that gender is in fact a *performance* that anyone, of either sexed body, is able to give:

> If gender is the cultural meanings that the sexed body assumes, then a gender cannot be said to follow from a sex in any one way. Taken to its logical limit, the sex/gender distinction suggests a radical discontinuity between sexed bodies and culturally constructed genders. Assuming for the moment the stability of binary sex, it does not follow that the construction of 'men' will accrue exclusively to the bodies of males or that 'women' will interpret only female bodies. Further, even if the sexes appear to be unproblematically binary in

> their morphology and constitution (which will become a question), there is no reason to assume that genders ought also to remain as two. The presumption of a binary gender system implicitly retains the belief in a mimetic relation of gender to sex whereby gender mirrors sex or is otherwise restricted by it. When the constructed status of gender is theorized as radically independent of sex, gender itself becomes a free-floating artifice, with the consequence that *man* and *masculine* might just as easily signify a female body as a male one, and *woman* and *feminine* a male body as easily as a female one. (Butler, 1990, p. 6)

However, in *Bodies that matter* Butler makes clear that when she argues that gender is performative, she does not mean merely 'performance', such as a drag show might suggest. She maintains that subjectivity or the sense of self is produced culturally through signs, behaviours and gestures that are both gender*ed* and gender*ing*, so that one enunciates one's gender by doing it or being it, and vice versa—that is, to say or be something with a strong gender content or bias is to announce/enunciate one's gender.

Butler also suggests that such gender-performativity is related to two other elements in the way that gender is both defined and enacted. The first has to do with the notion that gender is constructed, by which she does *not* mean that one has the liberty and free play to do what one likes with one's gender: one does not, and cannot, 'construct' one's own gender, for there are always already in the culture certain constraints which limit one in terms of sex and gender.[13] However, this should not be understood to mean that gender is therefore, to all intents and purposes, natural or innate, but rather that one construction is not necessarily more or less inevitable, in a logical or philosophical sense, than any other. The only necessity or necessities constraining the way gender may be constructed, for men or women, will be determined by historical contingencies operating in the culture. These may function to make such construction appear natural or inevitable; but, as contingencies, they are themselves neither. One of those cultural-historical constraints on the construction of gender, of course, and a very powerful one is what Butler, borrowing the term from Adrienne Rich, terms *the law of compulsory heterosexuality*, which defines, via sex and sexuality, the gender roles deemed appropriate to male and female bodies and subjectivities.[14]

Bernadette, then, by her very being in the strongly masculine world of Coober Pedy, as represented by the drinking party, issues a challenge to the assumptions of the men there: she is able to perform *both* genders *simultaneously*, since she is both male and female, and displays both masculine and feminine behaviours. She is thus more troubling to the culture's sex-gender system than her companion drag queens, for they *are* male, though they may behave in feminine—or at any rate effeminate—ways. However, we should not therefore discount them: to cloak the male body with the signs of femininity and to use the body's language of gestures to suggest femaleness is also to challenge the sex-gender system, which seeks to restrict the signs of gender to the appropriately designated sex.

If *Priscilla* may be said to deal with the sign systems and trappings of homosexuality—drag, glamour, effeminacy and so on—while glossing over the issue of male–male sexuality itself, *The sum of us* deals rather with the substance of homosexuality, namely, the issue of gay sex. This film tells a threefold love story: the principal strand deals with Jeff (Russell Crowe), gay son of Harry Mitchell (Jack Thompson), and the development of his relationship with Greg (John Polson), whom he has met in a bar; the second strand presents Harry's relationship with Joyce Johnson (Deborah Kennedy), a middle-aged divorcée whom Harry meets through an introduction agency; and the third, the story of the lesbian relationship of Harry's mother and her friend Mary.

The course of true love, however, runs rough for all couples. At the end of the intercut story of Gran and Mary, filmed in black and white, the two elderly women are taken from one another and sent to different homes, on the grounds that they are no longer capable of looking after themselves or one another. Harry and Joyce split up over Joyce's inability to accept either the homosexuality of Harry's son or Harry's own acceptance of it; and later Harry suffers a stroke and becomes incapacitated, relying on his son's help even for such basic necessities as emptying his bowels. Joyce, coming to see Harry to make amends after his stroke, meets Jeff for the first time, and changes her opinion of him (and presumably of all homosexuals), though it is now too late for her relationship with Harry.

Jeff and Greg split up because Greg, a very closeted gay man at the beginning of the film, cannot deal with Harry's hail-fellow-well-met approach to Jeff's lovers. By the end of the film, however, Greg has inadvertently come out to his family (they have seen him on a float in a televising of the annual Sydney Gay and Lesbian Mardi Gras), and is now living on his own. Jeff, who wanted the relationship with Greg to continue, runs into him in the Botanic Gardens, where Greg works as a gardener, and a tentative resumption of social relations takes place—much to the satisfaction of the now-invalid Harry.

Like *Priscilla*, *The sum of us* has also been subject to criticism. Many members of the audience, for instance, find the easygoing, apparently unproblematic relationship between Jeff and his father so idealistic as to suggest a sort of fantasy. Others have found Joyce's sudden change of opinion about gay men—a veritable conversion on the road to Damascus—equally unbelievable. The Gran–Mary strand in the film's narrative has struck some viewers as intrusive. Moreover, since one of its functions is to allow Harry to speculate whether homosexuality is a recessive gene that has skipped his own generation only to affect his son, many viewers regard this particular narrative thread as both providing a specious explanation of Jeff's homosexuality and feeding unhelpfully the debate about whether the homosexual is born or made, or whether she or he has a choice in the matter.

For many theoreticians of sexuality, and of homosexuality in particular, this is a particularly difficult issue. If homosexuality is indeed genetic, then a homophobic culture will seek ways and technologies to eradicate it genetically. If, by contrast, the homosexual is created by upbringing and other environmental factors, then, homophobes will argue, there must be ways of re-conditioning individuals so that what has been constructed may be reconstructed along the lines approved ideologically by the culture. And if the homosexual makes a choice about her or his sexuality (as a number of religious groups maintain—the idea, for instance, that it is a sin implies that one has elected to commit it), then the argument is advanced that that choice can surely be unmade.

The implicit presence in the film of this normalising impulse in the culture also underlies a criticism about the film's narrative technique. Though the device of direct address to the camera is used with both Jeff and Harry, the latter's perspective appears to dominate the narration, so that the exploration of gay subjectivity and the unfolding of the gay love story seem to be authorised by a patriarchal figure (Harry is, after all, a father) from the dominant heterosexual community (Harry is, after all, a *father*—he has reproduced); and if so authorised, then in some way also appropriated and domesticated.

Nonetheless, *The sum of us* may be said to queer a number of conventional ideological assumptions. Two instances will suffice. The first of these is the presentation of the two gay characters Jeff and Greg as indistinguishable from other, heterosexual men.

Far from being a flamboyant drag queen making large, theatrical and effeminate gestures, Jeff, when we first see him as an adult, is in the middle of a football scrum. Nor is he a hairdresser, an actor, a waiter, a fashion designer, or a member of any other profession which the culture conventionally associates with gay men: Jeff is a plumber. Similarly, Greg is a gardener. The film in fact foregrounds the sheer 'normality' of these two, as the culture understands men to be. And herein lies its queerness. If the gay man cannot be picked in a crowd, if indeed he is indistinguishable from other men, this has a number of important implications. First, it emphasises the notion of gender behaviour as both perform*ance* and perform*ative*: 'acting like a man' is a role that an individual male can take on, and in so doing, he is perceived 'to be a man'. Second, if the gender performance of a gay man can be indistinguishable from that of a straight man, what guarantee is there that the latter might not also have feelings of same-sex desire, or the former of other-sex desire? The ideological categorisation of sex identity and gender role in terms of sexual orientation is thus confounded and rendered unstable.

The other instance of a queering tendency in *The sum of us* is furnished in Harry's relationship to his son and to his son's lover. It is not merely that Harry accepts both men, but that he also attempts to enter into the discourse of the non-heterosexual, with his toast of 'up your bum'[15] and his narrative about asking his son to take him on an instructional pub crawl through the gay bars of Sydney so that he might learn about homosexuals and homosexuality:

> I got talking to a couple of blokes, you know, a bit nancy, but really a lot of fun. And one of them, he must have thought I was that way inclined, he asked me my name and when I said 'Harry', he said 'Oh no, that doesn't suit you at all. You'll always be Harriet to me.' Well, 'Harriet' is not a name I've ever been fond of, so I said, 'Harriet, never! Call me Henrietta!' (Stevens, p. 34)

Though Harry's 'he must have thought I was that way inclined' suggests the complacency of a heterosexual speaking from a place of privilege about someone else's error of judgment, the remark also indicates the provisional nature of gender assignments and assumptions, and that it is, after all, possible to mis-take the sex, gender and sexuality of another person. At the same time, Harry's plunging himself into a world which he does not know and of which he is not an intrinsic part, together with his jovial 'Call me Henrietta!', suggests that even one's assumptions about one's *own* sex, gender and sexuality may be thought of as provisional only. If Harry can allow himself to be called Henrietta and be thought gay, why might he not, at some time, in fact *identify*—temporarily, anyway—as homosexual?

The other chief way in which one might queer cultural representations is by reading other-wise: that is, first, by reading against the grain, contrary to the preferred meaning of the text; and, second, by reading from the position of the Other, the subject who is denied subjectivity or whose subjectivity is marginalised and inferiorised. In *Making things perfectly queer*, Doty suggests that it is thus possible to read cultural texts in ways that provide those in marginalised positions with a point of anchor, though one that is always shifting and therefore always provisional only. Thus, he proposes that to read the TV series 'Laverne and Shirley' as articulating a potential lesbian relationship between Laverne di Fazio (Penny Marshall) and Shirley Feeney (Cindy Williams) does two things. In the first place, it reads the series against the grain, against the dominant, and thus shows that the excluded and the marginalised, like the repressed of the human psyche, always return, even though those involved in making the series might have had not the slightest intention that it be read this way. As we saw in our discussion of ideology and discourse, for the dominant to be dominant, the subjugated and the subordinated must also be present, even if only by absence or in the most rudimentary form. This creates the possibility of resistance; and 'queer' is, perhaps above all else, a strategy of resistance.

In the second place, Doty's reading highlights the fact that the heterosexual man or woman is represented in countless texts. These representations thus function as role models, if one likes, for people in the culture; certainly they interpellate readers and viewers as ideological subjects, so that they 'recognise' themselves and one another in the text. The homosexual, bisexual, transvestite or transsexual person, however, is not so easily to be found in textual representations, and where such representation does take place, it is often in a negative or pejorative light. When such a person reads the culture and its texts queerly, then, she or he finds qualities, structures, events, behaviours and attitudes consonant with her or his sense of self; and since this requires reading against the grain—that is, against the dominant reading preferred by the culture—it is not only a resistant or guerrilla reading of the culture, it is also calculatedly *dissonant*. Queer pleasure thus is created by such reading, which is not merely perverse—if it were, it could be easily dismissed out of hand. Rather, it is to understand the text both *according* to the preferred, dominant reading and *against* it at one and the same time. A queer reading of 'Laverne and Shirley', therefore, is not simply or wilfully ignorant of the possibility of a non-lesbian relationship between the two characters; it is *also* to be aware of the possibility of a lesbian one. To read 'Laverne and Shirley' as a lesbian text is thus to read riskily, daringly and confrontingly. The pleasures that such a reading might produce merge with the pleasures of identification which a marginalised viewer, especially a lesbian, might derive from such a reading. It is to defy the text's attempt to constrain and control its own meaning; it is to subvert the text despite itself (Doty, pp. 39–62).

The television series 'Absolutely fabulous', a more recent cultural production and one that is much more aware of gender-theoretical issues, can also be read queerly. The series is set in an all-female household, with an age that ranges from Edina's mother (June Whitfield) to her daughter Saffron (Julia Sawalha). Thus, though the two central female characters are continually represented as heterosexual, and as engaging in heterosexual episodes, their manner of living is much closer to that of the women's commune, with its undertone of lesbian or quasi-lesbian relationships.

Patsy (Joanna Lumley) and Edina (Jennifer Saunders) are represented as having a friendship in which Patsy is the more aggressive, masculine partner—she smokes continually, drinks heavily, frequently dresses in a mannish style, and is dismissive of persons and ideas in ways that suggest the way men respond in similar situations. Moreover, she is sexually promiscuous, a trait traditionally associated with men in our culture. We are even casually informed, in the episode set in Morocco, that Patsy was a female-to-male transsexual, but 'it was only for a year and then it [the penis, presumably] fell off'.[16] (In this same episode the epicurean pervert Humphrey keeps referring to Patsy as though she were a man.) Eddy, on the other hand, is softer, more passive, dependent and easily led—in a word, feminine, as patriarchal ideology would have it. (Yet, we might note that Eddy is also the breadwinner and car-owner in her family, and appears able to support Patsy financially, all attributes which might be considered masculine.) In addition, Patsy loathes the manifest sign and result of Eddy's heterosexuality: her daughter Saffy, who into the bargain represents an interruption in the life-long association of Patsy with Eddy.

Doty suggests that everyone, whatever the sex, gender identity and sexual inclinations, experiences queer moments, moments when one finds oneself reading texts or understanding situations *from a reading position which one would not normally occupy.* To read 'Laverne and Shirley' or 'Absolutely fabulous' as a lesbian text, then, is to read it differently depending on whether you are a straight man, a gay man, a straight woman, a lesbian, a bisexual or a transsexual. However, in the array of possible reading positions, and subjectivities implicit in this, one or two are not reading particularly queerly. To see the series as purely heterosexual in import if you are heterosexual yourself is not to read it queerly. On the other hand, if you are female heterosexual but you read a particular episode of either show as susceptible to a lesbian reading, then you are experiencing a queer moment.

We can see this working too in the way that individual viewers might read the Underdaks commercials discussed in an earlier chapter. Because of the way that the narrative of these commercials is constructed, we, as viewers, are expected to see the male model's body first as the female officer sees it, desires to see it, desires it. At the same time, however, if we are male, we are expected to see/desire that body either as a heterosexual woman does or, alternatively, as a gay man does—this possibility is catered for in the version which ends with the sigh, 'He's probably gay'. This is particularly foregrounded in two shots which frame the male model's genital region for us—when he removes his trousers, and when he passes by the officer. At one level, of course, this moment serves to advertise to the viewer the make of underwear, since it is woven into the elastic band supporting the man's briefs; but since the viewer has, by this point in the commercial, been positioned alongside the officer, the close-up functions also as evidence of her desirous scrutiny, and as viewers we find our attention also focused there, and by implication also in desire. For the heterosexual woman watching the commercial, this must seem relatively unremarkable, aside from the objectification and commodification of the male body, which is a fairly recent phenomenon (women's bodies, of course, have been objectified and commodified for centuries). For the gay or bisexual man, too, staring at a man's crotch so conveniently and thoughtfully enlarged and framed for us must not seem particularly out of the ordinary. But what of the heterosexual male viewer or the lesbian, for whom—officially at any rate—such objects of desire are out of bounds and defined as irrelevant, at best, and dangerous at worst? These viewers may be said to experience a queer moment.

Many of the respondents who called Holeproof's toll-free line said approving things about the so-called 'gay' version. Interestingly, most assumed that the passenger *is* gay, though his sexuality is only surmise on the female officer's part and is, of course, totally opaque to us, the viewers. In that sense, therefore, this is a queer reading of the commercial—and we might categorise those responses which excoriated both Holeproof and the advertising company for 'promoting' homosexuality as an inverse, because homophobic, queer reading.

One male respondent objected to the 'He's probably gay' remark because he identified his own body with that of the male model in the commercial, and did not wish to be called gay by women and other men. The identification here is most interesting. Evidently, to possess the same physical body type is to run the risk of being characterised gay—and yet, as we have seen, there is no indication in the commercial that the passenger *is* gay: it is merely the female officer's guess, from which we may deduce both her sexual desire and frustration, on the one hand, and her need to find an external reason for the passenger's failure to respond to her desire. The caller on this occasion was clearly made anxious, not by a challenge merely to his sexuality, but rather by one to his masculinity, which he saw as vested both in his body and, particularly, his body type. This is a clear instance of the way that sexuality is closely implicated in masculinity, at least in our culture; that is, the masculine is generally held to be heterosexual, though it is not always sufficient to be heterosexual to be considered also masculine.

Michael Warner, in his introduction to *Fear of a queer planet*, suggests another dimension to the resistive reading afforded by queer theory. This is to demonstrate continually to the culture *that it is always-already queer*, and that it has chosen merely to suppress that queerness in an effort to make it invisible, 'not there'.[17] The essays in his collection read and re-read various texts to demonstrate how the presence of 'queerness' and the fears that it engenders are always mediated through the text, which attempts to smuggle them out of sight in varying ways. He also points out how cultural histories may be re-read—and indeed *need* to be re-read—in terms of what they have to say, or more properly perhaps not say, about queerness, queer people, queer activities.

Thus, for instance, Andrew Parker explores Karl Marx's homophobia in part through the dependent relationship which Marx had with Engels, and which itself was potentially queer (that is, Marx, a man, financially dependent on another man who, in turn, regarded himself as privileged to have supported Marx).[18] Eve Kosofsky Sedgwick, to take another, interestingly inverted example, reads the work of two psychologists (one less authoritative than the other) on male homosexuality in the era after the American Psychiatric Association struck male homosexuality from the list of conditions designated psychiatric diseases.[19] Sedgwick discovers that while both of the psychologists overtly affirm male homosexuality, they actually smuggle in the concept of disease by other means. Thus, while Parker's reading shows queerness as a repressed residue in Marx's personal life, Sedgwick shows how the announcement that the process of repression has been terminated needs to be examined carefully.

Queer theory and queer reading have much in common with deconstruction, a philosophical and language-based theory that enjoys less popularity now than it did a decade ago. However, where much deconstructionist theory sought to show that meaning in language is finally indeterminate, and indeed that it can recoil on itself until finally one stands upon the edge of an abyss of meaninglessness—this is the famous and perhaps rather overworked and misunderstood Derridean *mise-en-abyme*—queer reading seems to operate the other way: namely, to rework the idea of indeterminacy in order to reveal galaxies of potential meaning where before one might have anticipated a singular, consolidated one. We may observe how this works by briefly revisiting *Dracula*.

The Count's presence in the comfortable, middle-class lives of the Harkers, Van Helsing, Lord Arthur and Quincey Morris causes the death of Lucy Westenra and the various disruptions in the world of the 'normal' and the civilised. Stoker personally never visited the Count's native Transylvania, obtaining most of his material about it from various books by travellers to that quarter of the world. He sets it up as an area that is not merely foreign but actually odd, and getting odder with each mile that Jonathan Harker approaches his destination, Castle Dracula. The early entries in Harker's diary indicate certain 'un-English' features about this part of Europe: the failure of the trains to run on time, the peculiar language spoken—a language which Harker cannot understand at all—the superstitious behaviour of the folk, and so on.[20] The episode at the Borgo Pass, when the coachman and his passengers attempt to persuade Harker to continue with them, and the arrival of Dracula's coach and driver (who, it becomes evident, is Dracula in disguise) heighten the sense of oddity; but the ensuing episode of the nightmare journey that seems to repeat itself as Harker and the coachman circle about the countryside, the presence of the wolves, the strange flames flickering on certain places on the ground, and the coachman's behaviour should all alert us to the fact that things are not only wrong here—quite sinister, in fact—but that conversations, events and personages seem to mean much more than might appear on the face of things (Stoker, 1979, pp. 14–24).

We can say, then, that we have arrived in the country of queerness, where the rules and taboos of civilised society—England—are neither observed nor respected. It is this principle of social, moral and theological anarchy which Harker inadvertently lets loose in his homeland when he closes the real estate deal with the Count. Dracula's depredations, first in Whitby and then elsewhere, including the metropolis London, may be understood as not merely Gothic, dark and horrid, but as a different system of behaviours and meanings for which England has no guide, and over which it apparently has no control. It is significant, therefore, that Dr Seward must have recourse to Van Helsing, who, like the Count, comes from outside of England—from the realm of the increasingly queer Europe—and also like the Count, has no difficulty crediting the unusual, the extraordinary, the metaphysical and—if one likes—the queer.

The English characters are all drawn from the middle class, even Lord Arthur, despite his title. They are all also representatives of the institutions that constitute and shore up middle-class society: Seward and Van Helsing are both medical men (doctors, as Foucault reminds us in the first volume of his *History of sexuality*, became the high priests of science in the nineteenth century, and often replaced the actual priest); Van Helsing functions, at least in relation to the hunt for the vampire, also as a priest—he brings back the Host from Holland and administers it as appropriate; Harker is a solicitor; Mina a solicitor's wife; Lucy, a young lady of good family and ready for marriage; Lord Arthur represents the rulers of the society; Morris, though an outsider, being American, represents wealth (how this has been acquired remains somewhat obscure, though we are told that he has been an adventurer, a sort of nineteenth-century Indiana Jones [see, for instance, Stoker, 1979, p. 79]). In addition, we are left in no doubt about the sexes or their sexualities. It is this clear division of classes, functions and sexualities that the Count disrupts. (Lucy Westenra, however, is already signalled as sexually 'different', in that in a conversation with Mina she protests the limiting of women to only one husband [Stoker, 1979, p. 76]. This 'free thinking' was associated at the time with the emergent New Woman and her scandalous sexuality; and it prepares us for her later sexual aggressiveness upon her transformation into a vampire.)

To discuss how and why the figure of the Count upsets particular ideological structures, I will use a series of headings whose form I have modelled on the title of a 1980s TV cartoon series, 'Count Duckula', which enjoyed a certain cult status and which is singularly appropriate to the present discussion: Count Duckula himself may be thought of as an icon of queerness, being a vegetarian vampire duck. These headings are intended both to schematise the elements of queerness in Stoker's vampire, and to indicate the often confrontational but also often playful nature of queer criticism.

*Count Suckula.* Traditionally blood has signified life and it is what the vampire feeds on. But as we have seen in our earlier discussion of the novel it may also, in some readings of *Dracula*, symbolise femininity through menstruation, and a particular inflection of femininity at that. In Judaeo-Christian culture, menstruation has long been thought of as unclean; it also signals, under phallocentric patriarchy, the openness and penetrability of the feminine, its inability to close itself against and from the outside world like the masculine, and hence its lack of self-sufficiency.

Thomas Laqueur, in his *Making sex*, points out that the notions of human anatomy put forward by the Greeks continued to influence notions of the body, sexuality and gender virtually until the eighteenth century.[21] One of these was that the superior heat of the male body, when subjected to the further heat of sexual excitement, caused the blood to froth and then to be ejected from the body as a foamy white fluid; namely, semen. In any event, a case can be made for all bodily secretions to be made equivalent to one another, so that saliva, sweat, blood, semen and menstruum can be read as mutually transferable symbols. Logically, therefore, this allows us to read the vampire's feeding habits 'queerly': though the vampire feeds ostensibly on blood, she or he feeds symbolically also on semen. The act of vampirism can be read queerly as an act of fellatio, an idea made almost explicit in the scene in

*Dracula* in which Mina is forced to drink the Count's blood (Stoker, 1979, p. 336 and pp. 342–3).

*Count Dickula.* The association of the vampire with semen is made a little clearer in the episode in which Harker visits for the second time the Count's resting place in Castle Dracula. Harker removes the lid of the box:

> There lay the Count, but looking as if his youth had been half-renewed, for the white hair and moustache were changed to dark iron-grey; the cheeks were fuller, and the white skin seemed ruby-red underneath; the mouth was redder than ever, for on the lips were gouts of fresh blood, which trickled from the corners of the mouth and ran over the chin and neck. Even the deep, burning eyes seemed set amongst swollen flesh, for the lids and pouches underneath were bloated. It seemed as if the whole awful creature were simply gorged with blood; he lay like a filthy leech, exhausted with his repletion. I shuddered as I bent over to touch him, and every sense in me revolted at the contact . . . (Stoker, 1979, p. 67)

The description of the Count here, grotesque and repugnant as it may be at the level of the Gothic narrative, is also a description of the erect penis, likewise 'gorged with blood'. Like the erect penis, too, the Count has filled out, become more youthful-looking (unlike the wrinkled, flaccid penis), and hence more powerful. One might say that at this point the distance between the physical penis and the all-powerful, eternal symbolic phallus is diminished: the vampire, penile, powerful, invigorated, also becomes phallic. No wonder Harker is 'revolted at the contact': whatever Victorian sensibilities may have been violated by the attention to a penile symbol (and we might note in passing that the novel excites many Victorian anxieties), all men are threatened in their efforts to claim masculinity when one male individual seeks to engross the phallus and to become one with it.

As to the 'gouts of fresh blood' trickling down the chin and neck, we might think of this image as suggesting that anomalous, even monstrous thing, the menstruating penis. Alternatively, we might consider the blood as a displaced signifier for semen: the trickling fluid then represents ejaculate (we recall the image of the Count as like a leech 'exhausted with his repletion'). If we consider it to be the residue of the 'ejaculation' of the Count-as-penis, we are confronted by a further perversity, namely, the engorgement of the penis-figure *after* ejaculation, rather than its detumescence. On the other hand, if we consider the 'ejaculate' to be that of another male, we return to the image of vampirism as (homo)erotic and (homo)sexual.

*Count Wankula.* In his description of Dracula, Harker remarks of the Count's hands: 'they had seemed rather white and fine; but seeing them now close to me, I could not but notice that they were rather coarse—broad, with squat fingers. Strange to say, there were hairs in the centre of the palm. The nails were long and fine, and cut to a sharp point' (Stoker, 1979, p. 28). At one level, this description hints that the Count has a bestial side to him, and in this respect the mention of hairs in the centre of the palm is intended simply to strengthen the simile with an animal's paw. However, as Leonard Wolf notes in his commentary on the novel, the description also suggests the folklore of masturbation, certainly amongst adolescent boys. Wolf then quotes a nineteenth-century work on sexual functions and disorders, in which the effects on a child of masturbation are described:

> However young the children may be, they become thin, pale and irritable, and their features assume a haggard appearance. We notice the sunken eye, the long cadaverous-looking countenance, the downcast look which seems to arise from a consciousness in the boy that his habits are suspected, and, at a later period, from the ascertained fact that his virility is lost . . . Habitual masturbators have a dank, moist, cold hand, very characteristic of vital exhaustion; their sleep is short, and most complete marasmus [wasting of the body] comes on; they may gradually waste away if the evil passion is not got the better of, nervous exhaustion sets in, such as spasmodic contraction, or partial or entire convulsive movements, together with epilepsy, eclampsy, and a species of paralysis accompanied with contraction of the limbs.

Wolf adds:

> If this is a portrait that does not suggest the power that Dracula manifests, one needs only to remember the inert, pale cataleptic figure of the vampire in his daytime coffin.[22]

Thus, a further perversity is added to the figure of the vampire, for the masturbator may be understood not merely as a self-abuser or for some other sexual pathology, but rather also as the self-pleasuring, autonomous subject who needs or uses others only insofar as they feed his erotic fantasy. The erotics of self-pleasure here draw close to the vampire's imperious hunger for others only as a means to feed himself and to give himself prolonged life and renewed youth.

*Count Dragula.* This brings us to the next point, namely, the Count's ability to change shape. We have seen, of course, how he is able to rejuvenate himself; but he is also able to disguise himself in human form—the coachman with the 'long brown beard and a great black hat' who comes to meet Harker at the Borgo Pass is none other than Dracula himself (Stoker, 1979, p. 19), and we learn later that he is able to metamorphose into a bat, a great dog, even a mist or fog. To this we might add the Count's ability to crawl down a wall face down, which Harker characterises as the way 'a lizard moves along a wall' (Stoker, 1979, p. 47).

These changes of shape may be likened to the queer theoretical analysis of drag. Such an analysis sees drag not merely as female impersonation but rather as interrogating the division of gender itself, together with the ways that clothing, make-up, gesture and stance are used as the signifiers of gender. In similar fashion, Dracula's transformations refuse any stable signified: when we ask who the vampire is and what his form might be, we are left only with the traces of what shapes he has taken—not with any clear and stable definition of The Vampire.

Unlike drag artists, however, Dracula's abilities with transformation are both reflexive—he can change himself—and transitive—he can change others, by causing them to metamorphose into vampires themselves. This, of course, makes available to them a further repertoire of changes of form. In this connection, we might recall how, in his second encounter with the vampire women, Harker sees them materialising from motes of dust dancing hypnotically in the moonlight (Stoker, 1979, pp. 59–60).

*Count Dadula.* As we observed in our earlier reading of this novel, in his creation of new vampires the Count actualises and fulfils a dream of phallocentric patriarchy: the fashioning of new life without the need of woman as mother. This is, among other things, what makes Dracula's disposal of the baby to the vampire women so horrific: while it grotesquely parodies motherhood (we recall that he gives the child to the women not to feed, but to feed on [Stoker, 1979, p. 53]), it is also a clear gesture that the normal way of reproduction is not his. Similarly, Lucy's preying on children also signals a repellent parody of the mothering instinct and, at the same time, the absence of the (feminine) instinct to conceive, bear and nurture. The enormous seductive power of the vampire is oriented neither towards sex nor towards conception, but rather towards recruitment.

Structurally, the Count's victimisation of women serves to

provide a heterosexual cover. Were he to prey also on men the homoerotic potential in the vampire narrative would become manifest, as it is in Anne Rice's vampire novels, where the homoerotic element is exploited. (The first of these, *Interview with the vampire*, was made into the film *Interview with the vampire: the Vampire Chronicles*, which preserves the sexually ambivalent relationship between the vampires Lestat, Louis and Armand; but the film's cast list, which includes Tom Cruise, Brad Pitt, Antonio Banderas and Christian Slater, reads like a queer Who's Who of pin-ups admired and desired by men, women and those in between.)[23] At the same time, despite the horror of the Gothic narrative, there is something rather camp in the dark promises and sinister activities of Stoker's Count, as though he were acting a part, just as the drag artist often camps it up in his performance.

*Count Titula/C(o)unt Dracula.* In our earlier consideration of this novel, we noted that the scene in which Mina is forced to drink blood from Dracula's breast resonates with significations that go beyond the merely grotesque and the Gothic. Among other things, it presents an image that parodies motherhood and nurture, but also shockingly and impossibly suggests female-to-male cunnilingus, which in turn echoes the possibility of male-to-female fellatio. Thus it blurs the usual distinctions regarding sex, gender and sexuality. The Count is not only patriarchal and phallic (a preferred reading) but here also becomes mammarian and vaginal (a queer one). Moreover, the episode confuses the suckling of a child with non-procreative sexual activity, and in so doing shocks Victorian sensibilities by wedding the sacred notion of the family and especially of the child with unholy images of sensual abandon and blood lust.

We have not explored these possibilities of reading the figure of Dracula merely to show how inventively one might read, nor how perversely, but rather to make a number of points. The first of these is to demonstrate how a text may already be queer; that is, how that which is repressed by ideology and the culture necessarily—by virtue of that repression itself—remains present though hidden and/or transformed in the text. What *Dracula* attempts to repress, then, is not merely the possibility of the homosexual in the presence of the heterosexual; it is also the possibility of a refusal of gender distinction or of a variety of sexualities. The Count is constructed as truly *bi*-sexual, that is, as made up of two sexes, though that is characterised as grotesque, horrific, frightening and unacceptable, and finally is concealed under an overwhelmingly phallocentric and patriarchal identity.

As well as this, reading a canonical text from the position of a marginalised subjectivity and/or sexuality—what I have called reading 'other-wise'—may produce meaning that in some way validates or affirms that subjectivity and/or sexuality. In the case of *Dracula*, a preferred reading validates heterosexuality and the destruction of the horror—for which read: perversity—that the vampire represents. However, a queer reading might look at what is destroyed and why it is destroyed. What makes the Count horrible is not merely the fact that he is undead, nor that he subsists on human blood—these, if you like, are merely the pretexts, the surface reasons which the narrative offers. Rather, it is the fact that the vampire coalesces out of a range of possibilities—of sex, of sexuality, of gender identity and of gender role—and thus produces an excess of meaning. Those possibilities and meanings the culture refuses and therefore they cannot be allowed to remain or to go unpunished.

Thus, the presence of two medical men, one of whom also functions as the representative of religion, serves to provide the excuse of authority for the containment and/or destruction of those possibilities and meanings. Accordingly, the vampire is characterised on the one hand as unnatural, like a disease: he must therefore be checked before the whole of humanity (read: society) is infected. On the other hand, the vampire is constructed as a defiance of God's will, and must therefore be eradicated, lest he lead others also to challenge divinity itself. Both of these, of course, are arguments used to repress and suppress sexualities and gender identities other than those approved by the culture.

We should recall, however, that disease is, of course, also a part of nature, but in an ideological economy which allows culture to nominate health not merely as the *normal* state but also the *natural* one, it follows that disease will be constructed as unnatural. Similarly, the authority of divinity is established only through the possibility of its being questioned and challenged. The vampire's seductiveness, then, is not merely erotic; it invites us to contemplate the possibility of being Other. Herein lies its danger to the social fabric and to structures like patriarchy, whose very existence is threatened because these are predicated on a set of assumptions, of norms, which have been taken as universal, inevitable and natural.

Yet even the novel's attempt to annihilate these possibilities remains ambiguous: we are told at the end that Dracula's body 'crumbled into dust and passed from our sight' (Stoker, 1979, p. 447). On the face of it, then, society has been saved and the threat eradicated. But dust is not *nothing*: the vampire women in Castle Dracula materialise out of motes of dust dancing in the moonlight, after all. The fact that the vampire's body has passed from sight might mean merely that those troubling identities, functions and roles have once again become invisible, but not that they have been done away with altogether.

Imag(in)ing the masculine, then, is not merely to capture the male body photographically, as it were, and present it to a viewer or a reader. The process is freighted with a great deal of ideological weight, and mined with all sorts of traps. Reading queerly, as Doty suggests, not only brings apparently mainstream texts within the experiential reach and interest of those excluded from the mainstream—lesbians, gays, bisexuals and others; it also exposes the fragilities of masculinity and of the male body, and makes us aware of how carefully, powerfully, indeed even insidiously, ideological operations in the culture limit our vision.

The queer reading of a text in order to test the latter's representation of the masculine may be likened, therefore, to the materialisation of the vampire women before the horrified eyes of Jonathan Harker, once complacent in the knowledge that he knew how the world worked. Such a reading tracks down and makes manifest motes of meaning, fragments that have been ignored or banished, and pulls them into shapes which trouble and terrify the culture, yet at the same time thrill and seduce it with scandalous possibilities, significations that the culture has compelled to the margins, convinced that its dominant ideological 'truth' is the *only* truth there is.

# *Notes*

## Preface

1 M. H. Abrams, 'The deconstructive angel', *Critical inquiry*, vol. 3, no. 3, 1977, p. 431.

## Chapter 1—Fabulous monsters

1 L. Carroll, *Alice in Wonderland: authoritative texts of Alice's adventures in Wonderland, Through the looking-glass, The hunting of the Snark. Backgrounds, essays in criticism,* ed. D.J. Gray, W. W. Norton, New York, 1971, p. 175.
2 W. Shakespeare, *The Arden edition of the works of William Shakespeare: Macbeth,* ed. K. Muir, Methuen, London, 1962.
3 W. Shakespeare, *The Arden edition of the works of William Shakespeare: The tempest,* ed. F. Kermode, Methuen, London, 1958.
4 A. Sinfield, *Faultlines: cultural materialism and the politics of dissident reading,* University of California Press, Berkeley, 1992, p. 32.
5 L. Althusser, 'Ideology and state ideological apparatuses (notes towards an investigation)', in *Essays on Ideology,* Verso, London, 1984, pp. 48–9.
6 R. Williams, *Marxism and literature,* Oxford University Press, Oxford, 1977, pp. 121–7
7 T. Eagleton, *Marxism and literary criticism,* Methuen, London, 1976, p. 14.

8 M. Foucault, *The order of things: an archaeology of the human sciences,* Random House, New York, 1970, p. xxii.
9 E. M. W. Tillyard, *The Elizabethan world picture,* Penguin, Harmondsworth, 1963.
10 T. H. White (ed. & trans.), *The bestiary: a book of beasts, being a translation from a Latin bestiary of the twelfth century,* Putnam's, New York, 1960, p. 187.
11 T. Laqueur, *Making sex: body and gender from the Greeks to Freud,* Harvard University Press, Cambridge, Mass., 1990.
12 M. Foucault, *The history of sexuality, volume 1: an introduction,* trans. R. Hurley, Random House, New York, 1978, p. 94.
13 W. Shakespeare, *The Arden edition of the works of William Shakespeare: Othello,* ed. M. R. Ridley, Methuen, London, 1962.
14 See, for instance, H. Cixous, 'Sorties', in *New French feminisms: an anthology,* eds E. Marks & I. de Courtivron, Harvester, Brighton, 1981, pp. 90–8; L. Irigaray, *This sex which is not one,* trans. C. Porter with C. Burke, Cornell University Press, Ithaca, 1985; On *écriture féminine,* see, for instance, H. Cixous, 'The laugh of the Medusa', in *New French feminisms: an anthology,* eds E. Marks & I. de Courtivron, pp. 245–64; X. Gauthier, 'Is there such a thing as women's writing?', in *New French feminisms: an anthology,* eds E. Marks & I. de Courtivron, pp. 161–4. (This collection provides many other examples of feminist writing which centre on issues of female sexuality and desire.)
15 J. Weeks, *Sex, politics and society: the regulation of sexuality since 1800,* 2nd ed., Longman, London, 1989; see especially pp. 19–37 and pp. 38–56.
16 Quoted in Weeks, 1989, p. 40.
17 A. Sinfield, *Cultural politics—queer reading,* University of Pennsylvania Press, Philadelphia, 1994, pp. 3–4.
18 D. Buchbinder, *Masculinities and identities,* Interpretations series, Melbourne University Press, Carlton, 1994, p. xiv.
19 R. W. Connell, *Masculinities,* Allen & Unwin, St Leonards, 1995, p. 64 and *passim.*

## Chapter 2—A man among men

1 T. Parsons & R. F. Bales, *Family, socialization and interaction process,* Routledge & Kegan Paul, London, 1956. For a summary, analysis and critique of a range of sociological theories of gender and sex roles (including that of Parsons), see T. Carrigan, R. W. Connell & J. Lee, 'Hard and heavy: toward a new sociology of masculinity', in *Beyond patriarchy: essays by*

*men on pleasure, power, and change*, ed. M. Kaufman, Oxford University Press, Toronto, 1987, pp. 139–92; R. W. Connell, *Masculinities*, Allen & Unwin, St Leonards, 1995, pp. 21–7; J. H. Pleck, *The myth of masculinity*, the MIT Press, Cambridge, Mass., 1983; and L. Segal, *Slow motion: changing masculinities, changing men*, Virago, London, 1990, pp. 65–9.

2 R. Bly, *Iron John: a book about men*, Element, Shaftesbury, Dorset & Rockport, Mass., 1992.

3 I. & P. Opie, eds, *The Classic Fairy Tales*, Granada, London, 1980, pp. 32–3.

4 J. Weeks, *Coming out: homosexual politics in Britain, from the nineteenth century to the present*, Quartet Books, London, 1977, p. 3.

5 M. Foucault, *The history of sexuality, volume 1: an introduction*, trans. Robert Hurley, Random House, New York, 1978, p. 43.

6 See J. Boswell, *Christianity, social tolerance, and homosexuality: gay people in western Europe from the beginning of the Christian era to the fourteenth century*, University of Chicago Press, Chicago, 1980; A. Bray, *Homosexuality in Renaissance England*, Gay Men's Press, London, 1982.

7 Bray's *Homosexuality in Renaissance England* traces, among other things, the relationship between secular and ecclesiastical laws and responses to the issue of homosexual acts in Renaissance England.

8 R. J. Stoller, *Sex and gender: on the development of masculinity and femininity*, Science House, New York, 1968; A. Oakley, *Sex, gender and society*, Temple Smith, London, 1972.

9 G. Rubin, 'The traffic in women: notes on the "political economy" of sex', in *Towards an anthropology of women*, ed. R. R. Reiter, Monthly Review Press, New York, 1975, pp. 157–210.

## Chapter 3—Strictly ballsroom

1 R. Dyer, 'Male sexuality in the media', in *The sexuality of men*, eds A. Metcalf & M. Humphries, Pluto Press, London, 1985, p. 30.

2 It may be objected here that the equation does not work this way for men belonging to certain ethnic or racial groups, for instance, black men, most of whom could not be said to exercise a great deal of social power as individuals. However, it is worth bearing in mind, in this connection, that the myth of the virility of the black man, together with fables of the size of his penis, suggest that the *possibility* of phallic power

persists, and becomes a cause of anxiety in racist discourse, prompting calls on the one hand to protect 'our women' from black sexual predators, and on the other to ensure that the latter are kept subjugated and contained in some way. (See P. Hoch, *White hero, black beast: racism, sexism and the mask of masculinity,* Pluto, London, 1979.)

3 A. Flannigan-Saint-Aubin, 'The male body and literary metaphors for masculinity', in *Theorizing Masculinities,* eds H. Brod & M. Kaufman, Sage Publications, Thousand Oaks, CA, 1994, pp. 239–58.

4 P. Crayford, 'More than just song and dance'; D. Jones, 'Waltzing out of the outback into the ballroom'; and an editorial in the *Australian*, 11 Sep. 1992, 'Film's success is strictly wonderful'; in B. Luhrmann & C. Pearce, *Strictly ballroom,* from a screenplay by B. Luhrmann & A. Bovell, Currency Press, Sydney, 1992, pp. viii–xi, xiii–xiv, xv.

5 E. K. Sedgwick, *Between men: English literature and male homosocial desire*, Columbia University Press, New York, 1985, p. 1.

## Chapter 4—Degen(d)erates

1 L. Woodbridge, *Women and the English Renaissance: literature and the nature of womankind 1540–1620,* Harvester Press, Brighton, 1984, p. 169.

2 L. Jardine, *Still harping on daughters: women and drama in the age of Shakespeare,* 2nd edn, Harvester Wheatsheaf, New York, 1983, pp. 154–5.

3 See, for example, D. Buchbinder, 'Some engendered meaning: reading Shakespeare's *Sonnets*', *Works and days 14: essays in the socio-historical dimensions of literature and the arts,* vol. 7, no. 2, 1989, pp. 13–16.

4 W. Shakespeare, *The Arden edition of the works of William Shakespeare: Antony and Cleopatra,* ed. M. R. Ridley, Methuen, London, 1965.

5 E. Partridge, *Shakespeare's bawdy: a literary and psychological essay, and a comprehensive glossary,* E. P. Dutton, New York, 1969, p. 187.

6 See, for instance, D. Buchbinder, 'Some engendered meaning', pp. 13–16.

7 B. Stoker, *Dracula*, Penguin, Harmondsworth, 1979.

8 M. Foucault, *The history of sexuality, volume 1: an introduction,* trans. Robert Hurley, Random House, New York, 1978, p. 35.

9 C. Craft, '"Kiss me with those red lips": gender and inversion

in Bram Stoker's *Dracula*', in *Speaking of gender*, ed. E. Showalter, Routledge, New York, 1989, pp. 217–18.

10 K. Gelder, *Reading the vampire*, Routledge, London, 1994, p. ix.

11 R. Dyer, 'Children of the night: vampirism as homosexuality, homosexuality as vampirism', in *Sweet dreams: sexuality, gender and popular fiction*, ed. S. Radstone, Lawrence & Wishart, London, 1988, pp. 47–72.

12 See also K. Gelder, pp. 70–1.

13 See, for instance, J. Weeks, *Sex, politics and society: the regulation of sexuality since 1800*, 2nd edn, Longman, London, 1989, pp. 128–38.

## Chapter 5—Porn: where men meat

1 M. S. Davis, *Smut: erotic reality / obscene ideology*, University of Chicago Press, Chicago, 1983, p. 280, note 5.

2 But for some discussion of these matters, see, for instance, L. Williams, *Hard core: power, pleasure, and the 'frenzy of the visible'*, Pandora, London, 1990.

3 A. Dworkin, *Pornography: men possessing women*, E. P. Dutton, New York, 1989.

4 L. Segal, *Slow motion: changing masculinities, changing men*, Virago, London, 1990, pp. 237–8.

5 S. Gubar, 'Representing pornography: feminism, criticism and depictions of female violation', *Critical Inquiry*, vol. 13, no. 4, 1987, p. 740.

6 For discussion of the feminist debate both for and against pornography, see, for instance, L. Segal, pp. 205–32; A. Assiter, *Pornography, feminism and the individual*, Pluto, London, 1989; L. Williams, *Hard Core*; B. Ehrenreich, E. Hess & G. Jacobs, *Re-making love: the feminization of sex*, Anchor Books, New York, 1986; and A. B. Snitow, 'Mass market romance: pornography for women is different,' in *Powers of desire: the politics of sexuality*, eds A. Snitow, C. Stansell & S. Thompson, Monthly Review Press, New York, 1983, pp. 245–63.

7 G. Hawkins & F. E. Zimring, *Pornography in a free society*, Cambridge University Press, Cambridge, 1988, pp. 53–6.

8 J. Derrida, '". . . That dangerous supplement . . ."', *Of grammatology*, trans. G. C. Spivak, The Johns Hopkins University Press, Baltimore, 1976, pp. 141–64.

9 H. Brod, 'Eros thanatized: pornography and male sexuality', in *Men confront pornography*, ed. M. S. Kimmel, Crown Publishers, New York, 1990, pp. 192–3.

10 R. Girard, *Deceit, desire, and the novel: self and other in literary*

*structure*, trans. Yvonne Freccero, The Johns Hopkins University Press, Baltimore, 1965.

11 E. K. Sedgwick, *Between men: English literature and male homosexual desire*, Columbia University Press, New York, 1985, pp. 21–7 and *passim*.

12 S. MacDonald, 'Confessions of a feminist porn watcher', *Men confront pornography*, ed. M. S. Kimmel, p. 39.

13 D. M. Halperin, 'Why is Diotima a woman?', in *One hundred years of homosexuality, and other essays on Greek love*, Routledge, New York, 1990, p. 145.

14 See, for example, D. Zillmann & J. Bryant, 'Pornography, sexual callousness, and the trivialization of rape', in *Men confront pornography*, ed. M. S. Kimmel, p. 207–18; E. Donnerstein & D. Linz, 'Mass media, sexual violence, and male viewers: current theory and research', in *Men confront pornography*, ed. M. S. Kimmel, pp. 219–32; L. Segal, *Slow motion*, pp. 223–5.

15 See A. Easthope, *What a man's gotta do: the masculine myth in popular culture*, Paladin, London, 1986, pp. 51–4.

16 R. Barthes, *The pleasure of the text*, trans. Richard Miller, with a note on the text by Richard Howard, Hill & Wang, New York, 1975, pp. v–vi.

## Chapter 6—Do men have a gender?

1 R. Barthes, *The pleasure of the text*, trans. R. Miller, with a note on the text by R. Howard, Hill & Wang, New York, 1975, pp. 6–7.

2 J. Butler, *Bodies that matter: on the discursive limits of 'sex'*, Routledge, New York, 1993, pp. 12–16 and *passim*.

3 See R. Barthes, *Mythologies*, ed. and trans. A. Lavers, Paladin, Frogmore, St Albans, 1972, p. 138.

4 Cf. J. Butler, *Gender trouble: feminism and the subversion of identity*, Routledge, New York, 1990, p. 18.

5 E. K. Sedgwick, *Epistemology of the closet*, University of California Press, Berkeley, 1990, p. 1.

6 See, for instance, J. Boswell, *Christianity, social tolerance, and homosexuality: gay people in western Europe from the beginning of the Christian era to the fourteenth century*, University of Chicago Press, Chicago, 1980; J. Boswell, *Same-sex unions in pre-modern Europe*, Villard Books, New York, 1994; A. Bray, *Homosexuality in Renaissance England*, Gay Men's Press, London, 1982; K. J. Dover, *Greek homosexuality. Updated, and with a postscript*, Harvard University Press, Cambridge, Mass., 1989; D. F. Greenberg, *The construction of homosexuality*,

University of Chicago Press, Chicago, 1988; D. M. Halperin, *One hundred years of homosexuality, and other essays on Greek love,* Routledge, New York, 1990.

7 E. K. Sedgwick, *Between men: English literature and male homosocial desire,* Columbia University Press, New York, 1985, pp. 1–5.

8 L. Irigaray, *Speculum of the other woman,* trans. G. C. Gill, Cornell University Press, Ithaca, NY, 1985.

9 E. K. Sedgwick, *Between men: English literature and male homosocial desire,* Columbia University Press, New York, 1985, pp. 2–3.

10 G. Rubin, 'The traffic in women: notes on the "political economy" of sex', in *Toward an anthropology of women,* ed. R. R. Reiter, Monthly Review Press, New York, 1975, p. 165.

11 A. Easthope, *What a man's gotta do: the masculine myth in popular culture,* Paladin, London, 1986, pp. 51–2.

12 G. Hocquenghem, *Homosexual desire,* trans. Daniella Dangoor, Allison & Busby, London, 1978, p. 83.

13 J. Cleland, *Fanny Hill, or memoirs of a woman of pleasure,* ed. Peter Wagner, Penguin, Harmondsworth, 1985, pp. 193–4.

14 D. Buchbinder & B. H. Milech, 'Construction site: the male homosexual subject in narrative', *Works and days 18: Essays in the socio-historical dimensions of literature and the arts,* vol. 9, no. 2, 1991, pp. 80–1.

15 J. Rutherford, 'Who's that man?', in *Male order: unwrapping masculinity,* eds R. Chapman & J. Rutherford, Lawrence & Wishart, London, 1988, pp. 58–9.

16 M. M. Bakhtin, 'From the prehistory of novelistic discourse', in *The dialogic imagination: four essays,* ed. M. Holquist, trans. C. Emerson & M. Holquist, University of Texas Press, Austin, 1981, p. 61.

17 M. M. Bakhtin, 'Discourse in the novel', in *The dialogic imagination: four essays,* pp. 262–3.

18 For a fuller etymological discussion of 'homophobia', see D. Buchbinder, *Masculinities and identities,* Melbourne University Press, Carlton, 1994, pp. 55–6.

## Chapter 7—And then a queer thing happened . . .

1 J. Winterson, *Written on the body,* Vintage Books, London, 1993.

2 W. Shakespeare, *The Arden Edition of the Works of William Shakespeare: Othello,* ed. M. R. Ridley, Methuen, London, 1962.

3 C. Chawaf, 'Linguistic flesh', in *New French feminisms: an anthology,* eds E. Marks & I. de Courtivron, Harvester Press, Brighton, 1990, p. 178.

4 K. Bornstein, *Gender outlaw: on men, women and the rest of us,* Rouledge, New York, 1994, p. 24.

5 A. Jagose, *Queer theory,* Melbourne University Press, Carlton, 1996. See pp. 78–83 for her analysis of the Marxist, psychoanalytic, structuralist and Foucaultian contributions to queer theory.

6 A. Doty, *Making things perfectly queer: interpreting mass culture,* University of Minnesota Press, Minneapolis, 1993; P. Brett, E. Wood & G. C. Thomas, eds, *Queering the pitch: the new gay and lesbian musicology,* Routledge, New York, 1994.

7 E. Williams, 'Priscilla, Ginger and Fred', in *Quadrant,* June, 1995, p. 53.

8 For a history of the representation of the homosexual, both male and female, in film, see V. Russo, *The celluloid closet: homosexuality in the movies,* revised edn, Harper & Row, New York, 1987.

9 S. Elliott, *The adventures of Priscilla, queen of the desert,* Currency Press, Sydney, 1994, p. 68.

10 For a summary of this debate in and around Butler's work, see A. Jagose, *Queer theory,* pp. 83–93.

11 J. Butler, *Gender trouble: feminism and the subversion of identity,* Routledge, New York, 1990, pp. 6–9.

12 S. Schama, *Landscape and memory,* HarperCollins, London, 1995.

13 J. Butler, *Bodies that matter: on the discursive limits of 'sex',* Routledge, New York, 1993, p. 94.

14 See A. Rich, 'Compulsory heterosexuality and lesbian existence', in *The lesbian and gay studies reader,* eds H. Abelove, M. A. Barale & D. M. Halperin, Routledge, New York, 1993, pp. 227–54.

15 D. Stevens, *The sum of us,* Currency Press, Sydney, 1995, p. 32.

16 J. Saunders, *Absolutely fabulous 2,* Penguin Books/BBC Books, London, 1994, p. 60.

17 M. Warner, ed., *Fear of a queer planet: queer politics and social theory,* University of Minnesota Press, Minneapolis, 1993, p. xxvi.

18 A. Parker, 'Unthinking sex: Marx, Engels, and the scene of writing', in *Fear of a queer planet,* ed. M. Warner, pp. 19–41.

19 E. K. Sedgwick, 'How to bring your kids up gay', in *Fear of a queer planet,* ed. M. Warner, pp. 69–81.

20 B. Stoker, *Dracula,* Penguin, Harmondsworth, 1979, pp. 9–11.

21 T. Laqueur, *Making sex: Body and gender from the Greeks to*

*Freud,* Harvard University Press, Cambridge, Mass., 1990, pp. 35–43.

22 B. Stoker, *The annotated Dracula: Dracula by Bram Stoker,* introduction, notes & bibliography by L. Wolf, New English Library/Times Mirror, London, 1975, pp. 22–3.

23 A. Rice, *Interview with the vampire,* Futura Publications, London, 1977.

# *Bibliography*


Abrams, M. H. 1977, 'The deconstructive angel', *Critical inquiry*, vol. 3, no. 3, pp. 425–38

Althusser, L. 1984, 'Ideology and state ideological apparatuses (notes towards an investigation)', *Essays on ideology*, Verso, London, pp. 1–60

Assiter, A. 1989, *Pornography, feminism and the individual*, Pluto, London, Mass.

Bakhtin, M. M. 1981, 'From the prehistory of novelistic discourse', *The dialogic imagination: four essays*, ed. M. Holquist, trans. C. Emerson & M. Holquist, University of Texas Press, Austin, pp. 41–83

—— 1981, 'Discourse in the novel', *The dialogic imagination: four essays*, ed. M. Holquist, trans. C. Emerson & M. Holquist, University of Texas Press, Austin, pp. 259–422

Barthes, R. 1972, *Mythologies*, ed. and trans. A. Lavers, Paladin, Frogmore, St Albans

—— 1975, *The pleasure of the text*, trans. Richard Miller, Hill & Wang, New York

Bly, R. 1992, *Iron John: a book about men*, Element, Shaftesbury, Dorset & Rockport, Mass.

Bornstein, K. 1994, *Gender outlaw: on men, women and the rest of us*, Routledge, New York

Boswell, J. 1980, *Christianity, social tolerance, and homosexuality: gay people in western Europe from the beginning of the Christian era to the fourteenth century*, University of Chicago Press, Chicago

—— 1994, *Same-sex unions in pre-modern Europe*, Villard Books, New York

Bray, A. 1982, *Homosexuality in Renaissance England*, Gay Men's Press, London

Brett, P., Wood, E. & Thomas, G. C. (eds) 1994, *Queering the pitch: the new gay and lesbian musicology*, Routledge, New York

Brod, H. 1990, 'Eros thanatized: pornography and male sexuality', *Men confront pornography*, ed. M. S. Kimmel, Crown Publishers, New York, pp. 190–206

Buchbinder, D. 1989, 'Some engendered meaning: reading Shakespeare's *Sonnets*', *Works and days 14: essays in the socio-historical dimensions of literature and the arts*, vol. 7, no. 2, pp. 7–28

—— 1991, 'Pornography and male homosocial desire: the case of the new men's studies', *Social semiotics: a transdisciplinary journal in functional linguistics, semiotics and critical theory*, vol. 1, no. 2, pp. 51–68

—— 1994, *Masculinities and identities*, Melbourne University Press, Carlton

Buchbinder, D. & Milech, B. H. 1991, 'Construction site: the male homosexual subject in narrative', *Works and days 18: essays in the socio-historical dimensions of literature and the arts*, vol. 9, no. 2, pp. 69–90

Burt, R. 1995, *The male dancer: bodies, spectacle, sexualities*, Routledge, London

Butler, J. 1990, *Gender trouble: feminism and the subversion of identity*, Routledge, New York

—— 1993, *Bodies that matter: on the discursive limits of 'sex'*, Routledge, New York

Carrigan, T., Connell, R. W. & Lee, J. 1987, 'Hard and heavy: towards a new sociology of masculinity', *Beyond patriarchy: essays by men on pleasure, power, and change*, ed. M. Kaufman, Oxford University Press, Toronto, pp. 139–92

Carroll, L. 1971, *Alice in Wonderland: authoritative texts of Alice's adventures in Wonderland, Through the looking-glass, The hunting of the snark. Backgrounds, essays in criticism*, ed. D. J. Gray, W. W. Norton, New York

Chawaf, C. 1980, 'Linguistic flesh', *New French feminisms: an anthology*, eds E. Marks & I. de Courtivron, Harvester Press, Brighton, pp. 177–8

Cixous, H. 1981, 'Sorties', *New French feminisms: an anthology*, eds E. Marks & I. de Courtivron, Harvester Press, Brighton, pp. 90–8

—— 1981, 'The laugh of the Medusa', *New French feminisms: an anthology*, eds E. Marks & I. de Courtivron, Harvester Press, Brighton, pp. 245–64

Cleland, J. 1985, *Fanny Hill, or memoirs of a woman of pleasure*, ed. P. Wagner, Penguin, Harmondsworth

Connell, R. W. 1995, *Masculinities*, Allen & Unwin, St Leonards, NSW

Craft, C. 1989, '"Kiss me with those red lips": gender and inversion in Bram Stoker's *Dracula*', *Speaking of gender*, ed. E. Showalter, Routledge, New York, pp. 216–42

Davis, M. S. 1983, *Smut: erotic reality/obscene ideology*, University of Chicago Press, Chicago

Derrida, J. 1976, '". . . That dangerous supplement . . ."', *Of grammatology*, trans. G. C. Spivak, the Johns Hopkins University Press, Baltimore, pp. 141–64

Dickens, C. 1966, *Oliver Twist*, ed. P. Fairclough, Penguin, Harmondsworth

Dijkstra, B. 1986, *Idols of perversity: fantasies of feminine evil in fin-de-siècle culture*, Oxford University Press, New York

Donnerstein, E. & Linz, D. 1990, 'Mass media, sexual violence, and male viewers: current theory and research', *Men confront pornography*, ed. M. S. Kimmel, Crown Publishers, New York, pp. 219–32

Doty, A. 1993, *Making things perfectly queer: interpreting mass culture*, University of Minnesota Press, Minneapolis

Dover, K. J. 1989, *Greek homosexuality. Updated, and with a postscript*, Harvard University Press, Cambridge, Mass.

Dworkin, A. 1989, *Pornography: men possessing women*, E. P. Dutton, New York

Dyer, R. 1985, 'Male sexuality in the media', *The sexuality of men*, eds A. Metcalf & M. Humphries, Pluto Press, London, pp. 28–43

—— 1988, 'Children of the night: vampirism as homosexuality, homosexuality as vampirism', *Sweet dreams: sexuality, gender and popular fiction*, ed. S. Radstone, Lawrence & Wishart, London, pp. 47–72

Eagleton, T. 1976, *Marxism & literary criticism*, Methuen, London

Easthope, A. 1986, *What a man's gotta do: the masculine myth in popular culture*, Paladin, London

Ehrenreich, B., Hess, E. & Jacobs, G. 1986, *Re-making love: the feminization of sex*, Anchor Books, New York

Elliott, S. 1994, *The adventures of Priscilla, queen of the desert*, Currency Press, Sydney

Flannigan-Saint-Aubin, A. 1994, 'The male body and literary metaphors for masculinity', *Theorizing masculinities*, eds H. Brod & M. Kaufman, Sage Publications, Thousand Oaks, CA, pp. 239–58

Foucault, M. 1970, *The order of things: an archaeology of the human sciences*, Random House, New York

—— 1978, *The history of sexuality, volume 1: an introduction*, trans. Robert Hurley, Random House, New York

—— 1979, *Discipline and punish: the birth of the prison*, trans. Alan Sheridan, Penguin, London

Frye, N. 1969, *Anatomy of criticism: four essays*, Atheneum, New York

Gauthier, X. 1981, 'Is there such a thing as women's writing?', *New French feminisms: an anthology*, eds E. Marks & I. de Courtivron, Harvester Press, Brighton, pp. 161–4

Gelder, K. 1994, *Reading the vampire*, Routledge, London

Girard, R. 1965, *Deceit, desire, and the novel: self and other in literary structure*, trans. Yvonne Freccero, the Johns Hopkins University Press, Baltimore

Greenberg, D. F. 1988, *The construction of homosexuality*, University of Chicago Press, Chicago

Gubar, S. 1987, 'Representing pornography: feminism, criticism and depictions of female violation', *Critical inquiry*, vol. 13, no. 4, pp. 712–41

Halperin, D. M. 1990, 'Why is Diotima a woman?', *One hundred years of homosexuality, and other essays on Greek love*, Routledge, New York, pp. 113–51

Hawkins, G. & Zimring, F. E. 1988, *Pornography in a free society*, Cambridge University Press, Cambridge

Hoch, P. 1979, *White hero, black beast: racism, sexism and the mask of masculinity*, Pluto, London

Hocquenghem, G. 1978, *Homosexual desire*, trans. Daniella Dangoor, Allison & Busby, London

Irigaray, L. 1985, *This sex which is not one*, trans. C. Porter with C. Burke, Cornell University Press, Ithaca, NY

—— 1985, *Speculum of the other woman*, trans. G. C. Gill, Cornell University Press, Ithaca

Jagose, A. 1996, *Queer theory*, Melbourne University Press, Carlton

Jardine, L. 1983, *Still harping on daughters: women and drama in the age of Shakespeare*, 2nd edn, Harvester Wheatsheaf, New York

Keen, S. 1991, *Fire in the belly: on being a man*, Bantam Books, New York

Kimmel, M. S., ed. 1990, *Men confront pornography*, Crown Publishers, New York

Laqueur, T. 1990, *Making sex: body and gender from the Greeks to Freud*, Harvard University Press, Cambridge, Mass.

Lodge, D. 1978, *Changing places*, Penguin, London

Luhrmann, B. & Pearce, C. 1992, *Strictly ballroom*, from a screenplay by B. Luhrmann & A. Bovell, Currency Press, Sydney

MacDonald, S. 1990, 'Confessions of a feminist porn watcher', *Men confront pornography*, ed. M. S. Kimmel, Crown Publishers, New York, pp. 34–42

Mulvey, L. 1992, 'Visual pleasure and narrative cinema', *The sexual subject: a Screen reader in sexuality*, eds J. Caughie, A. Kuhn & M. Merck, Routledge, London, pp. 22–34

Oakley, A. 1972, *Sex, gender and society*, Temple Smith, London

Opie, I. & P. (eds), 1980, *The classic fairy tales*, Granada, London

Parker, A. 1993, 'Unthinking sex: Marx, Engels, and the scene of writing', *Fear of a queer planet: queer politics and social theory*, ed. M. Warner, University of Minnesota Press, Minneapolis, pp. 19–41

Parsons, T. & Bales, R. F. 1956, *Family, socialization and interaction process*, Routledge & Kegan Paul, London

Partridge, E. 1969, *Shakespeare's bawdy: a literary and psychological essay, and a comprehensive glossary*, E. P. Dutton, New York

Pleck, J. H. 1983, *The myth of masculinity*, the MIT Press, Cambridge, Mass.

Rice, A. 1977, *Interview with the vampire*, Futura Publications, London

Rich, A. 1993, 'Compulsory heterosexuality and lesbian existence', *The lesbian and gay studies reader*, eds H. Abelove, M. A. Barale & D. M. Halperin, Routledge, New York, pp. 227–54

Rowan, J. 1987, *The horned god: feminism and men as wounding and healing*, Routledge & Kegan Paul, London

Rubin, G. 1975, 'The traffic in women: notes on the "political economy" of sex', *Toward an anthropology of women*, ed. R. R. Reiter, Monthly Review Press, New York, pp. 157–210

Russo, V. 1987, *The celluloid closet: homosexuality in the movies*, revised edn, Harper & Row, New York

Rutherford, J. 1988, 'Who's that man?', *Male order: unwrapping masculinity*, eds R. Chapman & J. Rutherford, Lawrence & Wishart, London, pp. 21–67

Saunders, J. 1994, *Absolutely fabulous 2*, Penguin Books/BBC Books, London

Schama, S. 1995, *Landscape and memory*, HarperCollins, London

Sedgwick, E. K. 1985, *Between men: English literature and male homosocial desire*, Columbia University Press, New York

—— 1990, *Epistemology of the closet*, University of California Press, Berkeley

—— 1993, 'How to bring your kids up gay', *Fear of a queer planet: queer politics and social theory*, ed. M. Warner, University of Minnesota Press, Minneapolis, pp. 69–81

Segal, L. 1990, *Slow motion: changing masculinities, changing men*, Virago, London

Shakespeare, W. 1958, *The Arden edition of the works of William Shakespeare: The tempest*, ed. F. Kermode, Methuen, London

—— 1962, *The Arden edition of the works of William Shakespeare: Othello*, ed. M. R. Ridley, Methuen, London

—— 1962, *The Arden edition of the works of William Shakespeare: Macbeth*, ed. K. Muir, Methuen, London

—— 1965, *The Arden edition of the works of William Shakespeare: Antony and Cleopatra*, ed. M. R. Ridley, Methuen, London

Sinfield, A. 1992, *Faultlines: cultural materialism and the politics of dissident reading*, University of California Press, Berkeley

—— 1994, *Cultural politics—queer reading*, University of Pennsylvania Press, Philadelphia

Snitow, A. B. 1983, 'Mass market romance: pornography for women is different', *Powers of desire: the politics of sexuality*, eds A. Snitow, C. Stansell & S. Thompson, Monthly Review Press, New York, pp. 245–63

Stevens, D. 1995, *The sum of us*, Currency Press, Sydney

Stoker, B. 1975, *The annotated Dracula: Dracula by Bram Stoker*, ed. L. Wolf, New English Library/Times Mirror, London

—— 1979, *Dracula*, Penguin, Harmondsworth

Stoller, R J. 1968, *Sex and gender: on the development of masculinity and femininity*, Science House, New York

Tiger, L. 1969, *Men in groups*, Random House, New York

Tillyard, E. M. W. 1963, *The Elizabethan world picture*, Penguin, Harmondsworth

Tolkien, J. R. R. 1983, *The lord of the rings: Part 1, The fellowship of the Ring; Part 2, The two towers; Part 3, The return of the king*, Unwin Paperbacks, London

Tucker, S. 1990, 'Radical feminism and gay male porn', *Men confront pornography*, ed. M. S. Kimmel, Crown Publishers, New York, pp. 263–76

Warner, M. (ed). 1993, *Fear of a queer planet: queer politics and social theory*, University of Minnesota Press, Minneapolis

Weeks, J. 1977, *Coming out: homosexual politics in Britain, from the nineteenth century to the present*, Quartet Books, London

—— 1989, *Sex, politics and society: the regulation of sexuality since 1800*, 2nd edn, Longman, London

White, T. H. (ed. & trans.) 1960, *The bestiary: a book of beasts, being a translation from a Latin bestiary of the twelfth century*, Putnam's, New York

Williams, E. 1995, 'Priscilla, Ginger and Fred', *Quadrant*, June, pp. 53–6

Williams, L. 1990, *Hard core: power, pleasure, and the 'frenzy of the visible'*, Pandora, London

Williams, R. 1977, *Marxism and literature*, Oxford University Press, Oxford

Winterson, J. 1993, *Written on the body*, Vintage Books, London

Woodbridge, L. 1984, *Women and the English Renaissance: literature and the nature of womankind 1540–1620*, Harvester Press, Brighton

Zillmann, D. & Bryant, J. 1990, 'Pornography, sexual callousness, and the trivialization of rape', *Men confront pornography*, ed. M. S. Kimmel, Crown Publishers, New York, pp. 207–18

# *Filmography*

*The adventures of Priscilla, queen of the desert*, 1994, Stephan Elliott, dir., with Terence Stamp, Hugo Weaving, Guy Pearce & Bill Hunter, Polygram Filmed Entertainment/Australian Film Finance Corporation/Latent Image/Specific Films

*The blue lagoon*, 1980, Randal Kleiser, dir., with Brooke Shields, Christopher Atkins & Leo McKern, Columbia/Randal Kleiser

*Casablanca*, 1942, Michael Curtiz, dir., with Humphrey Bogart, Ingrid Bergman, Paul Henreid & Claude Rains, Warner Brothers

*Dracula has risen from the grave*, 1968, Freddie Francis, dir., with Christopher Lee, Rupert Davies & Veronica Carlson, Hammer

*Easter parade*, 1948, Charles Walters, dir., with Fred Astaire, Judy Garland & Ann Miller, MGM

*The getting of wisdom*, 1977, Bruce Beresford, dir., with Susannah Fowle, Sheila Helpman & Patricia Kennedy, Southern Cross/AFC/Victorian Film Corporation/9 Television Network

*Interview with the vampire: the Vampire Chronicles*, 1994, Neil Jordan, dir., with Tom Cruise, Brad Pitt, Antonio Banderas & Christian Slater, Warner/Geffen

*The living end*, 1992, Gregg Araki, dir., with Mike Dytri & Craig Gilmore, Mainline/Strand Releasing/Desperate Pictures

*Picnic at Hanging Rock*,. 1975, Peter Weir, dir., with Rachel Roberts, Dominic Guard & Helen Morse, Picnic Productions/Australian Film Corporation

*Rebel without a cause*, 1955, Nicholas Ray, dir., with James Dean, Natalie Wood & Sal Mineo, Warner Brothers

*The sound of music*, 1965, Robert Wise, dir., with Julie Andrews & Christopher Plummer, TCF/Argyle

*Star wars*, 1977, George Lucas, dir., with Mark Hamill, Harrison Ford & Carrie Fisher, TCF/Lucasfilm

*Strictly ballroom*, 1992, Baz Luhrmann, dir., with Paul Mercurio, Tara Morice & Bill Hunter, Rank/M&A/Australian Film Finance Corp.

*The sum of us*, 1994, Kevin Dowling & Geoff Burton, dir., with Jack Thompson, Russell Crowe & John Polson, Australian Film Finance Corporation/Southern Star

*Thelma and Louise*, 1991, Ridley Scott, dir., with Susan Sarandon, Geena Davis & Harvey Keitel, UIP/Pathé Entertainment

# Index